Web Search Savvy

Strategies and Shortcuts for Online Research

LEA'S COMMUNICATION SERIES
Jennings Bryant/Dolf Zillmann, General Editors

For a complete list of titles in LEA's Communication Series, please contact Lawrence Erlbaum Associates, Publishers at www.erlbaum.com

Web Search Savvy

Strategies and Shortcuts for Online Research

Barbara G. Friedman

*University of North Carolina
at Chapel Hill*

LAWRENCE ERLBAUM ASSOCIATES, PUBLISHERS

2005   Mahwah, New Jersey   London

Lawrence Erlbaum Associates, Inc., Publishers
10 Industrial Avenue
Mahwah, New Jersey 07430

Cover design by Sean Trane Sciarrone

Library of Congress Cataloging-in-Publication Data

Friedman, Barbara G., 1963–
  Web search savvy : strategies and shortcuts for online research / Barbara G. Friedman.
    p.   cm. — (LEA's communication series)
  Includes bibliographical references and index.
ISBN 0-8058-3859-7 (cloth : alk. paper)
ISBN 0-8058-3860-0 (pbk. : alk. paper)
1. Internet searching. 2. Journalism—Data processing. I. Title. II. Series.
ZA4230.F75   2004
025.04—dc22   2003064267
                                                              CIP

Books published by Lawrence Erlbaum Associates are printed on acid-free paper, and their bindings are chosen for strength and durability.

Printed in the United States of America
10 9 8 7 6 5 4 3 2 1

Contents

Preface

We are in the midst of the most significant communications revolution in centuries. New technologies are changing the ways people talk to each other, what we know, and how we think about and relate to the wider world. Wireless communications is credited with saving lives[1] and ousting politicians.[2] The World Wide Web (WWW) fosters democracy[3] and circumvents censorship;[4] and electronic mail is both a matchmaker[5] and a hatemonger.[6] "The World Wide Web has touched or has promised to alter ... virtually every aspect of modern life,"[7] a writer suggested in the *New York Times.* Consider that:

---

[1]For example Gillian Harris, "Mother's Mobile Call Rescue," *London Times* (5 January 2001), www.timesonline.co.uk or "Girl in Bali Sends Text Message SOS," *London Telegraph* electronic edition (15 February 2001), www.telegraph.co.uk

[2]See for example David L. Marcus, "Indonesia Revolt Was Net Driven," *Boston Globe* (23 May 1998), 1 or "Estrada Losing Hold in Philippines as Allies Abandon Him," *New York Times* (20 January 2001), A3. The *Times* reported that Filipinos used text messaging on mobile phones to summon others to join in public demonstrations against the current president. "If Joseph Estrada is forced out of power, it will be due in no small part to an unglamorous but politically potent technology known as text messaging," the newspaper offered.

[3]See for example Tiffany Danitz and Warren P. Strobel, "The Internet's Impact on Activism: The Case of Burma," *Studies in Conflict and Terrorism* 22 (July–September 1999), 257; or Jon Sawyer, "The Internet May Prove to be the Greatest Threat to Chinese Communism," *St. Louis Post-Dispatch* (24 May 2000), A7.

[4]See for example Bob Schmitt, "An Internet Answer to Repression," *Washington Post* (31 March 1997), A21; Elisabeth Rosenthal, "Detained Editor's Brother is Arrested in Beijing," *New York Times* (19 August 2000), A5.

[5]For example Barton Gellman, "A Modern Screen Romance," *Washington Post* (20 November 1988), A20; Janelle Erlichman, "Matchmaker, Matchmaker, E-Mail Me a Match," *Washington Post* (2 August 2001), C8; Lesley Dormen, "E-Mail Romance: Can the Internet Help Your Love Life?" *Glamour* (February 1996), 108; "New Internet Site is Aimed at Young Couples," *Wall Street Journal* (13 May 1996), B5.

[6]Robert Sheppard, "Patrolling for Hate on the Net," *Maclean's* (11 January 1999), 64; Steve Friess, "Virtual Animosity," *The Advocate* (10 December 1996), 40; "The Internet: Downloading Hate," *The Economist* (13 November 1999), 30; John Schwartz, "Thinking About Hate Messages and Limits of Resistance," *Washington Post* (4 March 1996), WB17; Deborah Sontag, "Israelis Grieve as Youth Who Was Lured to His Death on the Internet is Buried," *New York Times* (20 January 2001), A4.

[7]John Markoff, "Fast Changing Genie Alters the World," *New York Times* (11 December 2000), C1.

- *In Politics*: Bill Clinton's 1992 campaign, which used electronic mail to reach voters and shape the news, prompted a change in the way politicians disseminate their messages. Ironically, we learned later that Clinton sent only one e-mail during his administration.[8] By 1998, 75% of senatorial candidates had Web sites and most congressional candidates now say they consider the use of Web sites an essential component of the modern political campaign.[9] In 1999, Clinton's participation in a "virtual town hall meeting" was touted as a modern version of Franklin D. Roosevelt's fireside chats[10] and in 2000, the Democratic candidate for Ohio governor ran his ad campaign almost exclusively on the Internet. "When Eisenhower ran his first television ad in 1952, people thought he was crazy, but this is where we are now with the Internet," said his campaign manager.[11] E-mail is now being used along with more traditional means to mobilize political supporters and urge them to the polls.[12] Furthermore, the Internet has proved an effective forum for antigovernment protest as in China[13] and the United States,[14] and to circumvent government secrecy as in publication of the Environmental Protection Agency's secret "worst case scenarios."[15]

- *In Religion*: Pope John Paul II, who has traveled to more countries and met more Catholics than all of his predecessors combined, began broadcasting his public appearances on the WWW in 1998 in an effort to reach still more worshipers. That was the year the Vatican went online with its Web site powered by three host computers aptly named Raphael, Michael, and Gabriel (www.vatican.va). "The church has to take advantage of all technologies to spread the good news," said a papal spokesman.[16] In 2001, the Vatican named Saint Isidore of Seville the Patron Saint of the Internet.[17]

- *In Business*: "Dot com" businesses are credited (and blamed) for a dramatic upswing (and then downturn) in the stock market.[18] The number of commercial networks tied to the Internet increased some 300% in a 3-month pe-

---

[8]See for example Dee Dee Myers, "New Technology and the 1992 Clinton Presidential Campaign," *American Behavioral Scientist* 37:2 (November 1993), 187.

[9]David A. Dulio et al., "Untangled Web: Internet Use During the 1998 Election," *Political Science and Politics* 32:1 (March 1999), 53.

[10]"First Online Chat by President Clinton," *Time* (4 November 1999), www.time.com

[11]Dennis Cauchon, "Ohio Candidate Runs Entire Ad Campaign on Web," *USA Today* (18 October 2002), A16.

[12]See for example Nicole Ziegler, "Net Value: Constituents Can Compute Rather Than Commute," *St. Louis Post Dispatch* (1 June 1997), 4C or Leslie Wayne, "E-Mail Part of the Effort To Turn Out the Voters," *New York Times* (6 November 2000), C6.

[13]Barbara Crossette, "The Internet Changes Dictatorship's Rule," *New York Times* (1 August 1999), 4:1.

[14]Amy Harmon, "Protesters Find the Web To Be a Powerful Tool," *New York Times* (21 November 2001), B8. In October 2001, while the U.S. led a bombing campaign in Afghanistan, dissenters used the Internet to circulate petitions and to "weave their fragmented constituents into a movement."

[15]See also "'Worst Case Scenarios' Kept Secret by EPA are Published on Internet," *St. Louis Post-Dispatch* (12 September 1999), A5.

[16]"Pope John Paul Takes to the Internet to Spread His Message," *St. Louis Post-Dispatch* (16 August 1998), C3.

[17]Bess Twiston Davies, "Catholics Search for Internet Patron Saint," *London Telegraph* (13 June 2000), www.telegraph.co.uk

[18]James Cramer, "Bubble Trouble," *New York* (1 May 2000), 30.

riod in 1993.[19] Hundreds of thousands of shoppers skipped the malls and bought holiday gifts online, to the tune of approximately $8 billion in 1999, twice as much as in 1998.[20] In real estate prospective buyers are offered "virtual tours" of properties, along with online data to compare costs, neighborhoods, and school districts. Banks have turned to Web sites to expedite loan applications and approval.

- *In Education*: According to a Department of Education survey, half of U.S. classrooms are now hooked up to the Internet. Small schools and schools in isolated settings can network with organizations around the world, gaining access to more and improved resources.[21] Some universities have offered Web-based courses and forums for years[22] and now high schools have joined in, expanding the range of course content and opportunities for teenage students.[23] High school graduates in search of scholarships can scour the Web for possibilities.[24]

- *In Medicine*: Online health information allows medical professionals to reach people who lack computers or easy access to medical care;[25] and although concerns abound over medical advice proffered online,[26] the Internet is home to a myriad of support groups, databases of medical literature, and sites that allow users to check clinical trials[27] and even a doctor's credentials.

- *In Entertainment*: New technology offers numerous ways to fill leisure time. In addition to communicating with others via chat rooms, you can buy movie and concert tickets,[28] tune in to radio broadcasts from all over the world,[29] and make travel arrangements. When popular author Stephen King offered a new book exclusively for Internet download, more than 400,000 copies were sold or requested in the first 24 hours.[30] And more than 50 million users were swapping music files on Napster before a court order shut the music site down, and even then numerous similar sites

---

[19]Charles Babcock, "Internet and Beyond," *Computerworld* (30 August 1993), 35.

[20]Silvia Sansoni, "Santa Flaws," *Forbes* (27 December 1999), 282.

[21]See for example Barbara Kantrowitz, "Big Surf in a Little School," *Newsweek* (20 September 1999), 64.

[22]See for example Lisa Guernsey, "A Student-Run Technology Forum Where Even Web's Creator Speaks," *New York Times* (18 January 2001), D4.

[23]See for example Lisa Guernsey, "School Time, Minus the Face Time," *New York Times* (15 February 2001), D1.

[24]Elizabeth Stanton, "Prospects Look to Net, Hoping to Get a Look," *New York Times* (18 January 2001), D7.

[25]Joan Stephenson, "National Library of Medicine to Help Consumers Use Online Health Data," *JAMA* 283 (5 April 2000), 1675.

[26]See for example Vincent Kieran, "Study Finds Errors in Medical Information on the Web," *Chronicle of Higher Education* (2 June 1998), http://chronicle.com or Donald A. B. Lindbergh et al., "Medicine and Health on the Internet: The Good, the Bad and the Ugly," JAMA 280 (21 October 1998), 1303.

[27]Joan Stephenson, "National Library of Medicine to Help Consumers Use Online Health Data," *JAMA* 283 (5 April 2000), 1675.

[28]For example MovieLink (www.movielink.com) and Ticketmaster Online (www.ticketmaster.com).

[29]Eric A. Taub, "New Format For Radio: All Digital," *New York Times* (25 January 2001), D1.

[30]Dru Sefton and Jacqueline Blais, "Frightfully Slow Download at 'Bullet' Speed, Stephen King's Digital Tale Becomes a Net-only Nightmare," *USA Today* (16 March 2000), D1.

rushed to take Napster's place. The "peer-to-peer" software used by these
file-sharing sites promises to be a model for businesses of the future. In
sports, fans can follow games and players online. One sportswriter called
the Internet "the talk radio of soccer, providing statistics, chat rooms and
Web sites dedicated to individual players."[31]

- *In Art*: The Web has become a veritable gallery of art, ranging from the mundane to the extravagant.[32] On the Internet, you can tour the Louvre in Paris
(www.paris.org/musees/Louvre) and gaze at London's Tate collection
(www.tate.org.uk). In 1999, an online auction from New York's Plaza Hotel
included a rare 1887 Impressionist painting valued at $25 million.[33] Paint-
ings, crafts, and antiques are now routinely bought and sold via online auc-
tions (www.Sothebys.com or www.eBay.com, for example).[34] Even graffiti
has an audience in cyberspace long after it's been scrubbed from subway
walls.[35]

Although this new technology is quickly transforming every aspect of life, from
the way people do business to the way governments are supported or toppled and
the way we shop for groceries, the average Internet user's needs remain simple:
the skills to find information held on the World Wide Web.[36] And until that funda-
mental need is met, the most profound of technological advances are of little use
or interest to him. That is the basic premise of this book.

Maybe you've just been introduced to the Internet or you have achieved a comfortable level of proficiency. Maybe you've already used it for years. In either case,
this book will be of interest to you. Whether you have the latest technology, you're
working on secondhand equipment, or rely solely on the computers at the public
library, this book is for you. The book is for you, whether you have a warp-speed
broadband Internet connection or a takes-forever 28Kbps modem. Because beyond the basics, getting the most from the Internet is not about what you have,
but about how you use it. This book is not about keeping up with the Jones' RAM,
megabytes, or other Information Age accouterments. The most sophisticated,
fastest computer in the world won't do users any good until they have the skills to
find information on the Internet.

---

[31]Jack Bell, "On the Net, Soccer Waits for Prime Time," *New York Times* (24 August 2000), D6.

[32]See for example Matthew Mirapaul, "A Market for Flotsam and Jetsam as Performance Art," *New York Times* (5 February 2000), B2.

[33]Tara Wilfong, "Art in Cyberspace," *Art and Antiques* 22:4 (April 1999), 26.

[34]For example, Steven Ferguson, "E-Bay's $5,500 Modigliani," *Art and Auction* 22:5 (1 April 2000), 48. In this case, the authenticity of the painting was questioned by experts. See also Amy Page, "E-Bay: Sous la Responsabilite del'achetuer?" *Connaissance des Arts* 576 (October 2000), 36, in which the author debates the "buyer beware" policies of auction sites like E-Bay; Kelly Devine Thomas, "Collecting in Cyberspace," *ArtNews* 99:1 (January 2000), 131; "Sotheby's Launches New Online Auction Site," *Art Business News* 27:2 (February 2000), 70.

[35]Nina Siegal, "Extending the Life and Lore of Graffiti," *New York Times* (25 January 2001), D11.

[36]The Internet is a massive, global network of computers. The World Wide Web is the hypertext protocol or coding language that allows the information on those computers to be linked. The Internet
was originally conceived as a decentralized communications system for the military, enabling defense
centers to communicate in the event of a nuclear attack. The technology was eventually opened up to
civilian populations. Its most popular feature continues to be electronic mail (e-mail), messages sent
from one computer to another.

The purpose of this book is to:

- make your time online efficient, productive, and ultimately less frustrating
- show you what kind of information is available online
- show you the quickest, most effective ways to find and retrieve information
- provide you with the best techniques to make search engines work for you, circumventing distraction and advertisements
- show you the best ways to find people and find out about people, living or dead, famous or unknown
- guide you to online databases and other directories of information with an emphasis on free sites rather than on fee-based sites
- indicate where your privacy might be compromised by new technology and show you ways to protect yourself

I'm assuming certain things about the reader: that you're comfortable using a computer and mouse and have access to the Internet (home or elsewhere). Primarily, I'm assuming you're also short on time, and if you've already been online resent the time-consuming nature of most Web searches. You want breadth of information to enrich your life and nourish your mind, body, and soul but you don't want to wage a virtual war to find it. Neither your typing speed, your age, or your language is a barrier to searching the Internet efficiently. This book will provide you with the skills to do an efficient search.

Several years ago, I sat in on a lecture by our city newspaper's database manager, who demonstrated some of the ways newsrooms were using software and the latest computer resources to analyze large amounts of data. The results were impressive; the paper was able to publish more solid investigative types of series that were difficult or impossible before, including one on the quality of patient care in local hospitals and another on campaign finance. The process is called computer-assisted reporting (CAR) and the techniques used in CAR produce the stories that win Pulitzer Prizes for news organizations. It wasn't difficult to see that the skills a journalist uses to find online information would be just as helpful to those outside a newsroom. Students and scholars are rarely afforded the same resources of a top news organization, but their need to find reliable information online feels just as urgent when confronting a deadline.

I went straight home and loaded one of the many demonstration disks I'd gotten in the mail from America Online. But without anyone to guide me, I stumbled blindly through the wilderness of cyberspace. Online tutorials were no help because I did not know how to search and find them. All my attempts seemed only to lead to dead ends, or worse, advertisements. The manuals I located in the library or bookstore all seemed to be written in a foreign language. Finally, I signed up for an Internet workshop offered through a local writers' program. That workshop provided me with the push I needed to learn more; not long after that I initiated the first college level computer-assisted reporting classes in St. Louis, at Webster University and Washington University.

Since my introduction to the Internet, I've spent thousands of hours online and honed my skills with help from other journalists, computer programmers and librarians—three of the most appropriate and invaluable resources I can imagine. One author wrote that journalists can be the best guides to navigating the Internet's "lush jungles of information."[37] Why? Because reporters are trained to "ferret out what seems 'most important' ... and to present it in a language that average people can understand" she wrote.[38] I'd add, too, that journalists' ability to find information under intense deadline pressure also gives us an edge when it comes to Internet research.

Friends of mine have taken advantage of community workshops, which have become more available as the Internet is popularized. But those seem mostly geared toward introducing people to the most popular Web sites for genealogical research, vacation planning, and the like. I get impatient in those settings, which so often come across as interminable "surfing" sessions. I don't want to spend the day in front of a computer; there are too many things I enjoy doing more. When I go online, it's to find something specific, and invariably on a tight deadline. That motivated me to concentrate on refining my online research skills—and as a journalist I haven't yet missed a deadline. In this book, I've provided the tips and techniques I've picked up over the last few years to help you save time online and get back to the business of living.

The book is organized in a logical way to help you find information online but is not limited to search strategies. It's intended to maximize your proficiency to minimize your time online. Let me add that I'm not a computer expert. Rather, I'm trained as a journalist and I've written in straightforward language. If I use jargon occasionally it's because the Internet has created its own vocabulary, so I've also taken care to provide a glossary of terms at the end of the book. Certainly you'll get the most out of the book if you read it cover to cover. But, realizing that my goal here is to save time, the chapters have been organized for quick reference. Following is how the book is organized:

• **Chapter 1, Getting Started** tells you what you should consider in choosing an Internet Service Provider (ISP), how to connect to the Internet without paying a fortune, and what features are worth paying extra for. I also dissect a Web site and show you how a tool bar works (and moreover, how to make it work better). In addition, the chapter provides shortcuts for navigating the Internet and techniques for maximizing your browser, getting rid of advertising clutter, and maximizing screen space.

• **Chapter 2, When Seconds Count** offers strategies for locating what you want online and retrieving it in the most efficient way using search engines. This chapter also points out the critical differences between search engines and search registries, and ways to avoid the most common mistakes people make when trying to use search engines. As many search resources accept paid listings, I'll show you the ways to find what you want and how to get where you want to go online, not where advertisers would like to lead you.

---

[37]Doris Graber, *Mass Media and American Politics* (Washington, D.C.: CQ Press, 1997), 393.
[38]Ibid.

- **Chapter 3, Skipping the Middleman** shows a variety of alternate ways to find information should traditional searches fail. When you reach this chapter, you will already know something about the ways information is arranged and rearranged on the Web; searching is about more than typing a few keywords in a box. Want to find all the Web sites hosted by a certain corporation or network? Try a syntax search, described in this chapter. Looking for sites that reference computer programming, programmers, and programs? Try a wild card search, also described here, along with many other techniques for getting at the information you seek.

- **Chapter 4, Staying Connected** describes the pivotal role of newsgroups, mailing lists (also called listservs), newsletters, and Web logs (blogs) in finding information. The important differences between listservs and newsgroups (or electronic bulletin boards) are discussed, including the advantages and disadvantages of both. I'll show you the best ways to find these resources and their archives and discuss why it's a good idea to establish an online "beat." Finally, some advice on network etiquette and tips for protecting your privacy when you join online forums.

- **Chapter 5, Finding out About People** describes the myriad ways to gather information on individuals, from simple phone directories to details about their personal and professional lives. This chapter helps you find people and find out about people, but also to hide yourself. Read this chapter to understand where information is harbored online and how you can minimize the amount of personal information people can uncover about you.

- **Chapter 6, Finding and Using Databases** will direct you to large directories of information such as those maintained by the U.S. government and show you the best ways to retrieve it. The most common file extensions you'll encounter are identified here as is the software required to download and read the data. I discuss ways to keep up with information as it makes its way online and how to use your browser to create your own database. In addition, I've included some important considerations for judging the veracity of information you find online, and tips on protecting your privacy.

- **Chapter 7, Evaluating the Information You Find** gives you the tools needed to evaluate the information you find online. Start with your gut instincts, sure, but don't end there. How can you trust what you've found or verify the contents of a site? What will finding out who's behind a site tell you about the content?

- At the end of each chapter is a list of "tips for smart searches," reinforcing the best strategies for finding and evaluating information online.

Although it's true the Internet is with us to stay it's also a fact that individual Web sites come and go at a moment's notice. I cannot guarantee all the sites mentioned in this book will still be there when you seek them out, but I've tried to reference only sites that have a proven history of reliability.

In the midst of this book project, on September 11, 2001 the United States was attacked by terrorists who slammed four hijacked airliners into New York's World Trade Center towers, the Pentagon in Virginia, and a Pennsylvania field,

killing more than three thousand people. The tragedy of 9/11 marked a significant turning point in the way we view and use the Internet. It proved to be a tool
used by the terrorists to carry out their awful deed, and almost immediately was
a forum for anti-American and anti-Islam vitriol. Yet the Internet also brought
people together as it became an important news source, and a virtual space
where users could express individual memories and collective grief. Numerous
sites directed those in need to relief agencies, and others to how to donate toward
recovery efforts. Protesters also found the Web a powerful tool, a safe haven
where they could express their opposition to the war in Afghanistan. In the days
and weeks following the attack, the uses of the Internet, whether nefarious or
wondrous, were vividly rendered.

John Perry Barlow once wrote of the Internet as a "global social space ... that
all may enter without privilege or prejudice accorded by race, economic power,
military force or station of birth."[39] Barlow's (1997) "Cyberspace Declaration of
Independence" reflected the hope of many users that the Internet would be a
"home of the mind."[40] Yet just four years later, Stanford Law Professor Lawrence
Lessig wrote that the great promise of the early Internet, a haven for innovation
and creativity, had already been diminished by legal and technical changes. He
wrote, "The forces that the original Internet threatened to transform are well on
their way to transforming the Internet ... the future that promised great freedom
and innovation will not be ours. The future that threatened the reemergence of almost perfect control will."[41]

Still, Barlow's Electronic Frontier Foundation continues its important work as
a legal and information resource to protect free expression in this digital age. And
after all, Lessig isn't really so pessimistic. But they both warn us to tread carefully
or we will surely forfeit the public good that can come from this great technological tool. This then, is my small contribution. This book is full of practical tips to
make your experience online more efficient, but above all, it is meant to be em-
powering. The techniques described are intended to restore a measure of control
to computer users who share the belief that the Internet should be a marketplace
of ideas for all people, not just a marketplace.

ACKNOWLEDGMENTS

This book would not have been possible without the help of many others. At Lawrence Erlbaum Associates, I am grateful for my editor, Linda Bathgate, who encouraged my work from our first e-mail contact. My thanks to George Landau,
president of NewsEngin and Brant Houston, executive director of IRE/NICAR,
who guided my earliest attempts at Internet-based research. At the University of

---

[39]John Perry Barlow, "Cyberspace Declaration of Independence," 1997. Barlow, co-founder of the
Electronic Frontier Foundation wrote in part, "Governments of the Industrial World, you weary giants
of flesh and steel, I come from Cyberspace, the new home of the Mind ... You are not welcome among
us. You have no sovereignty where we gather." The organization's Web site is www.eff.org.

[40]Ibid.

[41]Lawrence Lessig, *The Future of Ideas: The Fate of the Commons in a Connected World* (New
York: Random House, 2001), vii.

Missouri School of Journalism, Professor Betty Winfield has been a great mentor and friend. Professor Charles Davis led me to the place where cyberspace, law, and creativity intersect, then inspired me with his wit and intelligence to linger and learn. Many of my classmates in the doctoral program at the University of Missouri generously shared their ideas and expertise. Meredith Austin was a capable research assistant and I am thankful for her attention to detail. Students and workshop participants provided me with many welcome opportunities to improve as a researcher and teacher. Finally, I'm especially grateful to my family for their continued support and encouragement.

—*Barbara G. Friedman*

1

Getting Started

THE LEARNING CURVE

Remaining committed to your manual or even electric typewriter isn't just folksy now, it's impractical. The reasons to become Internet proficient already outnumber reasons to the contrary. E-mail is the newest, simple way of communicating;[1] e-commerce is responsible for the latest investment opportunities as well as significant dips and peaks in the stock market;[2] and the Internet turns everyday people into instant celebrities[3] and millionaires.[4] Furthermore, the World Wide Web (WWW) is becoming the storage place for our nation's most important documents.[5]

The learning curve associated with the Internet is really more of a bend in the road. Here's the big secret: There's no reason to be intimidated. First, you need not be on the cutting edge of every technological advance. You can choose how many or how few bells and whistles you want to take with you on your online journey. It may seem like the technology changes at a rapid pace, but you need only acquire some basic skills and then refine them. A colleague said he understood why his young students picked up information technology so quickly: "They're not afraid of breaking the computer, whereas I am," he said. Be fearless—there are really very few things you can do that will absolutely wreck your

---

[1]John Schwartz, "Marketers Turn to a Simple Tool: E-Mail," *New York Times* (13 December 2000), E1.

[2]See for example Gregory Zuckerman and Greg Ip, "Nasdaq, Falling Again, is Now 50 Percent Below High," *Wall Street Journal* (20 December 2000), C1.

[3]For example, "Only in America," *New York Times Magazine* (26 November 2000), 38, which tells of Mike Collins, a 26-year-old engineer, whose design of a mock election ballot sent through e-mail resulted in myriad requests for publication.

[4]Johnnie L. Roberts, "All for One, One for AOL," *Newsweek* (20 December 2000), www.newsweek.com

[5]See for example Peter Shinkle, "Effort to Preserve Court Records of Dred Scott Case Moves to Web," *St. Louis Post-Dispatch* (14 January 2001), C1 and Katie Hafner, "Saving the Nation's Digital Legacy," *New York Times* (27 July 2000), E1.

computer. Software can be reinstalled (save the originals CDs and manuals, of course) and many items thought lost can eventually be retrieved from your computer's hard drive. For the average person, the Internet learning curve is relatively easy to overcome.

What is the Internet? The Internet is a huge network of computers. Connecting to it through your home or office computer, or with the newer wireless technology, provides users with access to a wide spectrum of documents, opinions, images, and sounds from individuals and organizations that have decided to share or make them public. Geographical boundaries are blurred, as you can communicate with or read documents from people and places around the world at any time of the day or night. The Web, or WWW, used synonymously with the word Internet, is the organizing system for all these documents. Each document is translated into a protocol or language (hypertext) that enables the user to view it through a *browser* (more on browsers to follow). Think of the WWW as an unprecedented repository of sources, both human and stored.

It may sound like the Internet is one-stop shopping for researchers, yet sometimes it is more productive to seek information in the library than online. Knowing the difference will save you considerable time. For example, if you're looking for information that predates 1985 you may have better luck at the library. Similarly, if the information is obscure, an experienced reference librarian is a better guide than the best search engine. Still, it is tempting to look for answers online. For a school assignment, my daughter was looking for information on the origins of cartoon animation, something her teacher assured her she could find online. Although she did find many sites related to animation, among the most valuable information were book reviews that pointed her to the most suitable references—in the library.

Getting Started

Although it may seem like the WWW is transforming on a daily basis, it is counterproductive to believe progress has passed you by. Although the Internet is less a novelty than it was in 1993, there are plenty of people who live quite well without it.[6] However, if you've decided to take the plunge but don't have much experience with computers or the Internet, following are some suggestions to ease the transition:

- Going online should not involve a big expense; take advantage of freebies. If your public library offers its patrons access to computers in order to search the card catalog or surf the Internet, plan to spend an afternoon there. A librarian can get you started. If the library imposes a time limit when someone else is waiting for the computer, use the break to look through computer magazines or how-to manuals, or to read the technology sections of various newspa-

---

[6]In a Pew Internet and American Life Project survey, one out of five Americans said they do not go online and have no plans to do so. They cited cost, complexity, and lack of interest as some of the reasons. See www.pewinternet.org.

pers. Then get back on the computer as soon as it's free. In the interest of saving space, some libraries are beginning to offer wireless technology, which allows patrons to check out laptop computers. It's a great opportunity to explore the Web at a leisurely pace, and in a comfortable setting. Best of all, it's free. Many libraries offer introductory classes free or at a nominal cost, geared to specific software (e.g., word processing) or Internet navigation (often targeted to genealogy research). Take advantage and if the classes are free, sit in on more than one. But use this only as a springboard to more targeted learning—more on that in chapter 2.

• Similarly, many community colleges or adult education programs offer computer classes for a nominal cost. Call the registrar's office and place your name on the schools' mailing lists to receive their schedules. If you decide the schedule doesn't work for you, or you don't want to learn in a group, contact the instructor through the college and see if he or she offers private lessons or can refer you to someone who does.

• Ask a friend who's computer proficient to spend an hour with you one afternoon showing you how to use basic software. If you feel uncomfortable asking them to do it for free, pay them a small fee or barter with a skill of your own. A freelance journalist new to town asked me to come to her house and show her some Internet search techniques. She offered to pay me, but I knew she was a gourmet cook, so I asked her to make lunch instead. We spent an hour at the computer, then another hour over lunch when she could ask follow-up questions to her "lesson."

• Along those same lines, invite a computer-familiar friend to accompany you to the computer store to check out the merchandise. The clerks will often try to sell you as much as possible and in most cases, more than you need. Take along someone who can help you understand what is necessary and what is overkill. And by all means, comparison shop since much of the computer software and hardware available are competitively priced. Don't rule out purchasing gently used or reconditioned equipment that may be available from many computer and office supply stores. Expand your search to the classified ads, including those of college publications. Students graduating or moving from dormitories would often rather sell their computers than pack them.

• Take advantage of the relaxed settings of many bookstores, where customers are invited to browse entire books in overstuffed chairs, even while they sip mocha lattes. Plant yourself in the computer section and go through every basic computer or Internet skills book on the shelf. You need not feel compelled to buy, and no one will look askance if you want to sit and take notes.

• Internet cafes are another kind of gathering place for tech-minded folks. Buy some time on a computer station, then don't be afraid to ask questions of either wandering clerks or nearby patrons, who may be more experienced than you in navigating the Web.

• Productive Internet navigation requires typing skills. If you've never used a keyboard or your typing skills are rusty, there are several good keyboarding programs available on CD-ROM. It's true that many are geared toward children, but at least they're entertaining. If you'd rather not purchase a tutorial, try the local library, video store, or even the grocery store, because stores offering video rentals may also rent CDs. You might even be able to borrow such a program from a local elementary school, where today keyboarding is taught as a basic skill to most students. Note: The CD-ROMs I have in mind will require your computer have a sound card and speakers, as much of the instruction is spoken. Most computers sold now include those. If not, a sound card can often be added for less than $100. Speakers range in size, style, and price, but a decent, basic pair should run less than $60.

• Practice, practice, practice. Unless you're a natural talent, mastering a skill takes patience and determination. My friends marvel at my typing speed, for which I give credit to my 9th-grade business skills teacher who encouraged us (only half-jokingly) to "type until your fingers bleed." And I navigate quickly on the Internet not just because of the particular skills I've acquired, but because it's something I do everyday. Practice won't ever make perfect in this rapidly changing medium, but it will definitely make your work faster, more efficient, and less frustrating.

When You're Ready to Venture Online

When you've built up some confidence and you're ready to search the Internet, you'll have to make some decisions on how to get there. An Internet Service Provider (ISP) is the gateway that most people use to connect. I encourage you to take advantage of the free software circulated by the major ISPs,[7] usually offering 100-plus hours of free access. Use it to get comfortable on the Internet, but try several before signing up with any particular one. Because some ISPs require you provide a credit card number to begin a trial membership, be sure to cancel it before the trial period ends or the provider will assume you wish to continue and will bill your credit card.

I learned on the earliest version of America Online (AOL) after receiving several free diskettes in the mail. I decided later I wanted something that allowed more direct access to the Internet. At the time, AOL was blocking access to many sites and I didn't care for all the fancy graphics that were intended to make it user-friendly. A friend refers to it as "Internet dumbed-down." In all fairness, AOL has made many improvements since then, and now that they've joined Time-Warner, they'll have even more to offer subscribers. Still, like me, you may prefer a provider that is "low frills."

Research suggests once computer users select an ISP, they tend to be loyal. But that's more for the sake of convenience than anything else. Changing your ISP usually means a change in your e-mail address; notifying your correspondents, reprinting business cards or stationery, may seem like too much trouble or expense. Thus, researching before you subscribe will save you time, money, and headaches in the long run. Many computer magazines rate ISPs, so you might skim some back issues at the library before choosing one. Unfortunately, there's

---

[7]America Online (AOL), Microsoft, and Earthlink, to name a few.

nothing yet like a *Consumer Reports* of computers, so pay careful attention to the source of a magazine's ratings to detect if advertisers are receiving preferential treatment. Online, *PCWorld* has rated ISPs (http://webcenter.pcworld.icq.com/). *Broadband Reports* routinely rates ISPs and you can search reviews by date, rating, or ISP reach (www.dslreports.com). To see the widest range of choices, check sites like The Directory (www.thedirectory.org), which offers a list of ISPs searchable by area code and ISP.com (www.isps.com), which has a list of national and international service providers.

You should consider the following when choosing an ISP:

Access.   Most home users connect to the Internet using a modem (modulator-demodulator); newer computers have them built in, but they are also available as external devices. As the technology improves, users have several choices in terms of access.

1. *Dial-up service*: This method allows the user to connect to the Internet through a conventional telephone line. Downloading and uploading data can be time-consuming, but dial-up service continues to be the least expensive and most popular way to get online. Ask your ISP if they provide a local number or if users have to dial long-distance (and pay those charges). This is an important, basic consideration. Many of the new, smaller ISPs offer attractive pricing (some as low as $5.95 a month), but you won't save much if you have to pay long distance charges to get online. Also, if you travel, find out if your ISP will let you connect to the Internet from distant locations. Again, some services require you dial and pay for long distance on the road when they really should provide you with a temporary local number. More hotels are beginning to offer dial-up access to their guests, but the cost can be an additional $10 to $20 per day.

2. *Broadband*: High-speed Internet connections used to be a perk of working in an office, but more home users are signing up for broadband connections (sometimes called pipelines) offered by telephone and cable companies. Broadband service is available through cable modem, digital subscriber line (DSL) or wireless transceivers. Currently, broadband connections are most popular in Korea and China, but by 2004, should outpace dial-up access in the U.S. These high-speed connections provide faster access to the Web and the ability to easily download data such as music, photographs, television and movies. Unlike dial-up service, a broadband connection is always open, that is, the user doesn't have to dial in through a provider. That means the phone line isn't tied up while you're online, and while traffic can be slowed, you won't encounter a busy signal. But that also creates more security concerns; ask your service provider about a firewall to protect your computer and data from hackers or other intruders.

3. *Wireless*: Also called WiFi for wireless fidelity, this service offers pockets of high-speed Internet access through radio transmitters and other wireless equipment. You'll still need software, hardware and a service provider in

most cases. But newer laptops come equipped with WiFi transceivers, as do palm devices. Hotels, airports, cafes and entire towns are providing wireless "hot spots" free or at a nominal charge. In fact, some McDonald's restaurants offer an hour of free high-speed wireless Internet access with the purchase of a value meal.

Speed. Most computers manufactured after 1998 include a 56Kbps (thousands of bits per second) modem. This refers to how quickly your computer can translate information transported across telephone lines. In other words, the modem speed regulates how quickly a Web site will appear on your computer screen or how fast you can send and receive electronic mail. However, that speed is affected by the phone line, so the first rule here is don't spend money for a faster modem if your connection method will not accommodate it. Anything slower than a 28.8Kbps modem is agonizing, downloads can seem to take forever. As the qualities of Web sites change (e.g., incorporating more sophisticated visual and audio components), a high speed is needed to view them in their entirety. Thus, Digital Subscriber Line (DSL) is gaining in popularity because it allows customers to connect to the Internet by high-speed cable or alternative phone lines. Pay rates can be twice as high as dial-up connections using a modem, but the difference in download and upload time is noticeable. You can find out more about DSL at www.dslreports.com. Before investing in a DSL consider the ways you'll use the Internet. Maybe something as simple as turning off the graphic components will speed your download time up satisfactorily (see How to get the most out of your browser, this chapter).

Pay Structure. How will you be charged for the time you spend on the Internet? There was once a proliferation of small ISPs that provided Internet access free of charge. But disproportionately active users forced many out of business and others to limit the number of hours users could spend online.[8] Among the bigger commercial ISPs, a flat fee (usually monthly) provides you with unlimited time, but if you only use e-mail, an hourly rate might make more sense. You can compose and read e-mail offline after all; the only time you need pay for is the time it takes to send mail or download the mail sent to you.[9] Should you opt for an hourly rate, keep track of the time you spend online to be sure you are charged correctly. When I was an hourly rate customer with a dial-up connection, I once received a bill that was twice what it should have been. When I contacted the ISP, I learned of something called "ghosting." When my modem dialed and failed to connect, I was in the habit of redialing immediately. In that case, the Earthlink system did not recognize the disconnect, and instead registered simultaneous connections, as if multiple people were connected to the Internet at my house, all at once. The result was an inflated bill.

---

[8]Bluelight.com, Juno Online, and NetZero are just three such companies. The latter recently announced it would charge subscribers $9.95 after they reach 40 hours in a given month. See Laurie J. Flynn, "Days of Plenty Are Over at Free Internet Services," *New York Times* (1 January 2001), C1.

[9]You can also cache sites to read offline, using your browser's options. More on that in the section, "How to Get the Most Out of Your Browser."

Flat fees are becoming more competitive, as more small ISPs enter the market. However, be sure to ask questions about service; it may be worth paying a little more to get 24-hour technical support. Juno Online Services offers a tiered pricing program, allowing better service and reliable connections to customers who pay $9.95 a month.[10] For further savings, inquire about discounts. For example, some ISPs offer discounted rates to seniors, students and educators.[11] Others may offer reduced rates or free service if you agree to view advertising when you log on.

Reliability.   If you use a dial-up connection, an ISP provides you with a phone number, which a modem uses to connect to the Internet. One of the early frustrations with AOL was the high frequency of busy signals users received when they were trying to connect. Find out from any ISPs you're considering how many phone numbers it uses to connect to the Internet, and about their call-failure and call-success rate. Upgrading to a broadband connection will eliminate this problem.

Support Services.   Most ISPs provide CDs or diskettes that will walk customers through the process of setting up their Internet connection. But once that's done, can you get help when you need it? Look for an ISP that offers around-the-clock help, preferably with a toll-free number. Just to be sure they offer more than lip service, try calling their help line at different times and see if you can get through. What is the average wait time for customers who call for help? Some ISPs, such as Earthlink, indicate the average wait time for customer service on their Web sites. Does the helpline employ a human staff? If so, what kind of training do their technicians receive? Or, does the ISP use an automated system that requires the customer to respond by touch-tone (as in "if you're calling about a problem with installation, press two")? One ISP I used began with a great technical staff, who seemed to actually enjoy working out problems with their customers. But they have since switched to inexperienced clerks who rely on a database of information to troubleshoot only the most typical problems.

Extras.   Some ISPs offer "extras" to attract customers, such as 100-plus free hours for subscribing or proprietary content (viewable by subscribers only). Some of the perks are great but others are unnecessary. If there are multiple people using your computer, you may lean toward an ISP that offers extra e-mail addresses. If you require the capability to receive and read messages in foreign languages, find an ISP that provides the support for that. If you want to create your own Web page, find an ISP that can provide you with software and server space. You'll want at least two megabytes, more if you plan on using lots of graphics. Still other extras include *chat rooms* where members can converse infor-

---

[10]Laurie J. Flynn, "Days of Plenty Are Over at Free Internet Services," *New York Times* (1 January 2001), C1.

[11]For example, when the *St. Louis Post-Dispatch* offered Internet service, educators paid a monthly rate of $12.95, compared to the regular $19.95 rate.

mally, instant messaging (IM), and spam[12] control. Again, it's important to consider how you'll spend your time online because you should not pay for features you don't want or need. And if there's something extra you'd like that is not offered, it never hurts to ask.

References.   Just as you'd expect a prospective employee to provide you with references, you should expect ISPs to do the same. Ask questions. How long have they been in business, for example, and how many subscribers do they have? If you're already online, but thinking about switching ISPs, contact people and organizations whose e-mail addresses reflect the name of the ISPs under consideration. For example, an e-mail address, janedoe@att.net tells you the individual's ISP is AT&T. An address that ends in "aol.com" indicates that America Online is the ISP. Contact other users and ask about their experiences with a particular ISP, or inquire among family, friends, and colleagues. Mailing lists and newsgroups are another useful way to get recommendations (more on that in chapter 4).

Browser Wars

In addition to an Internet connection, you'll need software that allows you to view and hear the content of Web sites. Most new computers are sold "bundled" with software that includes Web browsers, the client software that allows a user to navigate and view information on the World Wide Web. In addition, a browser allows you to copy and paste Web-based information into other programs (e.g., word processing documents). With a browser you can "bookmark" sites you want to return to regularly. Most browsers also allow the user to send e-mail.

Among browsers, the "big two" are Microsoft's Internet Explorer (IE) and Netscape Navigator. However, there are other choices, some available now, others in development. For example, Linux is a welcome alternative to the two big corporate entities; it shows great potential and programmers continue to refine its browser.[13] For PC users, Opera, written by Norwegian programmers, is growing in popularity and financial backing aside, has several features that give it an advantage over Explorer and Navigator. At www.Opera.com, you can download a free version or a $40 ad-free version. Mozilla is an open-source project developed and maintained by a community of enthusiastic programmers, many volunteers. The Mozilla browser is available at www.Mozilla.org. Another browser worth consideration comes from NeoPlanet and is free for download at www.neoplanet.com. However, NeoPlanet currently requires that you install Internet Explorer, as it uses that technology for its base.[14]

---

[12]"Spam" refers to unsolicited and typically high-volume "junk" e-mail. Although it's worthwhile to use an "anti-spam" program, many succeed in barring only a fraction of junk mail.

[13]For more on the Linux Operating System, see www.linux.org or for example Bill Laberis, "Linux is Full of Fanatics, Potential," *Computerworld* (2 July 2001), www.computerworld.com

[14]See for example, David Pogue, "Other Windows on the Web," *New York Times* (4 January 2001), D1.

Anatomy of a Web Site

What can you expect to see and hear when you begin to view documents on the Internet? A Web site is a multilayered document which, although often referred to as a "page," has no length limitation. It can be as long or as short as the programmer wants it to be and most contain a combination of text, images, and sounds. This is something to keep in mind when you print material from a site. Although you may only see a page length on your computer monitor, a print command can print the entire document, unless you limit it. One way to do that is to use the "print preview" option in the "file" pulldown menu on your browser. Note the page numbers that appear on the preview then return to "file" and "print," and select just those pages you want. Alternately, once a site begins to print, double-click on your printer icon to see how many pages are in the printer queue. There, you can purge (end) the print job at anytime.

A Web site is located or identified by a *uniform resource locator*, a URL—the address. URLs consist of several parts separated by dots (periods) or slashes, and characters indicating something specific about that site. For example, the URL for the White House is www.whitehouse.gov; the latter part of the address (.gov) indicates this is a government site. Web addresses begin with "http://"[15] as in http://www.whitehouse.gov, although with the latest versions of browsers this portion is assumed; you need not type it.

A Web site may contain pop-up or pull-down menus that transport you to another location on the site or to another site. Highlighted or underlined text on a Web site signals the user to a *link*. Clicking on the link transports the user to another location on the site, or to another Web site entirely. A link can also open an e-mail form, activate a graphic, audio or video component, or even download a program. When it's positioned over a hyperlink, your cursor arrow will change to a pointing finger.

Some sites have a link to something called a *site map*. This is basically a text-only version to all content on the page, including its link structure. It's a speedy way to zero in on specific information. For example, if you want to find a staff directory on an organization's site but there's no obvious link, look for a site map link and click that. Then from your browser's "edit" pulldown menu, choose "find" and type in "directory" (without quotation marks). That should locate the link that will take you to the staff directory and save you time searching the page's many links.

As an example, Fig. 1.1 is what you'll see when you visit the official White House site (www.whitehouse.gov).

An icon in the upper right corner of your browser screen indicates the status of your download as you move from site to site. While a page is still loading information or graphics, the icon remains in motion. Explorer shows a floating landscape, Navigator displays falling stars. The icon stabilizes once a page is fully loaded. The name or title of the site will appear across the top of your computer screen and the URL, or address, appears in the "location" box in Navigator; the

---

[15]*HTTP* stands for hypertext transfer protocol, which tells a browser how to display a page or record.

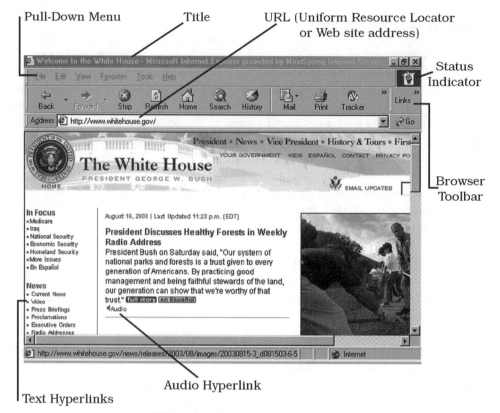

Pull-Down Menu   Title   URL (Uniform Resource Locator
                                                                              or Web site address)

Status
Indicator

Browser
Toolbar

Audio Hyperlink

Text Hyperlinks

FIG. 1.1.   Anatomy of a Web site.

"address" box in Explorer. At the bottom of the screen a security indicator icon, usually a key or padlock, indicates you are viewing a site that protects the information sent to and from it. The default setting on most browsers allows the computer to warn you when you're attempting to send information to an unsecure site. This is a critical consideration if you provide online retailers with your credit card information.

Each button on the toolbar has its own function. The examples described here work specifically with Internet Explorer, although Netscape Navigator works much the same way with slight variations.

• After you have viewed more than one page, the *back* key can be used to return you to the Web site you viewed previously. Imagine reading the first ten pages of a book, then returning to page five. Multiple mouse clicks will continue to "page" backward, until you reach the first page you viewed in a particular session. You can do the same using shortcuts if you prefer, or if a mouse is not available. For PC users, press Alt + left arrow or the backspace key. Macintosh users press the command and [simultaneously.

• Once you've moved backward, you can then use the *forward* key to progress. Again, this will only propel you forward to the last page you viewed in a given session. PC users can achieve the same by pressing Alt + right arrow; Mac users can move forward through sites by pressing command +].

• The *stop* key interrupts a transfer of information or stops a page from loading. PC users can press the ESC key alternatively. Mac users press command + .

• The *refresh* key reloads a page. This is useful if you suspect a page has been updated since you first loaded it (e.g., a news site) or if graphics fail to appear as expected. If a transfer seems to be taking an inordinate amount of time, it can also be helpful to stop the transfer, then press refresh. You can also click on the go key, located to the right of the address box. The shortcut for PC users is Ctrl + R.

• When setting the options for your browser, you can designate a starting place. This will be the first page you see each time you open your browser. Clicking on the *home* key during any session will return you to that page. You can change it easily and to any Web site available, by using the standard toolbar across the top of your browser. More on this later in the section, How to Get the Most Out of Your Browser.

• The *search* key will open a frame on the left side of your screen, displaying the Web site of a search engine or registry chosen by your software provider. Rather than use this key, it's best to find the search engine that you prefer and bookmark it instead or designate it as your starting place. The PC shortcut for the search function is Ctrl + E.

• Clicking on the *history* key will open the URL history folder in a pane or frame on the left side of your screen, allowing you to see the addresses of Web sites you've viewed on a given date. This is a means to find Web sites you neglected to bookmark, but want to revisit. Parents also find this an effective way to monitor children's use of the Internet. The PC shortcut is Ctrl + H. Your URL history is automatically deleted after a certain number of days, which you can set by using the "tools" pull-down menu on your browser. Select "internet options" and the "general" tab. Use the up and down arrows to designate how many days you want your URL history retained. Here, you can also empty your history folder and release hard drive space by clicking on "clear history."

• The *mail* button on the toolbar opens your browser's mail and news reader programs. (Microsoft Explorer's is Outlook Express.) You can use your browser's mail program or instruct it to launch a separate program, such as Eudora or Hotmail. This will save you the time of having to exit Explorer and open another program. This can be done using the "tools" pull-down menu on your browser. Select "internet options" and the "programs" tab. Click on the right arrow for e-mail and select the program you prefer.

• The *print* key will activate your printer. This option will print the entire contents of a Web page, graphics and all. As a Web page is not bound by the dimensions of your screen, this can wind up being labor-intensive for the average printer. If you're really after text and don't need to view the graphics, save your ink and use your mouse to highlight only the content you want. Then, move it to a word processing document using the "copy" and "paste" functions from the "file" pull-down menu.[16] This allows you to reformat the information to save ink and paper. In addition, some Web sites offer a "printer friendly" or "text only" link, which displays the page without additional graphics and allows faster printing. If that option is not readily apparent, use the "find" function of the "edit" pull-down menu, then type "text" in the dialog box. Click the "find next" button to see if the text only option link is available somewhere on the site.

• In Internet Explorer, the *translate* key opens the Web site for Alta Vista's Babelfish, which allows the user to translate text and Web sites into several languages. Although translation resources on the Web continue to improve, most have considerable limitations. Babelfish, for example, does not allow the translation of English-language sites to languages requiring distinctive characters (e.g., Korean or Chinese) without the proper support software. For example, if you opt to translate a page from English to Korean, you may end up with a screen full of unreadable symbols. In your browser, use the "encoding" function of the "view" pull-down menu, then click "more" to find the Korean option. Click that and you may get a message telling you to download the text display support software for that language. Even then, further effort is required, as the site's literal translations do not always yield intelligible results. Babelfish does not translate the advertising banners on a Web page.

• The address bar in your browser displays the URL of the Web site you're currently viewing. If you click on the arrow at the right hand side or press the F4 shortcut key, a list of recently viewed sites appears below. However, a more reliable way to see where you've been is to use the history button, or click on the small arrow situated between the back and forward buttons.

How to get the Most out of Your Browser

The default settings on your browser are not configured for maximum effectiveness, but rather seem designed to cram the greatest number of icons and brand names onto the computer screen. There are a number of ways you can make your browser work more efficiently. At the very least, learning to use the shortcut keys shaves seconds off the time it takes to navigate the mouse. Each of the suggestions that follow will save you time and improve your viewing.

• To load pages faster, turn off the graphics. If a page is taking too long to load, you can click on the *stop* key or press the ESC key. Sometimes this causes the text to appear quickly. If a graphic fails to download completely, place your cursor where the image was to appear. Right click your mouse and select "show picture" from the menu. You can also set your browser to display text only for all or part of an Internet session. To do that, use the "tools" pull-down menu on your browser and click on Internet options. Then select the

---

[16]Another option is to highlight the material, select "file" and "print" from your browser toolbar. Then under print range, choose "selection," then "OK."

"advanced" tab and scroll to "multimedia." There, you'll find an option for "show pictures." Click on it so the check mark disappears, then reload the page you're viewing. It should load quicker this time. An icon will still appear on Web sites where a graphic lurks. To view a graphic, right-click the mouse and select "show picture," as described above.

•   Get rid of advertisements that clutter the screen and distract you from your work. Pages will load faster if you block banner ads, animated images and music. One company, InterMute, offers an ad-blocking program free for home use, which can be downloaded at www.adsubtract.com. This program offers a further advantage to those concerned with privacy: it blocks cookies, which organizations use to track your Web use. InterMute also offers more sophisticated, paid versions of the software. Such programs help eliminate one of the most annoying innovations of late, pop-up and pop-under ads, which appear on top of your browser screen or as minimized windows as you're working online. Additionally, some ISPs such as EarthLink now offer free programs to block pop-up ads as a service to subscribers, and to lure customers away from the competition.[17]

•   Increase your cache. Your computer creates a temporary storage of pages you view on the WWW. That way, your browser doesn't have to download them anew each time but rather, reloads them from storage. Allowing the computer more space for that helps pages load faster. Use the "tools" menu on your browser, then select "Internet options." Under the "general" tab, you'll see a box for "Temporary Internet Files." Click on the button marked "settings." Then, under "amount of disk space to use," click the arrow with your mouse and slide it to the right, 30mb or higher. Be sure you also set your computer to check for newer versions of stored pages by clicking on the "automatic" option.

•   To move around a site faster, use shortcuts. The *home* key and *end* key on your keyboard will transport you to the top or bottom of a Web site, respectively. You can also use the *page up* and *page down* keys to move to the end or beginning of a Web document in large increments.

•   Don't wander. If you're looking for specific content on a Web site, don't get distracted by fancy graphics or links that transport you to irrelevant sites. At the site, use the "edit" option on your browser's toolbar, then select "find." Type in a keyword or the name you seek (in lowercase) and click "find next." Note however, that this searches only the open document, not the site's accompanying links. This technique is especially useful when you want to analyze search results efficiently (for elaboration, see chap. 2).

•   To see things more clearly, adjust the type size of many Web sites by using the "view" menu in your browser. Choose "text size" and then select "smallest" to "largest." The default setting for most browsers is "smaller." This is a handy trick, whether you want to make the text larger to reduce eye strain, or the width of a Web site's text exceeds your screen and you want to avoid having

---

[17]See for example, "Pop Go Those Blasted Pop-Up Ads, iVillage Decrees," *New York Times* (29 July 2002), C4; "EarthLink Upgrade Helps Kill Pop-Up Ads," *CNN* (20 August 2002), www.cnn.com

to scroll left and right to read it. However, adjusting the font size often means you won't see the sites exactly as their designers intended.

• Maximize the viewing area. If you're viewing Web sites on a small monitor (e.g., 15"), try hiding your navigation tools to add inches to the viewing area. The quickest way to do that is to press the F11 key on your keyboard to hide the toolbars. Press F11 again and the toolbars will reappear (see Figs. 1.2 and 1.3). If you prefer not to toggle back and forth, but want to continue navigating while the toolbar is hidden, use the right button on your mouse. This will allow you to move backward and forward, to bookmark sites, print, and reload.

• Open a window. To move between two or more sites without having to reload them each time, open a second (or third) browser window. To do this, use your browser's "file" pulldown menu, select "new" and "window." A new window will open (displaying the same page you're currently viewing), which you can then set to any other page you want. The bottom of your computer screen indicates your active windows; to open one, simply click on it to maximize the site.

• Change your home page. Most computer users find their starting page is automatically set as the one belonging to your ISP or software provider, but you can easily change that. It's better to identify the site you use most and make that your starting point, a search engine for example. Use the "tools" pull-down menu from your browser and select "Internet options." Then under the "general" tab, type in the URL of the Web site you wish to see when you launch your browser in "home page" (see Fig. 1.4).

FIG. 1.2.   Before maximizing the browser screen.

FIG. 1.3.   After maximizing the browser screen.

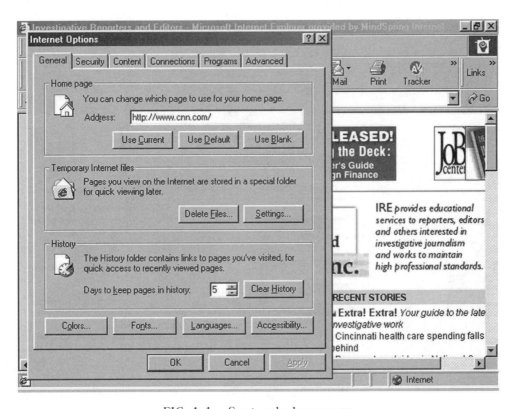

FIG. 1.4.   Setting the home page.

• Play favorites. Take advantage of one of the several ways you can "book-mark" sites you want to return to, without having to type in the URL each time. When you're viewing the page you want to mark, choose "favorites" on your browser menu, then select "add to favorites" from the pull-down menu. You'll be prompted to specify a folder, which you can label (search engines, for example) or the page can stand alone in your list of favorites (see Fig. 1.5). At the same prompt, you can also check the box that reads "make this page available offline." Doing that means you can read the page even when you're not connected to the Internet, although you will not see updated versions without connecting. If you also want to view its links, click on the "customize" button just to the right. Choose "yes" if you want to save the pages to which your favorite Web site is linked. But then specify that the computer save only those links one to two pages deep. This is great for users who pay an hourly rate to their ISPs for time spent online. You should be conservative though, as saving a site or sites offline uses space on your computer's hard drive; links take up still more space. Another way to bookmark pages is to click on the page icon to the left of the address bar, then drag it to the right and drop it in the "links" area in the Explorer toolbar. The next time you're online, click on the *links* button (or the arrow just to its right), then click on the bookmarked site you want to view.

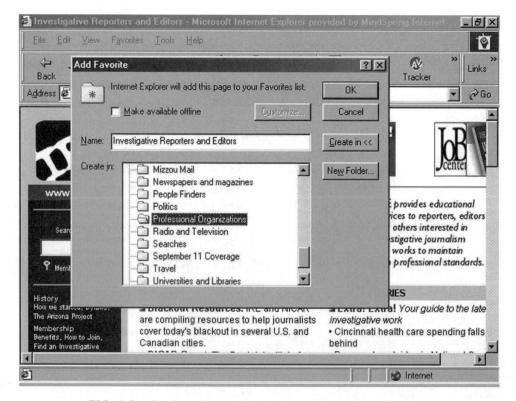

FIG. 1.5.   Bookmarking or designating a "favorite" Web site.

When the Honeymoon's Over

Research tells us that "newbies," those in the early stages of Internet experience, go through a brief period of euphoria, wandering about on the Internet with reckless abandon. Finally, they identify a few choice sites and settle into a routine. They avoid "uncharted territory" and stick with proven sites, returning again and again via bookmarks. In fact, a recent study suggested online sessions had decreased from 90 minutes to 83 minutes between March 2000 and March 2001— not because the users had become more proficient, but because the Web had gone from a "toy box to a toolbox."[18]

True, sites come and go and users naturally grow frustrated with error messages. The casual Web surfer finds the oddball pages harder to find. Or it might be that the user thinks he has come to understand all the Internet has to offer. As complacency sets in, users may find it easier to take advantage of many ISPs' offers to customize a start page, compiling content geared to a user's particular interests. After all, it's so much easier to have information served to you than having to hunt and gather for yourself. But complacency has no place online—it defies the changing nature of the technology and deprives the user of the Web's real potential. New sites are launched everyday; developments in software further enhance the Web experience. Many sites now offer streaming video, for example. Other sites allow users to download and view movies, read books or listen to the radio. If you do choose to let your ISP customize your start page, at least vary the categories of information you'll be served, and don't expect it to search the entire contents of the WWW for the information you request. Rather, what's displayed is only a small portion of what's available.

Just when you reach a certain comfort level navigating the Internet, the technology will progress still further and you'll fall behind. Don't be discouraged. As I've already stated, this book is intended to help you get the most out of your time online, regardless of the equipment you're using. There will always be someone else with the newest technology or the latest plug-ins. What's needed are some basic skills, and those can be learned with bare-bones software and hardware. Soon, you'll be in a better position to decide which changes are worth mastering, which accessories are worth having and which are passing fancies.

TIPS FOR SMART SEARCHES

*   ISPs are competitive; search for bargains before you sign a contract because changing will often mean a new e-mail address. Be sure to ask about the availability of technical support, and select a pay structure that matches your style of working online.
*   Neither getting online nor learning how to use the Web should be cost-prohibitive. In addition to searching for competitive bargains from ISPs, take

---

[18]Lisa Guernsey, "As the Web Matures, Fun is Hard to Find," *New York Times* (28 March 2002), D1.

advantage of access and instruction offered by libraries, or computer-proficient friends and colleagues.

• Become familiar with your browser's many shortcuts to navigate sites more quickly.

• To find content quickly on a Web site, look for a link to a "site map," a text-only version of the site's content and link structure. Use your browser's "edit" menu then "find" command, to zero in on specific information.

• Tweak the settings on your browser in order to make it work for you. For example, adjust the screen and text size for easier viewing of sites, increase your cache size for quicker downloading and get rid of advertisements.

• Don't leave it up to your ISP to customize your start page. Instead, choose the starting point that works best with what you want to do online and set that URL at your Internet options menu. A search engine's web site is a good choice for a start page.

• Accept that fact that you will never be ahead of the technology, and that you don't need excessive bells and whistles to enjoy all that the Web has to offer.

When Seconds Count:
Search Engine Strategies

SEEK AND ... YOU MIGHT FIND IT

The complaint I hear most frequently from those trying to navigate the World Wide Web is that their searches yield endless, and too often useless, results. "Why do I get so many results with my search terms, and how can I ever find what I want?" they ask. This frustration seems to characterize many Internet users' early experiences. One user compared looking for information online to going to a library, where the books are scattered all over the floor—without call numbers, categories or librarian to offer guidance.

This chapter provides you with the strategies to quicken your search time and improve your results. Follow these directions and you will find the information you want with a minimum amount of searching and scrolling. In fact, once you get the hang of these techniques, you can forget about scrolling altogether; you're likely to find what you want on the very first screen of search results.

For most searches of the Web, you'll rely on *search engines*. A search engine is simply a means to ask for information on the Web, a system for organizing the data held on the Internet. A search engine can be metaphorically compared to several activities: a miner panning for gold, a clerk searching for a document in a file cabinet, or as one of my students remarked once, like a game of Where's Waldo. In any case, there's a lot more information out there than you will need or want. Trying to locate specific kinds of information online can be an exercise in futility.

The needle-in-a-haystack feeling that so many people experience when they search for online information occurs for a couple of reasons. First, the search engine, or the mechanism being used to find information, is combing through millions of pages and billions of words, hence the bounteous results. Second, users generally fail to take advantage of the techniques that allow them to refine their searches and thus, yield fewer yet more practical results.

The frustration that many Internet users experience is often due to some common misunderstandings. Following are a few things that might be sabotaging your searches:

- *Great Expectations*. Whereas it is true the Internet is a wonderful tool for researchers, like anything, it has its limitations. I would never suggest an individual do all her research seated at the computer; we simply are not at the point where the information on computers can replace that found in traditional library research. Consider that one of the world's leading research institutes, Russia's Moscow State University, holds some eight million items in its library. Yet so far, less than 200,000 of those items have made their way onto the Web (www.msu.ru). And even when documents get posted online, it may be weeks or months before a site is picked up by a search engine's database. Other documents remain part of the *hidden Web*, beyond the grasp of most search engines.[1] Certain material, such as proprietary corporate information, may never be accessible online.[2] A recent study showed that despite the best efforts, search engines reach only a small percentage of sites on the Web. In other words, believing you can find everything and anything online is unrealistic.

- *You say Tomato, I say Tomatoh*. The diversity of cultures represented on the Web is an amazing and wonderful thing. But online searches are easily thwarted if the user fails to take into account the myriad spellings and meanings that accompany that diversity. As a basic example, in the United States, we spell "color" but in the United Kingdom the word is "colour." Searching for one will not find sites that use the other spelling, or for that matter sites containing misspellings. In addition, the same word can have alternate meanings even within a single language. A search effort should take that into account as well. For example, in English, the word "bank" has several definitions having nothing to do with money. In the U.S., the word "flat" can refer to a level surface, a musical note, or a deflated tire; whereas in Britain a "flat" might refer to an apartment. Unless you provide a search engine more exacting terms your results will be numerous, including sites containing all meanings.

- *Uppercase or Lowercase?* Some search engines are *case-sensitive*, that is, they recognize capitalization as part of your search. In those situations, a search in lowercase will typically result in more sites. For example, a keyword search for "Shark" on a case-sensitive search engine will return only those pages where the word shark is capitalized. On the other hand, "shark" will locate both uppercase and lowercase references. Using AltaVista's search engine, "great white" resulted in 134,126 related sites, whereas "Great White" returned 76,375 sites. Searching for a proper name (e.g., John Doe) using capitalization will minimize your results, leaving out any sites where the name is not capitalized.

---

[1]John R. Quain, "The Hidden Internet," *Popular Science* 258:2 (February 2001), 18.
[2]See for example Henry Kautz, et al., "The Hidden Web," *AI Magazine* 18:2 (Summer 1997), 27.

- *Avoiding the Advanced*. When offered a choice, too many users rely on a search engine's simple search, fearing an advanced search is too advanced. In fact, an advanced search is the best way to find information quickly and with few or no commercial intrusions. While the basics of the simple search are covered here, the superiority of the advanced search should be clear by the end of the chapter.

- *Engine vs. Directory*. Some computer users believe that the difference among the various search engines is how fast they work but in fact, the swiftness with which you can retrieve information depends more on your own connection or modem speed than on another's. The most important characteristics that distinguish one search mechanism from another are what it searches, or what is contained in its database, and how it allows the user to search.

The distinction between *search engines* and *search directories* is an important one. A search engine is one that attempts to gather the URLs of all Web sites on the Internet. It does this by sending out a robotic "spider" or "crawler" to scan the Web and return URLs to its database. Software then sorts and indexes it. In other words, it strives to be comprehensive, with the possible exception of John Q. Public's home page. You know the type of site, where the executive-by-day reveals his fondness for the hidden life of fungus. Use a search engine when you're conducting scholarly research, or looking for specific documents on the Web.

Unlike a search engine, a search directory (also called a registry or subject directory) like Yahoo uses humans and "bots" to gather URLs. By comparison, it is a selective directory, because it strives to include the best or most popular sites in its database, requiring subjective judgments. In addition, individuals can submit their personal Web site addresses to the directory, which then provides such URLs among search results.

What difference do these distinctions make, really? It comes down to quantity vs. quality. Search directories boast an impressive number of URLs, but so many belong to businesses selling products or to individuals' Web pages of narrow interest. If scholarly research is your goal, search engines are the better choice of the two. And while directories appear to do some of the legwork by clustering or categorizing results for example, they often deny users the tools to refine searches.

As an example, when you log onto the Go Web site (www.go.com), part of the Walt Disney Internet Group, you'll see a visual smorgasbord: brightly-colored links to news headlines and categories including food and drink, autos, health, finance, careers, and so on. Similarly, Yahoo (www.yahoo.com) and Google's Web directories (http://directory.google.com) offer links to categories such as education, recreation, arts and humanities, business and others (Fig. 2.1). At both sites, the links take you to more lists and for the most part, transmogrify into advertising, rather than the information you sought in the first place. Unless you've got time to kill, skip the registries' distractions altogether and concentrate instead on designing an effective search strategy. This chapter concentrates on helping you do just that.

FIG. 2.1.   Yahoo subject directory.

Search Basics: The Simple Search

AltaVista is a search engine preferred by many reporters and researchers, both for the way it searches and for its reliability. Google is another top choice. Although many of the examples in this chapter use AltaVista, other search engines (that's engine, not directory) do pretty much the same thing. And overall, search engines continue to improve daily. In October 2000, a columnist for *Yahoo Internet Life* raved about Google's search engine[3] (www.google.com), which claims to have over one billion Web sites indexed. "Expect the search engine size barrier to get broken again in the coming months," Danny Sullivan wrote.[4]

To use a search engine, you must first provide it with parameters for your search. At its home page (www.altavista.com), viewers are offered the option of a "simple" search or an "advanced" search. We'll start with the simple one. The AltaVista site offers you a choice of searching for Web pages, audio files, video files, or still images. The dialogue box asks for keywords, which at last count, could be in any one of 25 languages.

On the AltaVista site, type the word "architecture," without quotation marks, in the blank box (see Fig. 2.2). The results number in the millions. At the top of

---

[3]Google maintains, at separate URLs, a Web directory, and a search engine.
[4]Danny Sullivan, "Searchalert," *Yahoo Internet Life* (October 2000), 166.

FIG. 2.2.   AltaVista simple search for "architecture."

the list are distractions in the form of ads or what appear to be related content, but are not. Of particular irritation are ads that appear to be waiting messages: One flashes "Message Alert," but by clicking on it, the user is whisked to a commercial site for an ISP. Ignore those and instead scroll just a bit. You'll see that the first result (at least on this day) is an all-purpose site about architecture, followed by the site for a project that provides support for the Linux operating system (see Fig. 2.3). But what if you're only interested in the architecture of ancient Greece?

Simple searches tend to provide the user with miscellaneous results. Why? Think of going into a department store and asking the salesclerk to show you everything available in the color red. Without being more specific, the clerk will return with all kinds of red items from various departments: men's, women's, and children's clothes, shoes, linens, accessories, mixing bowls, and so forth. In this example, the search engine has done just what it was asked; it has combed through every word of every Web site in its database and returned those sites containing the word "architecture," but without regard to context—because you haven't provided any.

At the Google search engine site (www.google.com), users can perform a simple search using keywords, much like the earlier example. At the Google site, enter in lowercase and without quotation marks the name "hillary rodham clinton," the former first lady and current New York Senator (see Fig. 2.4), and your results

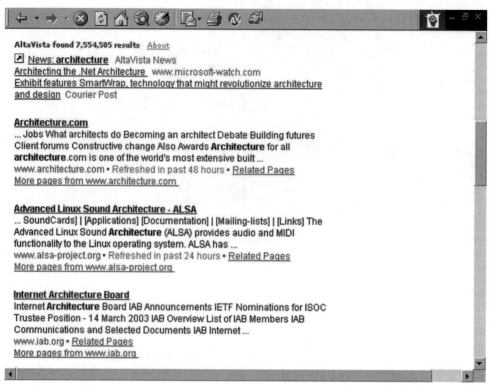

FIG. 2.3.   Results of an AltaVista simple search for "architecture."

number 108,000. The results in this case include sites related to Clinton's Senate race, her tenure as first lady, unauthorized biographies, a now-defunct quarterly newsletter, and a tongue-in-cheek essay about the Senator's sex appeal. Indented entries among the results indicate additional pages within a single site. By default, Google assumes you want pages that include all of your search terms, in other words, pages that cite Clinton using her first, maiden and married name. Such wide-ranging results are typical of simple searches (see Fig. 2.5).

Google's simple search offers users yet another option. Type in your keyword or keywords and click on "I'm Feeling Lucky." This opens a single Web page, based on the search criteria you've specified. The idea here is that you trust the search engine to know what you want. If you've followed along this far, the capriciousness of this option should already be clear. Still, the programmers at Google deserve credit for lending some personality to their search interface. By selecting the "preferences" link, users can specify results be returned in specific languages, including "Hacker," "pig Latin," and even something called "Bork, bork, bork."

Some search engines allow the user to execute a search by entering a question; this is a crude kind of search. If you choose this route, be prepared for similar, unwieldy results you'll get with a simple keyword search. Say you want to find a Web site that has an encyclopedia. For example, type "where do I find en-

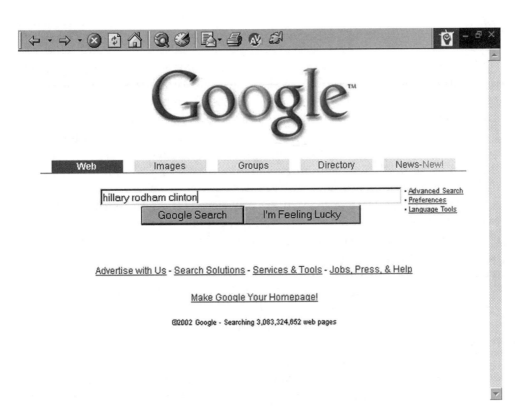

FIG. 2.4. Google simple search for "hillary rodham clinton."

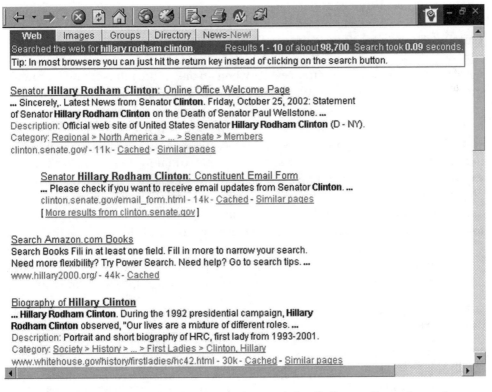

FIG. 2.5. Results of a Google simple search for "hillary rodham clinton."

25

cyclopedias?" at the AltaVista search page, in the dialogue box. This yields more than 100 million sites including, of all things, one for the U.S. House of Representatives. Likewise, typing "how is the electoral college selected?" yields 90 million Web sites, although these results were at least more on target. Still, that's far too many sites to trudge through. Searching with this technique will not work for specific questions, such as "how many televisions are contained in the average home?" That search netted a long list of sites (627 million), mostly those with televisions for sale.

Another popular Web site where users can search via questions is "Ask Jeeves" (www.ask.com), which works to understand semantic meaning and syntax in order to process a search request.[5] Users can pose questions such as "How do I improve my chess game?" and Jeeves will return links to Web sites, or more questions in the form of links, like "Where did chess come from?" or "Where can I buy toys and games online?" Again, the results are sometimes wide-ranging and very often lead the user to advertisers' sites.[6]

One way to improve a simple search is to rethink your keyword or keywords. Rather than typing in your subject, think of related words. You're looking for pages that contain text about your topic, so think of words that are sure to appear on the kind of site you want. For example, if you're searching for documents related to dinosaurs, don't use that alone as your search term. You'll surely get sites about the prehistoric critters, but also some about aging rock stars. Add to your search terms unique words that would appear on the pages you want, such as "cretaceous" or "dimetrodon."

Getting Closer to Your Target: The Advanced Search

A researcher will have far better results when an online search is refined, or made more specific. Returning to the department store analogy, once you articulate to the salesclerk you want to see only women's red low-heeled sandals in size seven, he is sure to return with a much smaller selection and you're more likely to find something that meets your needs. Likewise, most search engines offer ways for users to be more specific in their searches. Unfortunately, too few users take advantage of those options. It takes a little more effort to learn the particular methods, but once you do you shave hours off your search time. By learning a few simple techniques, you can hone in on your target information and avoid having to weed through or be distracted by useless or irrelevant items.

If a search engine offers an "advanced search" option (typically a link from the main, simple search page), use it to refine your pursuit. For example, at the Google advanced search page (www.google.com/advanced_search), we can fine tune that

---

[5]See Jenny Lyn Bader, "Searching for the Search Engines of Meaning," *New York Times* (28 November 1999), 4:4.

[6]Shinan Govani, "Dash It All, What a Bally Nerve!" *Toronto Globe and Mail* (29 February 2000), www.thegolbeandmail.com . The author posed the question to Ask Jeeves, "should I wear the red tie or blue tie?" and was referred to sites for the Cincinnati Reds and two Krzysztof Kieslowski films, "Red" and "Blue." Ask Jeeves' "most abiding value is an inadvertent feature on the site that allows you to see the questions that other people are asking … it's the greatest time-wasting diversion since the invention of thumb-twiddling," the author wrote.

earlier search for information on Hillary Clinton. Perhaps you want information related to her senate campaign, such as announcements or analyses, but nothing to do with the infamous White House intern Monica Lewinsky or the Senate Whitewater committee.

Four options on the Google advanced search page allow you to be very specific. For example, you can indicate what words the returned sites must have ("all the words"); what specific phrases they must contain ("exact phrase"); additional keywords of which the sites must include at least one ("at least one"); and words to exclude from search results ("without").

Figure 2.6 shows a search that uses all those options. I have asked Google to return pages that include all the words: hillary, clinton, senate, and campaign. I have not included her maiden name, "Rodham," because I remember she did not use it in campaign material, and it would limit my results. This way, Google will find sites that include her name either as Clinton or Rodham Clinton. I've also instructed the search engine that the Web sites must include the phrase "New York," and either the year 2000 or "Moynihan" (the last name of the retiring senator for whose seat she ran). The results should not include references to either "Lewinsky" or "whitewater."

Google limits its advanced search to 10 words, or I might consider adding more terms to better target my search. I have gone one step further by asking that the search engine return only those Web sites written in English, another option here.

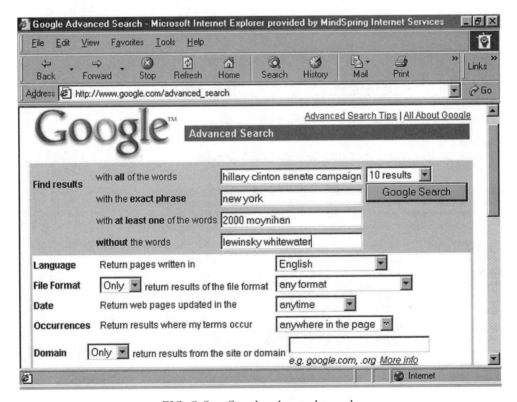

FIG. 2.6.   Google advanced search.

Figure 2.7 shows the results of this search. At the far right of the screen, the number of results are shown, about 28,000. At the top of the results page are sponsored matches (advertisers), in which I'm not interested. Scroll down just a bit and the sites include a series of research organizations and news coverage of Clinton's campaign.

Don't be put off by anything labeled an *advanced search*. That reflects the ability of the search engine, not the level of the user's expertise. I've always gotten the best results by going directly to Altavista's advanced search page (www.altavista.com/sites/search/adv, or link to it from the upper right hand corner of the simple search page). At the top of the advanced search page, you can build a query, much the same as Google's advanced option. But just below that, you can construct your own Boolean-expressed query.

Boolean Expression: The Web's Best Kept Secret

Boolean expression is the real power of the advanced search, and precisely why I prefer to skip the simple search altogether and start here each time. Boolean logic is named for George Boole, a 19th-century British mathematician who merged algebra and logic which, for our purposes, determines the way information on the Internet is searched for and retrieved. Boolean logic allows the user to include *operators* (also called *connectors* or *joiners*) in a search to retrieve fewer

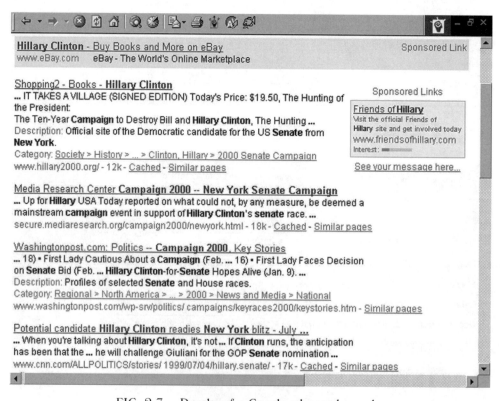

FIG. 2.7.   Results of a Google advanced search.

and more meaningful results. Boolean operators are: "and," "or," "not," and "near." The next section describes what each operator does:

"AND"

Putting AND[7] between words in your search tells the search engine you want it to return links to documents containing both (or all) words together on a page. For example, the names Laurel and Hardy would naturally appear together on some Web sites, since the two were a comedy team. Typing **laurel AND hardy** tells AltaVista you want all documents containing the words laurel and hardy. You may get links to pages about the comic actors Stan Laurel and Oliver Hardy, but by using lowercase letters you'll likely also get pages that make reference to bay leaves and hardy chrysanthemums. I searched this way, and got 27,000 results.

How might you narrow your search, then? Two options are worth trying. First, type your search using uppercase letters for the actors' names, as in Fig. 2.8. By capitalizing the names, you've indicated proper names are what you seek. The search engine seeks Web sites where only the two names appear together, as shown in Fig. 2.9. You could also enclose them in quotation marks, as in "**Laurel and Hardy**". By placing the names between quotation marks, you've instructed the

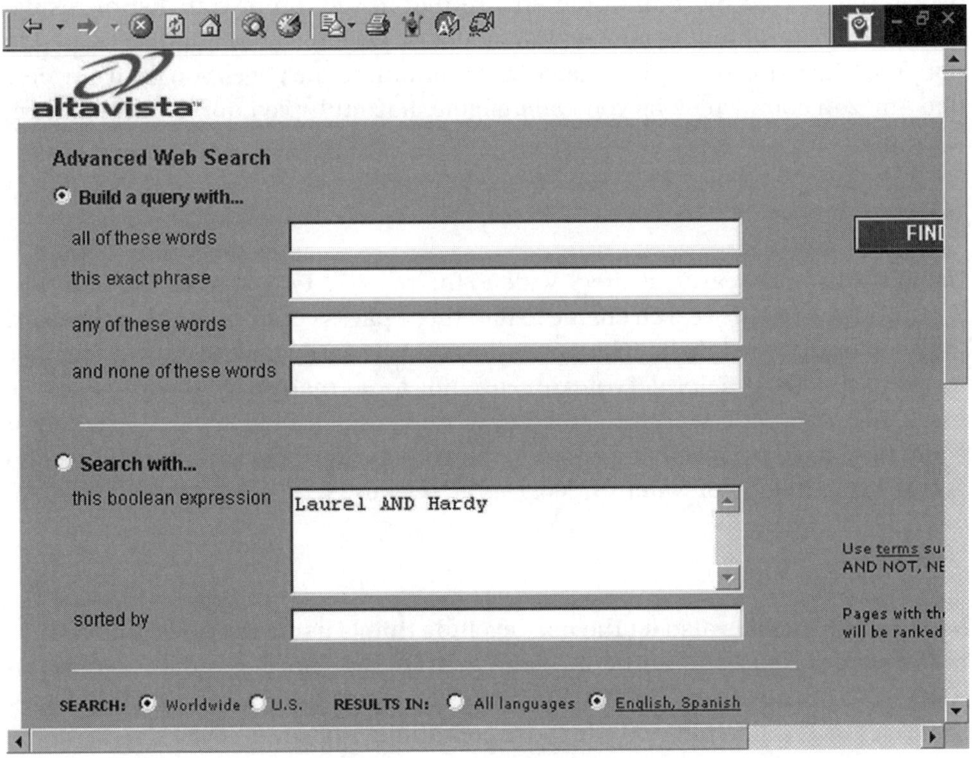

FIG. 2.8.   Boolean search using AND.

---

[7]It's best to capitalize the operators to make clear what is a query and what is meant as instruction to the search engine.

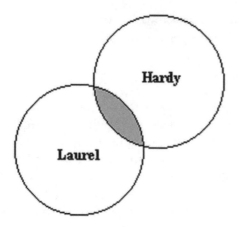

FIG. 2.9.   Detail of a Boolean search using AND.

search engine that the names must appear side by side, joined by "and," just as you've indicated. That search resulted in 6,477 related sites.

You could further minimize your search results by specifying language, a range of dates, or adding keywords that pertain to specific information. A movie title could be used in AltaVista's "sorted by" box to order your results, for example. Searching for "Laurel and Hardy," and including the film title, "Nothing But Trouble" in the "sorted by" box would ensure that at the top of your list of results would be sites containing information about or perhaps merchandise related to that film. Checking the "site collapse" box minimizes the pages you get from sites like Amazon.com, which as you can imagine, has multiple Laurel and Hardy related pages.

"OR"

Using OR in your search strategy widens the results. Type **sharks OR fish** (Fig. 2.10) and you tell the search engine to find those pages containing either the word "sharks" or the word "fish." The words do not necessarily have to appear together on the page. This is helpful if you are searching for as many pages as possible (see Fig. 2.11). This wide search resulted in more than 3 million sites. Alternately, it could be refined by specifying a kind of fish or shark, or perhaps sorting results according to a body of water or geographic region.

"AND NOT"

Most search engines also let the user exclude things using the operator NOT, or in the case of AltaVista "and not." For example, the search results for **Truman AND NOT Roosevelt** on the AltaVista page (see Fig. 2.12) would include pages that refer to Truman but exclude those containing Roosevelt, even if those same pages also contained Truman's name (see Fig. 2.13). A search for Truman AND Roosevelt returned 24,876 sites where the two men are mentioned together. This search returned 215,184 sites where Truman's name appeared exclusively, without Roosevelt's.

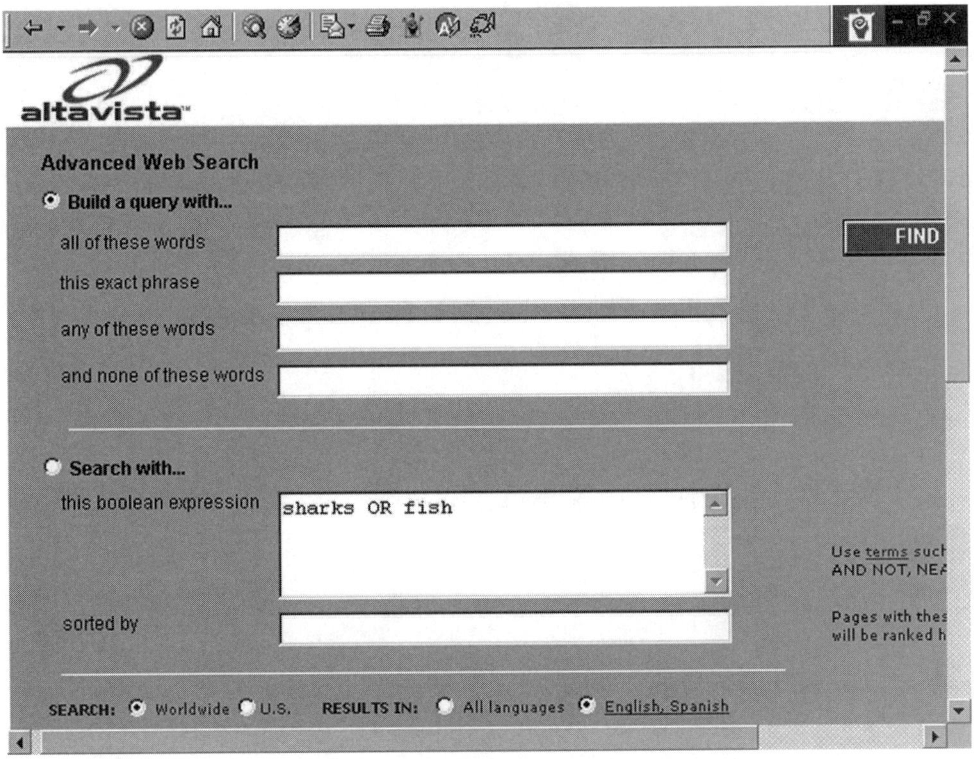

FIG. 2.10.   Boolean search using OR.

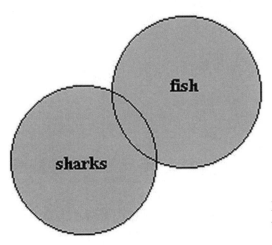

FIG. 2.11.   Detail of a Boolean search using OR.

"NEAR"

You may be able to call up a Web site by a identifying a combination of words and their proximity to one another. Say, for instance, you are looking for a site related to the professional golfer Tiger Woods. His first and last names are likely to appear on a wide range of sites. "Woods" could be on pages related to forests or parks and "tiger" might appear on pages related to wildlife, for instance. To avoid

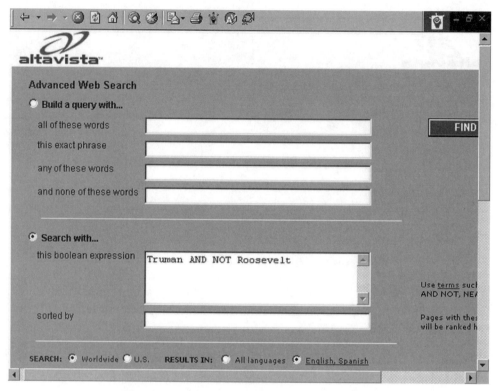

FIG. 2.12.   Boolean search using AND NOT.

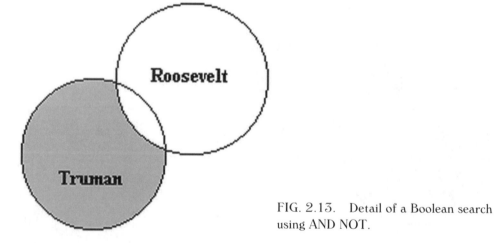

FIG. 2.13.   Detail of a Boolean search using AND NOT.

those kinds of sites, you can use the NEAR function of a search engine. AltaVista allows the user to identify sites where words appear within 10 words of each other. By typing **"Tiger Woods" NEAR golf**, you are telling the search engine to find sites where the name Tiger Woods (remember that by placing it in quotation marks or parentheses and using capitalization, you are asking for an exact match) appears within 10 words of "golf" (see Fig. 2.14).

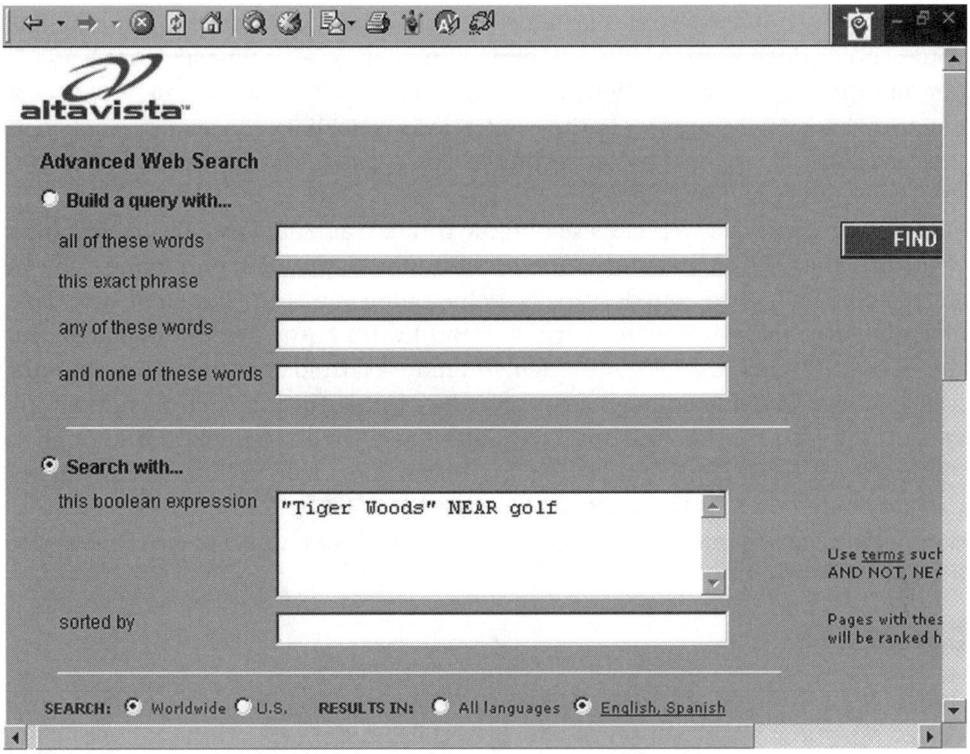

FIG. 2.14.   Boolean search using NEAR.

The NEAR operator is also quite helpful when you're looking for a person. Since proper names on lists are sometimes indexed by last name, use NEAR to find variations on a name. For example, a search phrased as **John NEAR Doe** will find Doe, John, and John Q. Doe.

Although I've recommended you use the advanced search option, some simple searches allow some use of Boolean logic using the plus sign (+) for AND, and the minus sign (-) for AND NOT. However, simple searches do not offer the additional strategies discussed above.

Once you've learned Boolean expression, you can apply it to almost any search engine that offers an advanced option. AltaVista's advanced search has even more ways to target information. Combined with Boolean expression, this is the fastest way to target what you're looking for online. Although the appearance of AltaVista's page has changed several times, the components remain the same. What the search options offer and how to use each one is detailed in the next section.

Language

AltaVista, along with several other search engines, allows you to search for information written in specific languages; there are about 20 from which to choose. Deciding whether to change the default setting, which is "any language" depends on what you are searching for. Is it likely to appear on a Web site originating from another country? If you're researching the rainforest, for instance, you may find some choice documents written in either Spanish or Portuguese. That leads to another question, however. Will you be able to read it? If not, do you have access to a translator? If the answer to these questions is no, better to specify English as your language of choice. That way, your search results will only include Web sites originally composed in English.

However, there are Web sites that allow you to translate foreign text, by either providing the URL or pasting in the text. AltaVista's Babel fish is one such site (http://world.altavista.com or http://babelfish.altavista.com). For single words or short phrases these translators are fine. But I would urge caution in translating the entire contents of a site. Although you may get an idea of the site's contents, none of these translators can be expected the capture the nuances of another language. A journalist, for example, wouldn't trust such a translation enough to quote from it. The example here (Fig. 2.15) was taken from a Canadian students' project posted on a university's site. I pasted the URL into the Babel fish introductory screen and although the translation was a bit clumsy, it gave me a good idea of the site's theme (see Fig. 2.16).

Sorted by

Journalism students are often taught to write news stories in a style known as *inverted pyramid*, which simply means providing readers with the most important

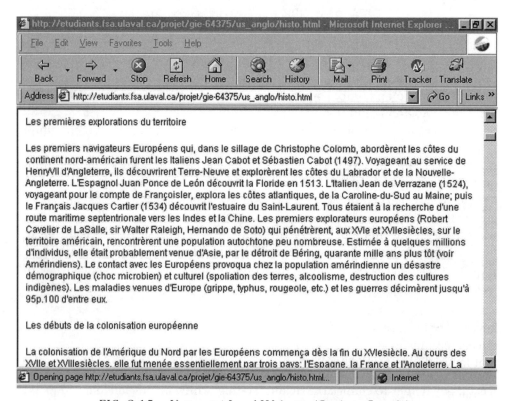

FIG. 2.15.   Université Laval Web site (Quebec, Canada).

FIG. 2.16.   Université Laval Web site, translated into English.

information about a story in its first paragraph and finishing with the least important information. Ranking your search results using the "sort by" option is a bit like this; it asks that the most "important" information, or sites you've distinguished as high priority, be returned at the top of your search results screen. Some search engines automatically rank, or prioritize, the results of a search in terms of relevance. That is, the more often your keyword occurs on a page, the higher the ranking. The engine recognizes that as a "good match."

However, as Tim Berners-Lee, the inventor of the World Wide Web, writes, search engines can be "remarkably worthless in that they have no way to evaluate document quality."[8] That kind of traditional ranking, in other words, tells you little about a document and is not always reflective of your priorities. For example, say you are researching an anthropological topic and you use the keyword "civilization" (although if you have followed this far in the chapter, you may be able to construct a more efficient search). The first page returned in your search may be a college professor's syllabus for a course in Ancient Civilization. It matches your keyword to be sure, but it is not the item for which you're looking. Further down the list, coming in at number 500, is a real gem. Few users would bother to scroll that far down the list, having given up long before. There is a better way.

---

[8]Tim Berners-Lee, *Weaving the Web: The Original Design and Ultimate Destiny of the World Wide Web by its Inventor,* (New York: HarperCollins Publishers, 1999), 177.

One of the reasons I like AltaVista is that it gives the user control over ranking, by allowing you to instruct the search engine in your priorities rather than leaving the computer to guess them. On the search page, for example, type between quotation marks "Harry S Truman" in the Boolean expression dialogue box. Then in the smaller ranking box ("sorted by") below that, type "foreign policy" as shown in Fig. 2.17. This tells the search engine you want all pages containing references to Harry S. Truman, and that links to pages referring to foreign policy should appear at the top of the results list. In other words, you are asking for a wide range of information by asking for Truman-related sites, but you minimize the amount of scrolling you will have to do by emphasizing or prioritizing those pages dealing with foreign policy. The kinds of sites you seek should appear on the first or second screen of results (see Fig. 2.18), just after the sponsored sites.

Date

AltaVista also allows you to narrow your search by specifying a time frame or range of dates. If you're only concerned with current information or know the information was posted on the Web recently, this information helps you to minimize your search results. Note that this indicates the date the information was posted online or updated in any way, and that may differ from a publication date. An article that appeared in the *New York Times* on December 10, 1998 may not have been posted until December 20. You'll want to be sure your range leaves

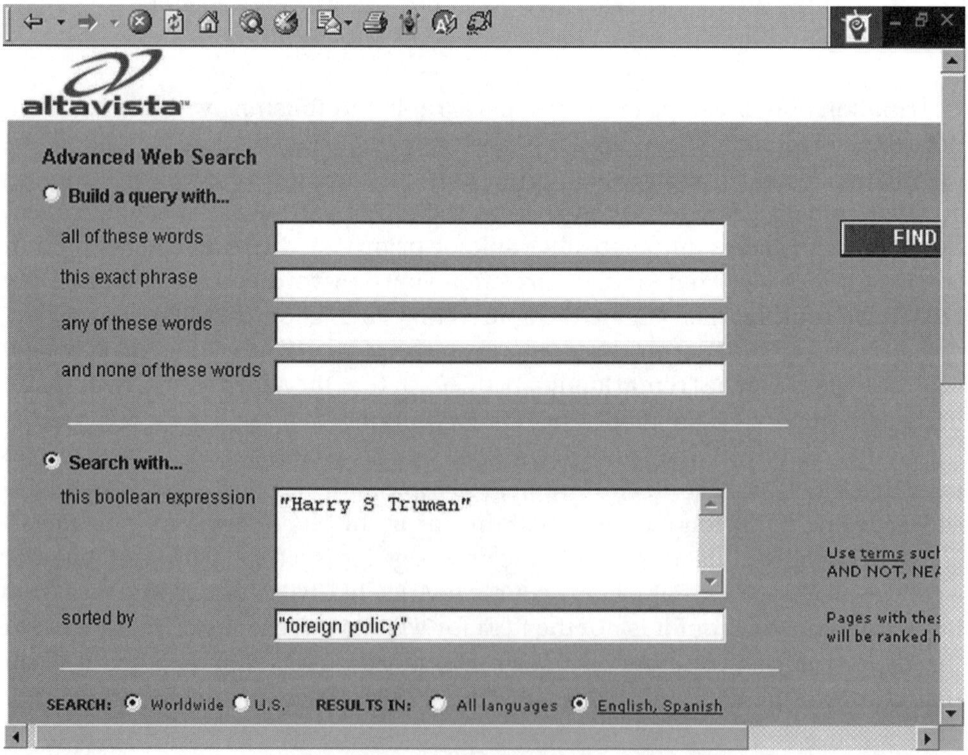

FIG. 2.17. Boolean search using "sorted by."

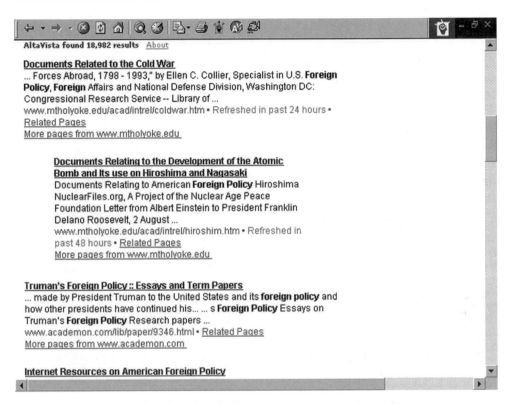

FIG. 2.18.   Results of a Boolean search using "sorted by."

room on either side—for instance, you might want to specify November 1, 1998 to February 1, 1998. Again, remember that the date range applies to when the page was placed on the Web, not necessarily the date a document was written. Thus, if you're doing historical research, you would not use the date range to find a document written in, say, 1776. Rather, you might use 1776 as a search term.

AltaVista's time frame option lets you expand or contract your search by the following time frames: one year, eight months, four months, one month, two weeks, or one week. If you do not fill in this information, the search engine will assume you want it to return all documents matching your search terms, regardless of when they were posted. Using the "anytime" default increases the number of pages your search will return.

Location

Another convenient feature of AltaVista's advanced search page is the option to specify or exclude sites within certain domains, originating from certain geographic regions, or hosts. A knowledge of domain names and what each denotes is an important way to master online searching; this particular technique is detailed in chapter 3.

Display

AltaVista lets you choose how many results you want to see displayed per screen. Clicking on the pull-down menu gives you a choice of either 10, 20, 30, 40, or 50 results. Whichever you choose, search results include links to sites, descriptions and URLs. In a simple search, no more than 200 total results will be displayed, even if the number of sites found by your search exceeds that. In an advanced search, you should be able to see them all, provided the system is not overly busy. The expectation is that ordinary users won't exceed more than 200 results before finding something of use, refining a search, or giving up and moving on to something else.

There is a default option here called "site collapse" and I encourage you to leave that box checked. Why? Because it limits the number of times a host or site appears on your results page. In other words, a search for "charles dickens" is sure to turn up multiple pages on a single bookstore's site; one link per book title. To avoid that and see more sites from a greater range of bookstores or other sites related to Dickens, check the "site collapse" box. When the site collapse is turned off (unchecked), you may be able to tunnel deeper into a Web site and see more pages, but ultimately, fewer hosts.

Now let's consider other ways to refine a search, save the user time scrolling and reduce the results.

Nesting the Commands

You can really see the mathematical properties of a Boolean search when you "nest" or structure the commands with parentheses or quotation marks. For example typing **(Roosevelt OR Truman) AND Eisenhower** at the AltaVista advanced search page, as shown in Fig. 2.19, instructs the search engine to first perform a search for the items grouped in parentheses and then finish by searching for the remaining item or items (you may experience deja vu about now, if your education included any algebra classes). Thus, the search engine first singles out those pages containing references to either Roosevelt or Truman. Then among those sites, the engine chooses the ones that also contain the name Eisenhower (see Fig. 2.20). In other words, each site will refer to Roosevelt and Eisenhower, or to Truman and Eisenhower. Among those results will also be pages where all three names intersect.

Ironically, some Web developers discourage their clients from offering Boolean capabilities on their sites. Why? Because some research has shown that few people know how to effectively use the techniques. Furthermore, these nay-sayers insist that mastering Boolean requires knowledge of debugging in order to master "query reformulation." One such consultant suggested Web developers intimidate users by calling Boolean searches "Advanced."[9] This is nonsense; Boolean

---

[9]Jakob Nielsen, Alertbox for July 15, 1997, http://www.useit.com.alertbox. Nielsen writes, "It is important to use an intimidating name like 'advanced search' to scare off novice users from getting into the page and hurting themselves. Search is one of the few cases where I do recommend shaping the user's behavior by intimidation."

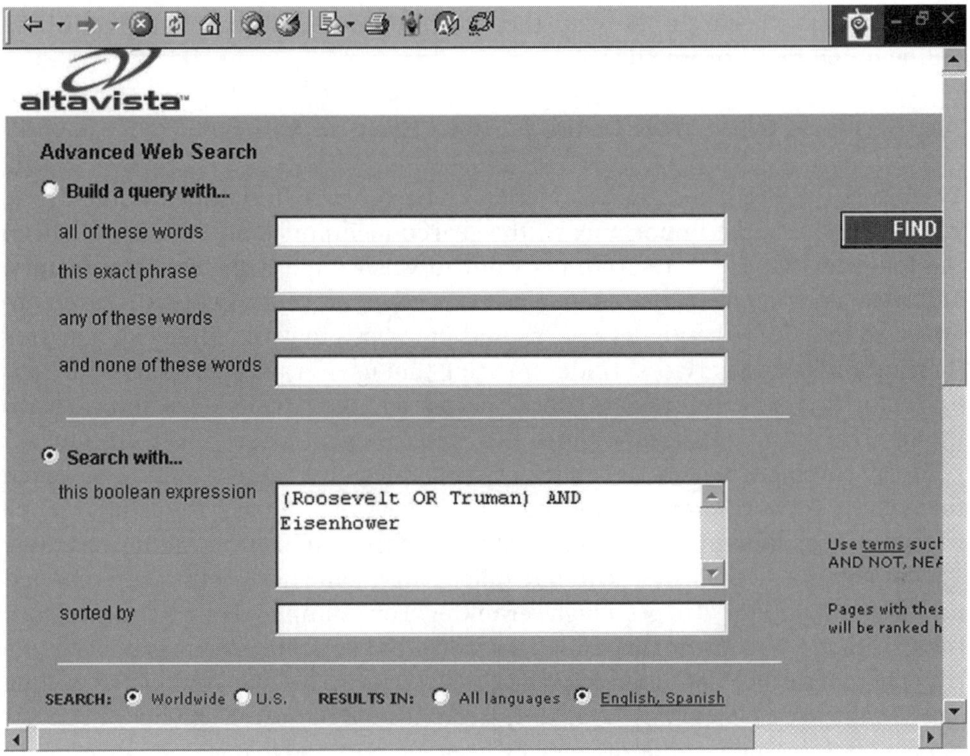

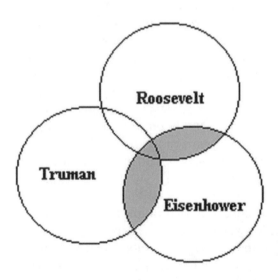

FIG. 2.19. Nesting commands in a Boolean search.

FIG. 2.20. Detail of a Boolean search using nested commands.

logic is not difficult to learn. More likely, the real reason developers discourage Boolean is because it serves the user, not the creator of the site or its advertisers. Constructing searches using Boolean logic lessens the chances of getting lost in wasteful information or advertising links and minimizes the time one spends wandering about. Calling them advanced searches is misleading. Think of it instead as a "smart search," as using these techniques results in making your time online much more productive.

As the World Wide Web Turns, How to Stay on Course

The bigger the Web gets, the more difficult it becomes to find things stored there, which reinforces the importance of the search techniques outlined here and in the following chapters. Users don't want to waste time with unwieldy results. Likewise, as content increases and users become more savvy about search engines, so too, do Web site developers find new ways to gain online exposure for their products and services. Understanding that users rarely scroll past the first screen or two of search results, developers may take advantage of several techniques to manipulate search engines and directories, in order to get top billing.

Most search engines identify sites by their titles and content, and then match them to the keywords you've provided. If those keywords appear frequently on one page and less often on another, the first page receives a higher ranking and thus, appears higher on the list of search results. Thus, some developers have resorted to "keyword stuffing"[10] to get a higher ranking. For example, the developer of ABC Landscaping's Web site might embed the word "house" multiple times on its home page, so that a search of "houses for sale" also picks up his site. Another technique calls for the use of "metatags," words that can be read by search engines but do not appear on the version of the site seen by users. In addition to metatags, developers might place "invisible" keywords on sites, by masking them in a color that is the same as the color of the page, according to a *New Yorker* article.[11] Some of the most commonly used metatags are "free," "shareware," "windows," and "adult." A search using any of those keywords will likely turn up many unwanted sites.

Even search engines that rely on link structure to produce results can be manipulated. Take for example the "I'm Feeling Lucky" option on Google's search page. When you enter a keyword and click you're led to the highest ranked or most popular page for that search. The more that other Web sites link to a particular page, the higher its ranking. In other words, popularity confers a certain value. Although link structure recognition has emerged as one of the best ways a search engine responds to a query, a clever individual could influence it by setting up multiple pages with links to each other, thus forcing his way into the rankings.

Still another way for Web site owners to gain a high ranking among search results is to create bridge pages. A single site can have multiple bridge or doorway pages, each emphasizing a different keyword—and each displacing more relevant pages that might otherwise appear in your search results. When users link to a bridge page, they are transported to the site owner's main page, which is usually a detour from the users' original search.[12]

---

[10]Robert Berkman, "Internet Searching is Not Always What It Seems," *Chronicle of Higher Education* (28 July 2000), B9.

[11]Michael Specter, "Search and Deploy: The Race to Build a Better Search Engine," *New Yorker* (29 May 2000), 91.

[12]Berkman, "Internet Searching is Not Always What It Seems," *Chronicle of Higher Education* (28 July 2000), B9.

Too, search engines are businesses that rely on profit to make their services available. As such, some search engines and directories, such as GoTo (www.goto.com), routinely accept payment from site owners for higher placement.[13] A developer might bid on a certain keyword—"pizza," for example. If no one bids a higher amount, that developer's site or sites will appear at the top of the list when a user searches for pizza on that search engine or directory. Then, each time a user clicks on that site's link, the developer pays the agreed amount to the search engine or directory. It's a nifty business arrangement, but one that tends to clog search result pages with sales pitches, and routinely sends searches off course. Similarly, a search on AltaVista will return two or three links to advertisers at the top of the page, and still more at the bottom. Although the links are designated "products and services," they look enough like the genuine results to mislead users. It's an unfortunate practice that is likely to dampen enthusiasm among users.

Most reputable search engines and directories frown on the machinations described here. But as quickly as they can identify and ban violators, site owners find new ways to fool them. What can you do about it? Try to maintain a measure of control over your searches by using the techniques available to target and prioritize your results. When you get a page full of results that seem off-target, open one more of the sites to gain clues and refine your search. In your browser, use the "edit" pull-down menu, then "find" to locate your keywords or phrases on a page that seems incompatible with your search. Consider context and placement, and fine-tune your search accordingly. You can also look at the page's source code (HTML, or hypertext mark-up language), by using the "view" pull-down menu. Click on "source" and look over the programming code. By using the "search" pull-down menu, you may find your keywords. How do they appear; were you duped by hidden text?

Try Something New

Once you've found a search engine you like, identified its particular quirks and optimized your search techniques, it's tempting to stick with it, if only for the sake of time. But search capabilities represent one of the fastest-growing features of the Web; programmers are frantically creating what they hope will be the next best thing. To wit, two sites are currently vying to be Google's successor, WiseNut (www.wisenut.com) and Teoma (www.teoma.com); the latter site shows great potential. Another contender is AlltheWeb (www.alltheweb.com), which recently added several finding aids to its advanced search.

Keeping up with the competition, understanding how the engines compare, is critical to successful Web searching. Thankfully, there are a number of sites that can help you do the work. The best by far is Danny Sullivan's Search Engine Watch (www.searchenginewatch.com), which provides tips for searching the Web, creating effective search engines, information about the industry and cri-

---

[13]Specter, "Search and Deploy: The Race to Build a Better Search Engine.

tiques of specific engines and directories. Another site, Search Engine Show-down (www.notess.com/search) publishes search engine reviews. Research Buzz (www.researchbuzz.com/news/index.html) was created to provide resources for online researchers, and provides information on new search sites and online databases. Each of these sites publishes a newsletter that can be delivered to you via e-mail. Certainly, another way to stay current in search engine development is by skimming the latest editions of Internet-related periodicals such as *Yahoo Internet Life* and *Wired*.

TIPS FOR SMART SEARCHES

- Know the differences between search engines and search registries or subject directories, to determine which is more likely to yield the information you seek. Engines catalog web pages; use them when you're looking for specific documents. Registries catalog sites; use them if you're looking for a range of the best or most popular sites on a given topic or general category. Scholars often favor search engines for their research.
- Simple searches often produce unwieldy results, as do sites that allow users to type in questions. Instead, look for an engine that offers advanced options to narrow and refine your search; AltaVista, Google, and Teoma are three good search engines.
- Learn Boolean logic and apply it to advanced searches.
- Type your search in lowercase to get more results.
- Use your subject as a keyword to search, but also unique words related to your subject that are likely to appear on the sites you seek.
- Look over the results of a failed search for clues to refine it, by opening a site and using the "find" menu to locate your search terms, or by viewing a site's source code. Checking over the source code helps uncover keyword stuffing or metatags that might be used to (mis)lead you to a particular site. Avoid searches that use the most common metatags, such "free," "shareware," or "windows."
- Because search software evolves quickly, keep up with developments in new technologies and new search engine sites by reading reviews online or in print.
- Consider putting a quick link to a search engine by dragging and dropping the URL to your browser's toolbar. Some engines offer a "make a shortcut" or "add a toolbar" option at their sites. Instead, you might want to make a search engine your start page. To do that, use the "tools" pull-down menu in your browser and select "Internet options." Then, at the home page or start page option, type the URL for your favorite search engine site and click "ok."
- Opening a second or third browser window allows you to perform multiple searches simultaneously.

3

Skipping the Middleman: Alternate Ways to Find Information

When a "traditional" search fails to turn up the documents you need, there are plenty of other ways to get at the information you want. Knowing where to search for information before resorting to a search engine is an important strategy to efficient online research. This is particularly true because a search engine may take weeks or months to locate online information and return URLs to its database.

To anticipate where information might be held requires a familiarity with domain names, described later in this chapter. In addition, syntax searches allow you to pinpoint sites by host organizations or by the pages that link to it. Thinking ahead allows you to "skip the middleman," to pass up the search engine altogether and go straight to the sites that hold the information you want.

LOCATION, LOCATION, LOCATION: SEARCH BY DOMAIN

It's said that location means everything in real estate and there's some truth to that on the Web, too. Location, better known as a Web address or URL, provides one way for researchers to find information online.

Before a site can be made available on the Internet, it must be assigned a URL or Web address. The organization responsible for overseeing the Internet address system is the Internet Corporation for Assigned Names and Numbers, known as *Icann*, established by the U.S. Commerce Department. Applicants must supply contact and technical information to a registrar; a list of Icann-accredited registration services can be found at www.internic.net/regist.html.

As the Internet gained in popularity, addresses were relatively inexpensive to purchase, some just $10 per year. That led speculators to grab up URLs that might eventually be worth more than the initial fee. Some traded on misspellings of celebrity names or entities to divert Internet users from their intended target and to advertising or pornography.[1] One vivid example is www.whitehouse.com, the URL for a pornographic site that many mistake for the official White House site, which is www.whitehouse.gov. Still another pornographic site raised eyebrows when it took over the domain of a children's financial site.[2] *Cybersquatting,* as this practice came to be called, made some people rich[3] but landed many more in court. Nintendo[©], for example, filed and won a mass domain name lawsuit against 22 defendants in October 2000 under the Anti-Cybersquatting Consumer Protection Act to recover 49 domain names, including pokemon-trader.com.[4] By March 2001, there were 700 federal suits filed over Web domain names,[5] and in September 2001, the World Intellectual Property Organization reported 259 ".info" domain names challenged.[6]

Sparring over Web addresses usually involves copyright infringement and illustrates an important point about searching for information online. Because most Web site creators want their sites to be found they try to make their URLs fairly obvious and easy to remember. Keep in mind the protocol of a Web address: most begin with "www" for World Wide Web, followed by a period ("dot"), a noun, another period, and an extension or suffix. For example, the online shopping site, Amazon, is found at www.amazon.com; Microsoft resides at www.microsoft.com. It's not always so easy, but being aware of the conventions of URLs provides one way to find sites when you lack the actual Web address to get there.

Every Web address or URL has a *domain* name embedded in it, to identify the organization responsible for the Web site and the type of site it is. Top-level domains are the extensions or suffixes on a Web address; the most recognized domain is ".com," as in http://www.microsoft.com, indicating this is a commercial site originating in the U.S. Again, once you know the conventions of a Web address and what each domain represents, it becomes easier to surmise what a URL might be and direct your browser to the site, skipping the search engine and saving time.

Following is a list of top-level domain names for sites originating in the U.S., and what types of sites they denote.

---

[1]Paul Bond, " 'Cyberscammer' Sites Crashed," *Hollywood Reporter* (2 October 2001), 8. A U.S. court shut down 5,500 URLs registered by John Zuccarini, a Pennsylvania resident accused of exploiting Internet users' inexperience or poor typing and spelling skills, to "trap them in a web of online advertising." Zuccarini had already been forced to relinquish some 200 domain names considered to be trademark infringements.

[2]Susan Stellin, "Pornography Takes Over Financial Site for Children," *New York Times* (26 October 2001), C5.

[3]"Domain Name Growth Slows Considerably," *CNN* (25 January 2002), www.cnn.com . According to this report, speculators resold the "business.com" domain for $7.5 million in late 1999, and "loans.com" for $3 million in January 2000.

[4]"Nintendo Wins US$560,000 in Mass Domain Name Lawsuit in U.S.," *AsiaPulse News* (14 November 2001), 732.

[5]Darryl Van Duch, "Cybersquatter Litigation Boom: Statute Prompts 700 Federal Suits Over Web Domain Names," *Los Angeles Times* (8 March 2001), C2. See also Alan J. Hartnick, "Cybersquatting: 'In Rem' Actions Against Domain Names," *New York Law Journal* 226 (30 October 2001), 3.

[6]The WIPO handles trademark disputes between organizations and individuals who have registered dot-info sites, one of the most recent additions to top level domain names. See Joanna Glaser, "Domains Delayed, Not Disputes," *Wired* (21 September 2001), www.wired.com .

.com	commercial sites, the most common domain name on the Internet. This includes most pay sites, and sites generated by private companies, individuals, and groups.
.edu	sites maintained at or by an educational institution including four-year institutions, community colleges, beauty, theological, and distance-learning schools. Ths sites are generated by faculty, staff, and students.
.org	represents mostly not-for-profit organizations but may include commercial sites.
.net	represents networks, this domain was traditionally used by organizations with Internet infrastructures and are not intended for the general public.
.gov	government sites
.mil	military sites, such as www.army.mil

International sites are indicated by country codes. For example, a site originating in Indonesia will contain "indo" in the path of its address; Russian is "ru," and Great Britain is "uk," as in www.guardian.co.uk, the site for London's *Guardian* newspaper. A complete list of country codes appears at the end of this book, in Appendix B. Country codes are not managed by Icann, but rather, by the governments of the countries represented. Rules vary, but in most cases country codes are reserved for citizens of that specific country. In February 2002, a Washington-based company, NeuStar, offered registration to Web site creators, for the United States' country code, represented by ".us," as in www.xyzcorporation.us. Some state governments have opted for this domain over .gov, as in www.state.va.us, the home page for the Commonwealth of Virginia. In addition, the U.S. House of Representatives approved the "Dot-Kids Implementation and Efficiency Act of 2002," which would mandate the creation of a .kids extension with the .us Internet domain.[7]

In late 2001, Icann introduced seven new domains in response to a high demand for .com addresses and to increase the pool of available names. But at approximately the same time, numerous .com addresses were relinquished because many dot-com businesses had failed. We're likely to see some of these new top-level domains in the coming years, particularly the .biz extension. But now that the dot-com frenzy has waned, most Web addresses include the original extensions, as detailed earlier. Among the new domains listed next, the first four are general domains, and the remaining three are represented by specific sectors:

.biz	business or commercial sites
.info	general use
.name	individuals, as in barbarafriedman.name

---

[7] David McGuire, "House Approves Dot-Kids Internet Domain," *Washington Post* (21 May 2002), www.washingtonpost.com. The Dot-Kids Implementation and Efficiency Act of 2002 is intended to demarcate a safe area online for young children, which would not allow instant messaging features or the posting of hyperlinks to content beyond the .kids.us domain. Washington, D.C.-based NeuStar would be responsible for maintaining the domain.

.pro	professionals, such as certified lawyers, doctors, and accountants
.museum	museums
.coop	co-operative businesses and organizations
.aero	air transportation industry

Once you familiarize yourself with domain names, you can find information without knowing a specific URL. Now you can skip the search engine and exercise an "educated guess" instead. For example, if you seek the Web site of the Department of Energy, a government agency often called by its acronym, DOE, a good (and correct) guess would be www.doe.gov. The University of Texas, an academic institution, would likely have a ".edu" extension, www.utexas.edu, and so on. Knowing domain names also helps you include and exclude certain Web sites from a syntax search, explained in the following section.

An interesting result of the Internet's growth is the introduction of multilingual domain names. Until recently, domain names were registered using only English characters, but now Web site creators can register for domains in any of 350 languages represented by 39 different writing systems including Russian, Chinese, and Tamil.[8] VeriSign, a domain registry, has a complete listing at http://global.networksolutions.com/en_US/name-it/languagelist.jhtml.

You've got the Apple, now Where's the Tree?

At some point, you may find yourself on a page that belongs to the site you seek, and yet is not the main page. Examine the URL (shown in the "address" box of your browser) for the top-level domain, position your cursor after that and delete any text that follows. Press enter or return, and you should find your way to the main page.

Another solution is to work your way backward gradually, by positioning your cursor at the end of the URL in the address bar, then typing CTRL + left arrow (Mac users type command + left arrow). This will move the cursor backward to the next logical break, allowing you to trace the path of a site. For example, a search for conservation projects leads you to a Web site that details the mission statement of something called the New Forests Project. You're intrigued, but want to know more about the organization and the foundation that houses it. There isn't a link offering to return you to its home page nor does the URL give any obvious clues. Put your cursor in the address box at the end of the URL and press the CTRL and left arrow keys simultaneously. Your cursor will move left to the next break. Delete everything after the break and hit return. Repeat the procedure until you reach the "root," or starting page, of the organization.

Syntax Searches

Syntax searches can be used in lieu of or in combination with more traditional searches. Here, you'll still use a search engine's advanced option, but by using

---

[8]"Domain Name Registration in Asian Languages," *New Straits Times* (4 April 2001), 15.

Boolean logic and a syntax search, you really zero in on content, either by context, host or hyperlinks, for example. This requires that you think beyond manifest content and ask questions such as "what words might appear in the title of the page?" or "what words might appear in the URL of the site I am looking for?" This technique can be extremely productive in narrowing your search, or getting at sites that might be overlooked by using other search tactics. Some of these techniques are useful in finding people, as is discussed in chapter 5.

The first group of syntax searches, domain, host, and URL offer ways to search by a computer's name. Following are several examples:

domain: This directive allows you to specify what kinds of sites you want to see, and is a sure way to minimize your results. For example, if you think the information you seek is likely to reside with a not-for-profit agency, then you might specify the ".org" domain in your search. At AltaVista's advanced search site, you can do this with a free-form Boolean search. Type your keywords, then the appropriate Boolean connector and your desired domain. A search might look something like this:

(adoptive parents) AND domain:org

Note that domain and org are separated by a colon, no spaces and no "dot"; that's important. The same kind of Boolean search could be used to exclude certain domains. Typing **(adoptive parents) AND NOT domain:org** will find sites that have the phrase "adoptive parents" among the remaining top-level domains instead: .com, .gov, and .net, for example. Alternately, AltaVista now has a specific option to include or exclude domains, just under the "Sort By" box. At "location," click on "domain" and type in the top-level domain name. If you want to include more than one domain, separate them by a comma; the order you type them will be the order the results appear. Google's Advanced Search also allows you to exclude and include certain domains. At the "domain" prompt, choose "only" (to include only certain domains) or "don't" (to exclude domains) from the pull-down menu, then type in the appropriate domain (see Fig. 3.1). You could also use this technique to find sites maintained on servers in other countries. For sites originating in the United Kingdom, try domain:uk. To use this syntax you must first familiarize yourself with the various domain names in use on the Internet; a list is included in Appendix B.

host: This search will find pages that originate with a particular host organization or computer server. For example, suppose I want to know what use my alma mater, the University of Missouri, is making of the Web. I could begin by searching **host:missouri.edu** at AltaVista's advanced search page. To narrow that search or to find only those sites used in the journalism program, I might try **journalism AND host:missouri.edu** in the free-form Boolean query box (Fig. 3.2).

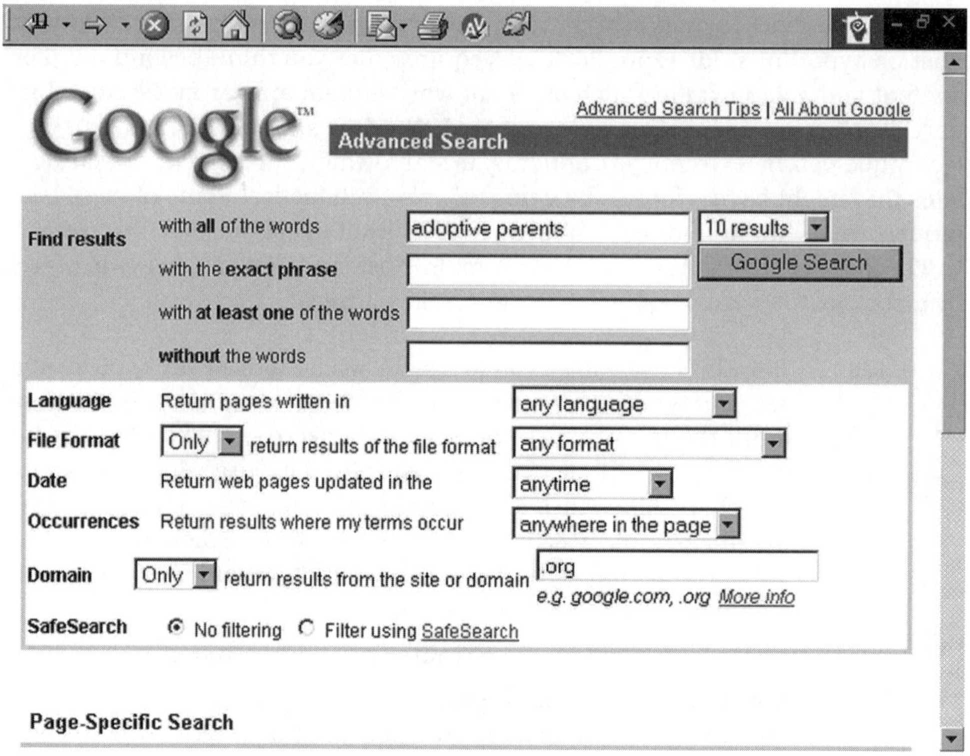

FIG. 3.1.   Google advanced search by domain.

AltaVista offers a host or URL search at the "location" prompt. However, if you type "journalism" as your keyword, and "missouri.edu" in the "only this host or URL" you'll miss many pages. In the latter search, AltaVista looks for sites among the University of Missouri's hosted ones that have the word "journalism" in the address or URL. You'll miss URLs that refer to the J-School, as it is usually called (e.g., www.missouri.edu/jschool), and the agricultural journalism program, denoted in some URLs as "agj." The former search looks for sites hosted by the University, with the word journalism as any part of the sites' contents (Fig. 3.3). To narrow down the search of a host's site even further, I could specify a professor's name, for example **(faculty name) AND host:missouri.edu.**

URL: Another type of syntax search looks for pages or sites that have a particular keyword or phrase embedded in the URL or Web address. For example, in the free-form Boolean query box, use **url:smithsonian** to find sites with the word "smithsonian" in the host name, path, or filename. This search finds the main index for *Smithsonian* magazine, articles from that publication, and an endangered species research project. A search for **url:NBC** will locate Web sites with "NBC" as part of the Web address, including numerous pages hosted by the National Broadcasting Corporation

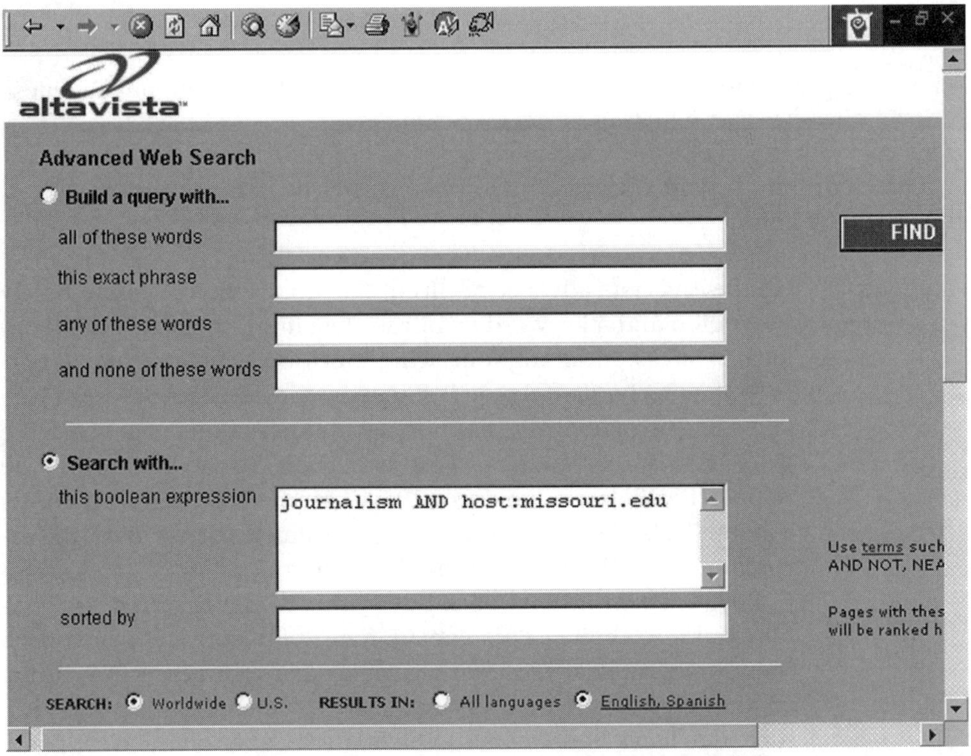

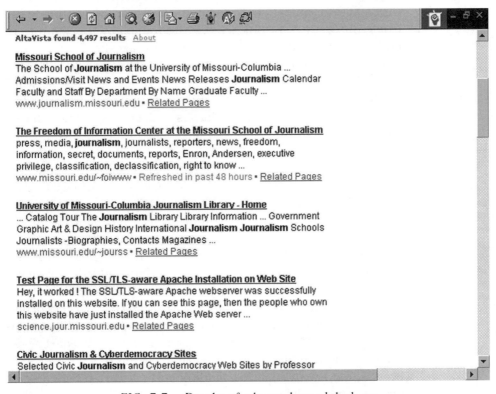

FIG. 3.2. AltaVista advanced search by host.

FIG. 3.3. Results of advanced search by host.

or sites of its affiliates, as well as sites of the National Business Center, which uses the same acronym.

Three additional syntax searches allow you to search using a Web site's text, hypertext, or links:

anchor: On the AltaVista advanced search, "anchor," followed immediately by a colon and a keyword or phrase (again, no spaces in between) locates sites containing your search term(s) in the text of a *hyperlink,* the mechanism that will transport the user to a different Web site. For example, typing **anchor:newspapers** finds pages with the word "newspaper" in the text of a hyperlink. To write a story on the popularity of professional wrestling, a student of mine used this as a means to find fans of the sport, by searching **anchor:wwf** (the acronym for the World Wrestling Federation).

link: Colleagues of mine have used this syntax to identify sites that contain links to theirs. This can be handy for copyright purposes (has someone else reprinted or plagiarized your research?) or for anyone concerned with privacy issues. One colleague was disturbed to learn her site was a link from a "Babes on the Web" page. For an investigative news story, a journalist I know used this technique to find out what groups and individuals were associated with a hate organization, by locating sites promoting links to the hate group's site. Type link:**www.whitehouse.gov**, for example, to find sites that link to the official White House site.

text: This results in fairly wide results but may still be worth a try. Using a text approach, the search engine retrieves pages with your keyword or phrase anywhere in the text, with the exception of the image tag, hyperlink, or URL. Try **text:"charles dickens"** (quotation marks tell the engine to retrieve that exact phrase) for sites containing Dickens' name in the text of any of its pages. It's similar to a keyword search, but concentrates solely on the visible text in the body of a document. To increase your chances of success, try using a thesaurus to find synonyms for the word or words you seek. *Roget's Thesaurus* is online at http://humanities.uchicago.edu/forms_unrest/ ROGET.html. Phrase Finder, a subscription service, does for phrases what Roget's does for words; it is online at http:// phrases.shu.ac.uk/index.html. Google recently added a synonym search to the simple search page. Inserting a tilde mark before a keyword instructs the engine to return sites with occurrences of that word and its synonyms (as Google understands them). For example, typing **~coffee** returns Web sites with the words coffee, cafe, caffeine or java in their pages. You can make this a Boolean search, by using the + and - signs to include or exclude words. Typing **~coffee -javascript** will find sites with coffee, cafe, caffeine, and java, but exclude those related to javascript programming language.

The following syntax searches allow you to search for a site or sites according to the name of the page or images included there. Both require some insight on the part of the searcher, who must try to intuit under what name a site or image might be held.

title: When Webmasters create Web sites, they typically (but not always) give it a name to indicate its primary content; the idea being that most site creators want their material to be found and seen by others. For example, a page on Web design will probably not be called "comic book heroes," even if there is a hyperlink to such a site. More likely, it will be something like "Jane Doe's Web Design Tips." In the free-form Boolean query box on AltaVista's advanced search, use a syntax such as **title:"web design"** (use parentheses or quotations) to find pages titled with that phrase. You can use Boolean connectors to look for multiple words or phrases in the title, although you must repeat the syntax. For example **title:"web design" AND title:java** will find pages with both the phrase "web design" and "java" in the title. Typing **title:"web design" AND NOT title:java** in AltaVista's free-form Boolean query box will exclude pages that include java in the title. Note also that the title of a site is not always the same as the headline. This search helps to weed out sites only loosely related to your keywords or phrase.

Finally, you can use a "wild card" to widen your search. The asterisk (*) is a wild card for several search engines. This provides for misspellings, alternate spellings, and word forms. For example, researching a story about adoption, a reporter also wanted to see sites related to "adoptive" parents. In AltaVista, she typed **adopti*** and the search yielded results with both forms of the word. The wild card must appear at least three characters into your search word, and the engines generally handle only one wild card per search. Try typing **poli*** and you'll get police, policy, political, and so on. Try poli**t*** **and** you'll get politics, political, polity, and so forth.

Image Searches

Perhaps your search is not for text, but for images—of people, places, objects, or documents. In that case, try an image search engine such as Picsearch (www.picsearch.com), which offers an advanced search option. Here, the user can specify what kind of image (e.g., photo or animation) and limit the size of the image file. Another site, Ditto (www.ditto.com), allows searches using Boolean logic. Enter your search words or phrases then select whether you want to see the results as thumbnail pictures, on which you click and be taken to the corresponding Web site, or with detail, which returns the file name, file size, and URL. Typing "russell crowe" (lowercase, no quotation marks) yielded 851 picture files of either Crowe or actors with whom he has appeared in movies.

As another tactic, you could start with AltaVista's basic search (www.altavista.com) and click on the "image" tab (there are also options for audio and video searches). To the right of the search button is a link to the advanced image search; click on that. Here, AltaVista allows you to search for images represented by .jpg, .gif, or .tif file extensions. There are options to search for images in color, black and white, or both and to include photos and graphics (sketches, documents, objects), or you may limit your search to one or the other. Checking the "buttons and banners" expands your search to include a Web site's advertisements or decorative elements. In most cases, you'll want to click on the pull-down menu next to "partner sites" and select "none" to exclude advertisements.

You can use Boolean logic to expand your search, in the same way as described in chapter 2. For example, if you want to find images of Albert Einstein, try typing **einstein OR "albert einstein"** in the image search box (Fig. 3.4). This tells the search engine to look for image files that have either the word einstein or the name "albert einstein" as part or all of the title. That search finds more than 27,000 photographs, sketches, paintings, and documents, with some duplication (Fig. 3.5). You're counting on the artist or archivist to have saved the file under an obvious name; you could expand your search by adding **OR genius OR relativity**. To minimize the search results, AltaVista allows you to specify color or black and white images, sources and size.

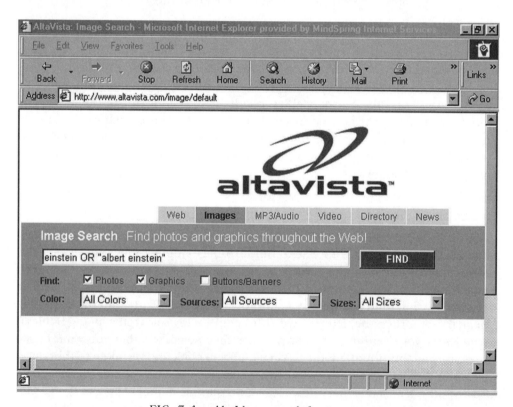

FIG. 3.4.   AltaVista search for image.

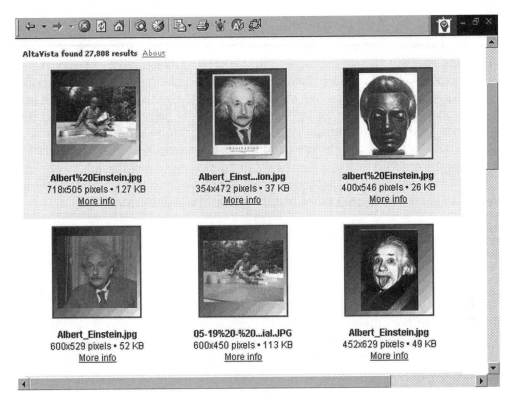

FIG. 3.5. Results of AltaVista search for image.

The "museum" domain has only recently been introduced, but soon it will allow you to narrow your search to images held in museums. For example, searching **"pablo picasso" AND domain:museum** at either AltaVista's advanced image search or in the free-form Boolean query box on AltaVista's advanced search page would locate works of Pablo Picasso held on museum Web sites. Currently, museums are represented by commercial (.com), not-for-profit (.org), and government domains such as the National Gallery of Art in Washington DC (www.nga.gov).

Be aware that many images on the Web are protected by copyright and trademark laws in the U.S. If you intend to reproduce the images you find online, you must contact the owner for permission.

Search by File Type

If you're looking for data on the Web and you know what kind of file type it's composed in, Google will help you find it. At the simple search page (www.google.com), type the prefix "data filetype," without quotation marks, followed by a colon and file extension. For example, typing **data filetype:pdf** returns more than 4 million portable document format files. Add a topic or keyword to target a search. For example, a search for the FBI Uniform Crime Report, a major national source of crime statistics, might look like this:

data filetype:pdf "uniform crime report"

Boolean connectors are not needed here, as Google assumes you want all words included, but I've enclosed the name of the report in quotation marks so the engine searches for that exact phrase. Google returns 1,600 files, including annual crime statistics from universities, municipalities, codebooks for deciphering reports, and government publications (Fig. 3.6). I could target the search further, by adding keywords to the search—the name of a particular city, for example.

This kind of search works for all types of files: spreadsheets (.xls), database (.dbf), and so on. But to keep your results to a manageable number, add keywords, phrases, or titles to a file type search. For a listing of file types and their abbreviations, try a site like AceNet (www.ace.net.nz/tech/TechFileFormat.html).

Foreign Language and News Searches

If you want to find Web sites composed in a specific language, there are few better search engines than AlltheWeb (www.alltheweb.com/advanced), which has consistently improved its advanced search. AlltheWeb can translate a query from English to find results in any one of 49 languages. Its site is well-designed, with many ways to refine a search and no ads. You can limit your search by file format, domain, host and even file size. AlltheWeb does accept paid submissions, but sponsored sites are labeled among the results. While you can also search by lan-

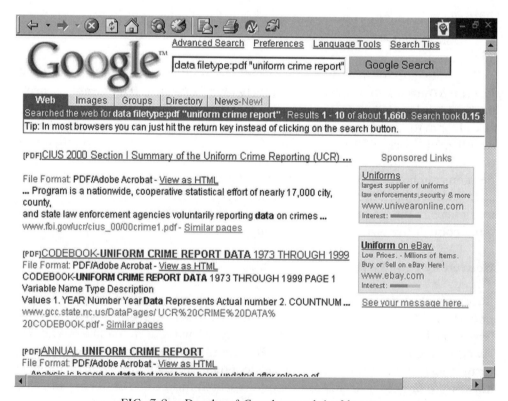

FIG. 3.6.   Results of Google search by file type.

guage on Google and AltaVista, AlltheWeb boasts more current content, and had fewer broken links (defunct sites) among its results for every search I performed.

You may also have good results using search directories or portals created for native language speakers. Remember that search directories are repositories of selected information and Web sites organized by category. A native-language directory is designed with a specific group of users in mind and so might yield a better and wider range of search results than a general purpose search engine. For example, to search Russian-language sites, you could refer to any of the following three portal sites: www.rambler.ru, www.omen.ru, or www.list.ru. As another example, Estonia-Wide Web (www.ee/www/index.html) searches for Estonia-related information and sites in the Estonian language. A Greek portal is www.protoselida.com; and one Asian portal is www.asiaco.com. A Spanish portal is www.typicallyspanish.com. Similar sites exist for searching current news related to particular regions and in native languages. For example, Newslook Magazine (www.newslookmag.com) provides links to current news related to Nepal. To search Moroccan and Maghreb's press, try www.marweb.net.

These sites are only a few of the many available online. Try Search Engine Colossus for links to search engines and directories in 195 countries and many languages (www.searchenginecolossus.com). Another way to find such sites is to conduct a Boolean search on Google or AltaVista for **(search engine) OR (search directory) AND (language here, no parentheses)**. Whereas these search directories can be very helpful when your search requires native-language sites, many have the same nuisance features of other sites. Advertising is prevalent both in the form of banners and links.

Where in the World? Searching by Location

Search engines often provide results from among U.S.-based sites, which is not necessarily helpful when you're seeking information about or originating from another country. Geographic search engines allow users to search other countries' sites more thoroughly. Some may be loaded up with sponsored results, but others provide the best way to search a country or continent's Web resources and local or regional news. One such site, the Engine Rooms (www.enginerooms.com), provides links to U.K.-related search engines and directories. Web Wombat (www.webwombat.com.au) searches only Australian sites, and also provides links to a variety of local services such as travel accommodations and phone directories.

Yahoo offers links to local search engines or directories in other countries, available at the bottom of its home page (www.yahoo.com). It's not comprehensive, in fact, there are entire continents absent here that boast a significant presence on the Web, though additions are expected. A better resource is AlltheWeb (www.alltheweb.com/advanced), which offers a domain filter on its advanced search page. A drop-down menu lets the user search among only those sites originating from a specific geographic region.

Another online source, Nielsen NetRatings (www.nielsen-netratings.com) rates search engines by popularity. At that Web site, click on the tab "top rankings" to see figures on the most-used sites in western Europe and Asia.

Finally, any search engine that allows a Boolean-language query will let the user limit search results to sites originating from a particular region. A syntax search, as described in this chapter, will allow you to search among a country's Web sites by specifying its domain name (e.g., country code as in "au" for Australia, "fr" for France).

Ask an Expert

Another way to shave time off a search is to let someone else do the legwork. If you're searching for sites on a particular topic, try using a "search guide," a self-described expert or aficionado on a given topic. Services such as About (www.about.com; formerly The Mining Company) put individuals in charge of finding and selecting the "best" sites in certain categories. The guides are introduced at the top of the Web page and their credentials are provided. Although each Web volunteer approaches the job a little differently, users can read about additions to the list of sites, changes, current debates, and so on. In some cases, the guide encourages users to e-mail questions and suggestions, or even to telephone so they can speak directly to one another.

Similarly, the Open Directory Project (www.dmoz.org) puts volunteer editors in charge of compiling and evaluating Web sites in some 46,000 categories. ODP aims to be the largest human-edited Web directory, and in fact, its database is part of what the bigger directories (Lycos, Google) search. Editors select sites based on strict criteria, so the incidence of "stray" sites among search results is lessened. Routine peer reviews ensure that editors stay on top of their categories, and jettison broken links quickly. The disadvantage to ODP is that sites are slow to be added, since humans, rather than robotic spiders, are retrieving and reviewing them.

Furthermore, the drawbacks here are the same as with any search directory. You can't know for certain how much of the Web the guide has actually scoured, or how often. Nor can you really be sure what criteria they've used to sort and rate sites—one man's trash is another man's treasure. But generally, if you're looking for a range of quality sites on a particular subject, using a guide might be a comfortable alternative to a standard search directory.

Meta Searches

Meta search engines are also known as "all in one" search sites, because they allow users to search using multiple engines and directories at once. I generally don't favor meta searches, because most fail to adjust queries to individual engines' preferences, so you won't get the same results as you would if you searched at each site separately. Advanced techniques are usually not available, so you're limited to searches using simple words or phrases. Furthermore, meta search sites can take longer to return results; if you have a slow connection speed, your queries may time out.

However, meta search engines do represent inroads in Web searching technology, so it's worthwhile separating the good from the bad. One of the best is

Ixquick, for example (www.ixquick.com), which searches across engines and returns unique sites with titles, descriptions, and popularity rankings. I like Ixquick for many reasons, including the fact that it shows you exactly what engines and directories it has queried and identifies sponsored sites. In addition, by clicking on "highlighted result," you can see exactly why you got the results you did, by looking at where your search terms occur on a site. Importantly, it offers multiple language versions of its search, so that queries are directed to native-language engines and directories, in addition to the usual bunch.

Another top choice for meta searches is Vivisimo (www.vivisimo.com), which uses document clustering or categorization software to organize results hierarchically. As examples, the site offers a collection of documents on anthrax, and another on Microsoft patents. A meta search for women's history yielded 137 results under a general heading, and offered on the left side of the screen expandable listings for numerous subcategories including science, aviation, women's studies programs, museums, and so on. Users also have the option to open any of the sites as a separate window or preview. Accompanying each result are their sources. Here you see the top result was found through a search using Yahoo, Lycos, and Looksmart (Fig. 3.7). Vivisimo offers an advanced search and does not accept advertising or payment for placement among results. That is not to say, however, that the engines and directories it searches do not engage in that practice.

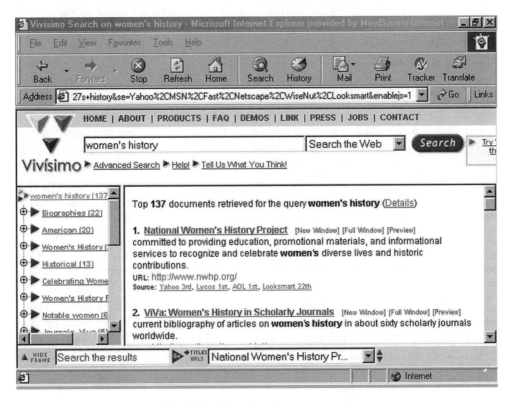

FIG. 3.7. Results of a meta search.

Several other meta searches are popular with users, but they're not the most efficient sites. Dogpile (www.dogpile.com), for example, claims to search "many top engines" and offers an advanced or "custom" search which lets users choose the search directories or engines to which a query will be sent. Results are shown by directory in groups of 10, although users can link to a longer set—many of the results are advertisers. A new all-in-one search site launched in July 2003, Yes Wacked (http://yes.wacked.us) lets you choose among engines, directories, and meta seacrhes using Boolean query language. Results are displayed as side-by-side panes.

Back to the Future

When you find a good site, you will want to be able to return to it quickly. But research suggests Web sites have an average lifespan of just 75 days.[9] What you retrieve today may not be there tomorrow. The Internet Archive Wayback Machine (www.archive.org) is a site dedicated to the preservation of Web sites. At this site, users can enter a URL, and be provided with stored versions of that page, or select from the Archive's collection listed in the site's left-hand column. This is a handy way to search for sites that have changed, moved, or been removed altogether. The Wayback Machine is a project of the Internet Archive, a not-for-profit organization committed to preserving digital materials for historical research. So far, about 10 billion sites have been archived, dating back to 1996. A search for www.whitehouse.gov resulted in approximately 450 links to the site since 1996 and indicated with an asterisk which links were updated versions.

Because the content on the Internet changes so often, you simply cannot rely on a search engine to turn up the same sites everyday, even if you use the same search techniques as the day before. Instead, take advantage of your browser's menu to mark the site so that you can easily return to it. When you have the site open in your browser, select in Microsoft's Explorer, "Favorites" and then, from the pull-down menu, "Add to Favorites." In Netscape Navigator, the same function is known as "Bookmark." At the same pull-down menu, both browsers also allow users to organize bookmarks. This is convenient, because it allows you to order sites by categories of your choosing and rename sites.

When you want to return to a site you've marked, open your browser and click on the pull-down "favorites" or "bookmarks" menu and click on the site you are looking for; the page will open automatically. Once it's open, you can click "refresh" or "reload" to be sure you have the most current version of the site.

That said, not all sites can or should be bookmarked. Search result screens usually cannot be bookmarked, nor can articles appearing in the daily edition of an online newspaper. Bookmarking the front page of the *St. Louis Post-Dispatch* Web site will allow you to return, but will display the current edition, not

---

[9]John Waggoner, "Information Age Losing Memory," *USA Today* (22 October 1999), B1.

the last page you read. In the case of evolving content such as newspaper sites, you'll want to highlight the desired text and save it to another kind of file, download the contents and save to your disk or hard drive, or print the information.

Another way to retrace your steps is to refer to your "URL history," which is automatically maintained on most browsers. In Explorer, the main toolbar at the top of the screen has a "history" button. Clicking on that opens a new window on the left side of the screen. The folders shown there are organized by date; clicking on each folder displays the URLs for sites visited recently. Clicking on a URL transports you to that site and keeps the history window open. If you're not sure where your URL history is located among your files, click on your "start" button on your desktop, then on "find," and type "URL history" or "history" in the "name" box, then click OK. When you see the folder or file showing your URL history or Web history, click on that.

To change the settings for your history folder, click on the "Tools" pull-down menu in Explorer, then on "Internet Options." At the bottom of the first screen, you have the option of changing how many days' worth of Web sites you want to cache—from 0 to 999. If you want to clear the history folder immediately, click on the "clear history" button.

Good News, Bad News

Researching on the Internet is somewhat of a good news-bad news scenario. The good news is that users have access to a phenomenal range of information. The bad news is that the WWW does not offer a panacea for your research needs. Search engines leave plenty of room for improvement, as suggested in recent studies that point out just how much search engines overlook on the Web.

As much as the Internet has made life easier for researchers, sometimes it is wiser to forgo it altogether and rely on traditional library or archival research. Those scenarios include:

- When you are searching for information that predates the mid-1980s— refers to when it was posted, not necessarily to the contents, because there are sites that contain amazing historical documents hundreds of years old. Some Web site administrators have seen fit to archive data, but that is a slow-going process.
- If your Internet Service Provider (ISP) charges an hourly rate. Given all the competition that has sprung up, users should be able to find an ISP that charges a flat monthly fee for unlimited Internet access. If not, users could pay dearly, particularly if their search skills are less than efficient.
- When the information is esoteric. As an example, for a research project I needed to know what newspapers were published in Kansas City, MO from 1938 through 1952. Furthermore, I needed to know exactly what kind of content they held. The answers were found in the local historical society and on microfilm at the Kansas City Public Library—not on the Web.

TIPS FOR SMART SEARCHES

When traditional searches disappoint, try these alternate methods:

- Use your knowledge of domain names to narrow a search or to go straight to an organization's site.
- Trace a site back to its source whenever possible.
- Use syntax searches to narrow a search and filter out unwanted sites.
- Use specialty searches for image and audio files.
- When searching for information in a foreign language, take advantage of native-language search engines and directories.
- When your search is for a range of sites on a particular topic, a guided search such as the kind offered by About.com, will save time.
- Search by file type.
- Meta searchers get better all the time, allowing you to search across many engines and directories. If you opt for a meta search, choose one that allows you to control what engines and directories it queries, and how to display results.
- Use your browser's bookmarking function to save sites you may want to return to later. If the content of the site is critical, save it onto a disk, or to your computer's hard drive. Take advantage of archive projects like the Wayback Machine to find sites that have changed, moved, or been removed from the Web.
- Know the Web's limits and use the library when appropriate.

4

Staying Connected: Mailing Lists, Newsletters, Newsgroups, and Web Logs

A police officer assigned to patrol a particular area refers to it as a *beat*. A beat cop, by traversing the same route regularly, quickly becomes familiar with the peculiar characteristics of an area and the people who live and do business there. That kind of familiarity allows the officer to locate resources and to recognize and respond quickly to changes.

Similarly, journalists assigned to cover specific industries or issues also refer to those assignments as beats: the city beat, sports beat, society beat, and so on. To cover their beats effectively, reporters cultivate human and stored sources they can return to on a regular basis to find out what's new, what changes they can anticipate, who the key players are, prevailing values, and preoccupations. Like the beat cop, a beat reporter becomes something of a specialist, familiar enough with an issue to recognize news, to know where information is likely to be found, and to recognize and anticipate changes.

For these reasons, I strongly encourage journalists and other researchers to establish Internet beats. For example, a reporter responsible for covering "family issues" could bookmark and drop in regularly on several family related sites, engage in Internet-based discussion groups, arrange to receive press releases via e-mail from a number of appropriate commercial or not-for-profit organizations, and download data from related government agencies. An online beat helps reporters and researchers to stay connected, to keep up with changes—an important ability when dealing with a medium that changes so frequently.

For a nonjournalist, an Internet beat still has plenty of advantages. At the very least, it encourages regular use and so makes it easier to keep up with changes. Beats are a natural choice if you want to keep up with news on a particular subject. They can also help you find and keep in touch with people working on similar projects, including those who have struggled and overcome the very challenges you may be facing. In some cases, it's the only way (or certainly the most affordable) to communicate with people you might not otherwise meet because of their location: the computer programmer in California, the software author in North Carolina, or the engineer in Brazil, for example. You'll see in chapter 5 how an online beat can help you locate specific people and organizations.

ESTABLISHING AN INTERNET BEAT

Bookmarks or favorites, discussed in chapter 3, are a starting point for establishing a beat, because they allow you to return to the same sites easily. Among my own bookmarks are several newspapers, magazines, wire service sites, and web logs. You could also take advantage of many newpapers' offers to customize electronic editions so that when you visit those sites, you see news only on the topics of your choosing. Web logs, also known as *blogs*, are a good way to follow very current debates. Not quite journals and not quite journalism, blogs are running commentaries—the "rapid-fire online jottings of political opinions, media critiques, and Andy Rooney-ish kvetches,"[1] according to one online publication. A blog that I visit regularly is that of Stanford Law School professor and author Lawrence Lessig, one of the most thoughtful voices on Internet regulation, at http://lessig.org/blog.

In addition, consider joining Internet-based communities—mailing lists or newsgroups. These informal means of online communication can be mined for all kinds of material: current research and critiques, expertise in many areas, leads on computer-based resources, technical advice, and social support and encouragement. In fact, discussion groups are perhaps the best source for tips on computer-based resources in development, as it's often where people congregate to announce the launch of new sites, and debate the quality of what they offer.

In this chapter I explain what each of these forums is and how you can locate and search their contents online.

Mailing Lists

An Internet-based mailing list is really an informal discussion group, dedicated to a given topic and distributed to subscribers via electronic mail. Also called listservs,[2] mailing lists have been organized by enthusiasts of a huge range of subjects: investigative reporting, computer programming, spoon collecting, klezmer music, anthropology, cooking, and book publishing, to name a few. According to one estimate, there are more than 100,000 lists currently in use. Mailing lists are often denoted by an acronym followed with the letter "L," as in "SPJ-L," a mailing list for the Society of Professional Journalists. Being part of a mailing list allows you to converse with people interested in a common topic through an exchange of

---

[1]James Wolcott, "Blog Nation," *Business 2.0* (1 May 2000), www.business2.com.
[2]"Listserv" refers to the software used to manage mailing lists.

messages routed through a central point and distributed to list of subscribers. If a list is moderated, messages are sent first to an individual, often the list owner, who then decides whether to forward them to subscribers or not. Messages may be rejected if they are obscene or off-topic. A "closed" list means subscribers must first be approved by the list owner, commonly a prerequisite for lists aimed at very specific audiences—the 1982 graduating class of John Foster Dulles High School in Sugar Land, Texas, for example, or university students enrolled in a particular course.

Some Internet users might choose to join a list based on a hobby, but I gravitate toward lists for professional, not necessarily personal, enrichment. For example, reporters might join mailing lists based on their current assignments. By temporarily subscribing to a parenting list, one journalist located valuable resources and families to interview for a story on international adoption. As a teacher, I have subscribed intermittently to lists centered on computer-assisted research, media literacy, and mass media history. Readers of this book might find it helpful to subscribe to a list that focuses on identifying and using computer-based resources. You need not be a reporter to belong to a journalism-related list, which can be a very helpful resource for online research tips and strategies. Mailing lists are easy to join (subscribe) and leave (unsubscribe), so when your interests change or the volume of mail becomes more than you care to handle, suspending or terminating a mailing list subscription is simple.

Newsgroups

A *newsgroup* is another way for people to congregate online to discuss specific topics. You may also have seen or heard them identified as Usenet,[3] net news, message boards, electronic bulletin boards, or BBS. They are a handy way to find like-minded people, gauge current thinking, pose conundrums, and get a range of solutions, or to gather information about individuals (more on that in chap. 5, Finding People). Some newsgroups are moderated, but most are not.

Newsgroups are categorized much the same way as mailing lists, around a central topic. The names of these electronic bulletin boards are hierarchical, and look like a series of abbreviated words separated by dots or periods. For example, talk.religion.buddhism is a discussion group related to the Buddhist religion. The newsgroup known as rec.juggling is a discussion related to the recreation or sport of juggling.

Rather than being sent to users' individual e-mail addresses like mailing lists are, newsgroups can usually be viewed at a central web site. As the conversation in a newsgroup develops, messages (or "posts") related to a specific topic proceed in a linear fashion and are referred to as "threads." Messages are typically displayed in your browser under columns that show the date, subject heading and author of each message. Clicking on the subject heading lets you view an in-

---

[3]Usenet is a UNIX-based electronic bulletin board network recognized as the largest public information resource in the world, about four times the size of the Web. By some estimates, there are more than 50,000 active newsgroups representing some 25 million users.

dividual message. There, messages appear in plain text (no frills here), and generally contain a hypertext link for the sender's e-mail address or newsgroup mailing address, and another back to the list of messages. Some authors like to include the subject line and text of message to which they've responded, either at the end of theirs or throughout to respond to specific points the previous writer has made. Ideally, the previous message is set off by bullets, brackets, or a contrasting font or color.

Newsletters

A *newsletter* is a kind of small newspaper, devoted to a certain subject and targeted to a specific group of readers. Online newsletters work much the same way as traditional ones except that they are delivered over the Internet. An electronic edition may have enhanced graphic features in comparison to a print version. Some newsletters require users to subscribe, by providing an e-mail address; others may be viewed on a Web site. An advantage to an electronic newsletter is that readers can get updated information quickly, and back issues may be available for search. A fine example of an electronic newsletter is Search Engine Report, a free monthly newsletter with content devoted to search engine tools, developments, and news delivered via e-mail by request (www.searchenginewatch.com/about/newsletters.html). Another example is Texas A&M University's Aggie Hotline, a daily news brief of university-related events and issues e-mailed to subscribers (www.tamu.edu/univrel/aggiedaily/news/Agg.html).

Web Logs

Personal Web logs, or *blogs* can be great sources of commentary and critique. Authors and editors are known as "bloggers," and they represent some of the Internet's most enthusiastic (dare I say compulsive?) users. Blogs are basically running commentaries, maintained as time-stamped entries on a Web site. A blogger responds to anything that strikes her on a particular day, providing links to all kinds of related information, and to other blogs. Organizations also maintain blogs, such as the one by the Electronic Frontier Foundation, which posts and comments on Web-related legal issues.

For research purposes, blogs serve two important functions. First, they provide an instant snapshot of public opinion, as bloggers tend to contribute one or more entries each day, often in response to breaking news.

Second, the link-driven structure of a blog means a certain amount of filtering is done by the time you get there. Bloggers scour the web and then, recommend or lambaste sites with their commentary, which can range from acerbic to sublime to ridiculous. For example, a recent blog illuminated contradictions in mass media coverage of a Moscow terrorist siege, with links to numerous news sites. Each link was introduced with substantive commentary.

The Right Tool for the Job

More and more frequently, I hear people use the terms newsletters, newsgroups and mailing lists interchangeably. That's unfortunate, because they are most definitely not the same. Just as knowing the differences between search engines and search directories makes online research more productive, knowing the distinctions among newsletters, newsgroups, and mailing lists can spare researchers precious time.

A more appropriate comparison to a newsletter is a newspaper or magazine—perhaps this is why they are sometimes referred to as *e-zines*, a category that also includes electronic editions of magazines, fanzines, comic books, and more. Readers are a vast, anonymous group; in fact, it's impossible for you to know who else is subscribed to or reading the same newsletter—something you *can* find out with mailing lists. Some newsletters provide links to related information but are generally for distribution only, with no interaction among subscribers. However, online newsletters typically offer some means for readers to provide feedback to the publisher (e.g., letters to the editor), usually a link to an e-mail form. As an example, the Journal of the American Medical Association publishes an online newsletter for people who suffer from migraine headaches and offers a link for readers to comment on the content and quality of the site through e-mail. That same site allows users to search past issues of the newsletter (www.ama-assn.org/special/migraine/migraine.htm).

Some newsletters offer readers the opportunity to leave comments on electronic bulletin boards, but because those messages and responses are rarely searchable, they hold little appeal for researchers. The content of such postings can be decidedly lowbrow and in some cases, have little or nothing to do with the publication on which they're hosted. A recent irate exchange on a bulletin board for *Slate*, a politics and culture magazine, responded to another publication's article about tennis star Serena Williams.[4]

Although newsgroups and mailing lists are often used interchangeably, they have some distinct differences. Think of a newsgroup as a bulletin board in a hallway; anyone with Internet access can post a message and anyone passing by can respond. If the messenger and respondent want to post their messages anonymously or pseudonymously, they can do so because there is usually no obligation (or incentive) to do otherwise. In fact, some newsgroups deal with alternative or risque subjects, and being able to post anonymous messages frees members to communicate with little fear of repercussion. Of course, that anonymity also makes it easy for participants to hurl insults and accusations at one another, which happens quite often.

There is no subscription required on your part to read the messages posted to a newsgroup, although some sites ask you to register by providing personal information. For privacy concerns, you may want to use a secondary mailing address

---

[4]See for example, "I am so offended," a bulletin board posting by "Maureen" at www.slate.msn.com, 12 September 2002. This thread responds to a newspaper article in which Serena Williams' attire was criticized as inappropriate.

reserved for bulk or junk e-mail. If you are opposed to your personal information being gathered for marketing purposes, you can always mask your identity by claiming a different gender and geographic region.

A mailing list, on the other hand, does require some disclosure on the part of subscribers and actually benefits from it. The substance and success of a list relies on not just the enthusiasm of its participants, but their expertise. Ideally, a mailing list is a thoughtful, generous exchange of ideas, problems, and solutions, with a minimum of posturing. Because contributions to list discussions are typically accompanied by the author's name, affiliation, and contact information, subscribers seem to take more care with what they post. Although debates can get heated, lists rarely degenerate into *flame*[5] wars, as newsgroups often will. The Investigative Reporters and Editors (IRE) mailing list is among the most civil, and as a result most productive, mailing lists to which I've ever been subscribed.

Also distinguishing mailing lists from newsgroups and newsletters are the delivery and search options. Some lists offer subscribers a digest form, meaning that rather than sending individual messages from subscribers on a daily basis, the list owner or moderator sends out a cumulative e-mail less frequently, perhaps once a week or monthly. A digest form is good for mailing lists that generate a high volume of messages. Furthermore, archives are often searchable by a variety of methods: sender name, subject line, date and message content, for example.

There has certainly been a blending of discussion groups and online forums—newsletters with electronic bulletin boards, for example—and perhaps that accounts for some of the confusion over definitions. But knowing what differentiates newsgroups, newsletters, and mailing lists saves research time. To find someone with a specific expertise, locate resources or keep up with changes in a particular industry; mailing lists and newsletters are a good bet. Newsgroups are helpful when you want to eavesdrop on or take part in a more casual, even impulsive, conversation. These discussion groups give you a sense of what a community of people are thinking and feeling at a particular moment, in other words, how an issue or event is being received by a group of people.

The Search Begins

To find out what kinds of mailing lists, newsgroups and newsletters are available online, start with a direct approach. If you want to find out if a specific organization hosts a listserv, begin with that organization's Web site, where you may find a link to subscribe. For example, at its Web site, Investigative Reporters and Editors has a link to its listserv, IRE-L, on the left side of the opening page (www.ire.org). The Foundation Center Web site has a link to a list of philanthropy related newsletters (http://fdncenter.org/newsletters), with subscription information. In the latter case, a direct approach is really best, as I find many newsletter databases lead the user straight to advertisements.

---

[5]*Flaming* is a term for an exchange of irate or abusive e-mails between newsgroup or mailing list participants.

Otherwise, your first stop will be a "list of lists," a Web site that serves as a clearinghouse of mailing lists, newsgroups and newsletters. Some sites are manually maintained, although many early ones were abandoned when keeping up with thousands of listservs became too much for their owners. Publicly Accessible Mailing Lists (PAML) is one such casualty. Other databases are automatically updated through special software programs. It's always a good idea to check a site for some indication of when it was last updated.

Listed here are some of the best sites for finding these sources. Some sites' databases include a little of everything: mailing lists, newsgroups, newsletters, and archives, with no immediate indication to the user which is which—that's when knowing the differences will serve you well. Although each site has its strengths and weaknesses, none are comprehensive so a combination of searches may be needed to find what you seek.

FINDING MAILING LISTS AND ARCHIVES

CataList

CataList, a database of public mailing lists (www.lsoft.com/lists/listref.html), calls its database the "official catalog of listserv lists." It's a fine site, although the search interface is a bit tricky. Searches of the database are not conducted by subject or description, but by list name, host name, or title. For example, searching with the keyword "journalism" did not yield information about the IRE (Investigative Reporters and Editors) mailing list, although it is in fact a journalism-focused list. Rather, that required that I search using the keyword "investigative." Neither keyword search returned the listserv for the Center for Investigative Reporting—a reminder that none of these sites is comprehensive.

Many reputable mailing lists are hosted by universities, meaning the discussions are university affiliated or list owners rent space on a university's server. CataList allows you to search by host. At the main page, click on the link for "Search for a mailing list of interest." Then try typing "Dartmouth" or "Dartmouth.edu" (either uppercase or lowercase works) in the "look for" box, then check the box for "host name." The other two boxes, for list name and list title will already be checked; you can leave them as they are (see Fig. 4.1). Click on "start the search" and you'll find that Dartmouth hosts about 106 lists, including discussions groups for current students and alumni, and others on the subject of Indonesian performing arts and another on freediving in New England (see Fig. 4.2).

Clicking on the host name of any list returns more information, such as the identity of the list owner, number of subscribers, and whether the list is moderated, among other features. A little further down that page is a link with instructions to subscribe. Most mailing lists require you send commands (subscribe, unsubscribe, suspend) to a central address. It's important that you not fill the body of your e-mail with any more text than is called for. Usually a computer is handling these commands, and any extraneous text results in your request not

L-Soft

List search

This form allows you to search the database for lists whose name (XYZ-L), host name (LISTSERV.XYZ.EDU) and/or title ("Central America Discussion List") matches your search string. You can search for multiple topics by separating them with a comma. For instance, a search on "opera,classical" will return all the entries containing the word "opera" OR the word "classical". To search for a topic that actually contains a comma, type two commas in a row.

Look for: dartmouth|

In: ☑ List name ☑ Host name ☑ List title
☐ Lists with web archive interface only

[Start the search!]

FIG. 4.1.   Searching for mailing lists or listservs.

Search results

1YEAR2GO@LISTSERV.DARTMOUTH.EDU
        Planning and information for upcoming weddings *(78 subscribers)*
57-BUSINESS@LISTSERV.DARTMOUTH.EDU
        57 Business *(190 subscribers)*
57-TEAM@LISTSERV.DARTMOUTH.EDU
        57-Team *(30 subscribers)*
9WEBSTER@LISTSERV.DARTMOUTH.EDU
        9Webster Ave Alumnae Association Forum *(16 subscribers)*
ALUMNI-ULTIMATE@LISTSERV.DARTMOUTH.EDU
        Dartmouth Ultimate Frisbee Club *(104 subscribers)*
BAHASA@LISTSERV.DARTMOUTH.EDU 👁
        Indonesian language list *(139 subscribers)*
BERRY@LISTSERV.DARTMOUTH.EDU 👁
        Berry Library Construction *(35 subscribers)*
CABIN-TRAIL@LISTSERV.DARTMOUTH.EDU 👁
        Cabin and Trail *(804 subscribers)*
CANDG-ALUMNI@LISTSERV.DARTMOUTH.EDU

FIG. 4.2.   Mailing list search results.

being processed. In Fig. 4.3, the user is given explicit instructions for subscribing to this Indonesian language list. On the same screen, just below subscription instructions, users are offered an e-mail link to contact the list owner, and an option to view other mailing lists hosted on the same server.

At its main page, CataList also offers an option for searching lists by host country. Unless you're studying patterns of cyberspace regulation, this option has limited benefits. In comparison to other countries, the United States imposes the fewest restrictions on computer-based communications. Thus, most mailing lists are hosted by U.S. servers whether or not the owners or participants actually reside there. Consider that CataList's database includes more than 50,000 U.S.-based lists compared to China's 39, or just four in the Russian Federation.

Tile.Net

A moderately-sized database of mailing lists, *Tile.Net* (http://tile.net/listst) allows users to search by list name and domain. Oddly, it also has a search by list description, though it's hard to imagine why. To use that option, you would have to know the first letter of the first word of the list description. Instead, use the search option located at the lower left of the Tile.Net Web site. Type either a subject keyword, proper name or list name in the box, then select "list" from the drop-down menu and click "search." This search is still a little clumsy, as typing

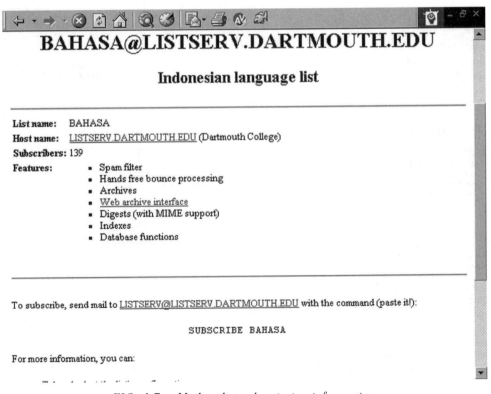

FIG. 4.3.   Mailing list subscription information.

"Missouri" netted listservs having to do with Missouri or hosted by Missouri-based servers, and perhaps most frustrating, results were not arranged alphabetically. Clicking on any of the lists takes the user to a description and instructions for subscribing.

Topica (Formerly Liszt)

One of the early and most popular sites, named for the composer Franz Liszt, has since been taken over by *Topica*, and not necessarily for the better. At the Topica site (www.topica.com), scroll down to the list of "newsletters and discussions." Here, a jumble of mailing lists, newsgroups and newsletters are organized alphabetically by category. If you're interested in discussion groups that help you use the Internet efficiently, try categories that are likely to address such research: journalism, libraries, computers, and so on. If you don't see the category listed, use Topica's search option near the bottom of the page. Search for "journalism" and you'll get a list of alternate categories (each a hyperlink), followed by descriptions of about 30 mailing lists (Fig. 4.4). Click on the name of the list that interests you, and Topica provides you with some basic information: For example, how many subscribers the list has and how many messages you can expect to receive daily or weekly. You'll also find out if the listserv hosts a Web site of its own, often the best place to look for archives of earlier messages. As an example, Fig. 4.5 shows the details for the listserv maintained by the Center for Investigative Reporting.

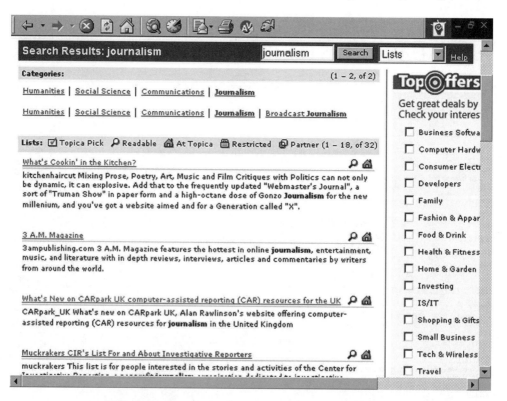

FIG. 4.4.   A search of mailing lists and newsletters.

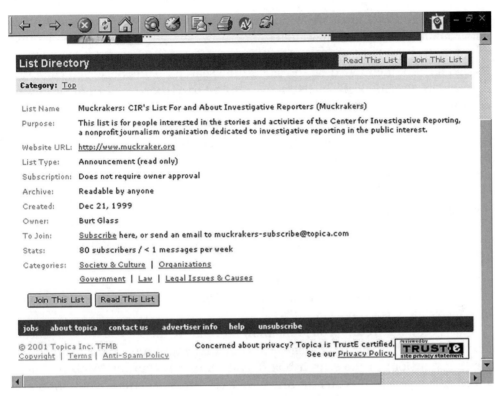

FIG. 4.5.   Mailing list details.

A great thing about Liszt was that it offered users powerful options for narrowing searches; unfortunately Topica retained few of them. Topica does allow users to search messages using keywords or phrases, but oddly that option only appears on the search results page. In other words, you have to first search lists by category. Then, at the right side of the search results screen is a pull-down menu that allows you to change your search from lists to messages. Click on the latter, and you can search the text of thousands of messages by keywords, names or phrases. At the search results page, click on the highlighted text to see the full message. At the bottom of the message are links to information about that listserv, or to join it.

In searching for messages or lists, Topica allows Boolean searches. For example, searching lists with the Boolean phrase journalism and computer will return lists that include both words in their descriptions. Searching messages with the phrase computers or news finds messages that contain either word, but not necessarily both. You can exclude terms by using the "not" joiner, although this worked better for searching messages than it did for lists. Using the phrase computers not news finds messages that contain the word "computers" but not "news." Topica does not allow wild cards, so you must choose your search words carefully. Although in one search I excluded the word "programming," it still returned messages from an Italian listserv with the word "programmatore." Similarly, although I excluded "news" in a search of listservs, it still returned many lists containing the word "newsletter."

Topica has another feature that online researchers are likely to find helpful, although it is not mentioned on the site. At the search results page, you can organize results alphabetically by list name, subject or author, or chronologically, by clicking on a column heading. For example, clicking on the "date" heading organizes the messages in ascending order, from oldest to the most recent. This is a good way to follow a message thread (a message and any subsequent responses from subscribers), or to find messages written by a particular author, even if they occur on different lists.

The Mail Archive

If you're looking for past mailing list correspondence, this is a choice place to start. The *Mail Archive* (www.mail-archive.com), gets high points for accuracy, although the number of lists it includes is minimal at this time—just 3,000. However, a wide variety of lists are represented and among them, many computer and Internet-related lists.

To use the Mail Archive, you must know the name of the list you want to search; it will not search through message text. Either type the name of the list (without the "L" extension) in the search box (Fig. 4.6), or click on the "Archives" link, which takes you to a roster of archived lists (Fig. 4.7). Here, you can scroll

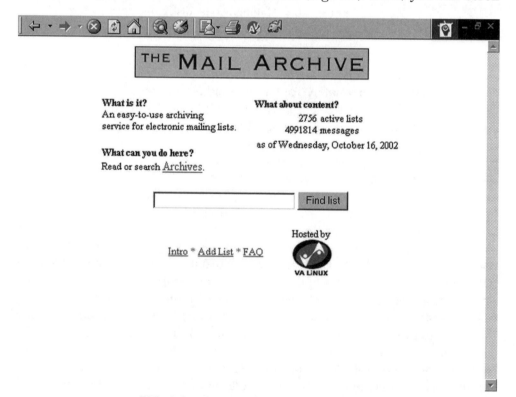

FIG. 4.6.   Search of mailing list archives.

FIG. 4.7.   A roster of mailing lists at The Mail Archive.

through an alphabetical listing, or use the "find" option under your browser's edit menu to find a particular list.

Clicking on a list name takes you to a screen of the list's most recent 100 messages, all denoted by subject lines and authors (Fig. 4.8). There is another option, at the upper left hand corner of the page, to organize messages by date, but this can result in some *threads* (messages and related responses) being separated. At this screen, you can use your browser's "find" option under the "edit" menu to locate messages on a particular topic or written by a particular individual.

Click on a message's subject heading to see the text (Fig. 4.9). In this example, a mailing list subscriber has responded to a post from another subscriber, regarding the editorial response time among certain academic journals. The author has pasted the original message at the bottom of his response, a courtesy to other subscribers, to keep the thread in context. The name of the list, *Armchair*, appears in the upper right corner.

Mail Archive has a nice, clean form, free of advertising. At the bottom of archived messages, links to the remainder of the thread are provided, as well as an e-mail link for the author (Fig. 4.10). In most cases, the authors identify themselves at the end of their posts but if that's not the case, an e-mail address can also provide identification. For example, clicking on this author's name opens an e-mail form with an address extension of "anu.edu.au." If I then go to my browser,

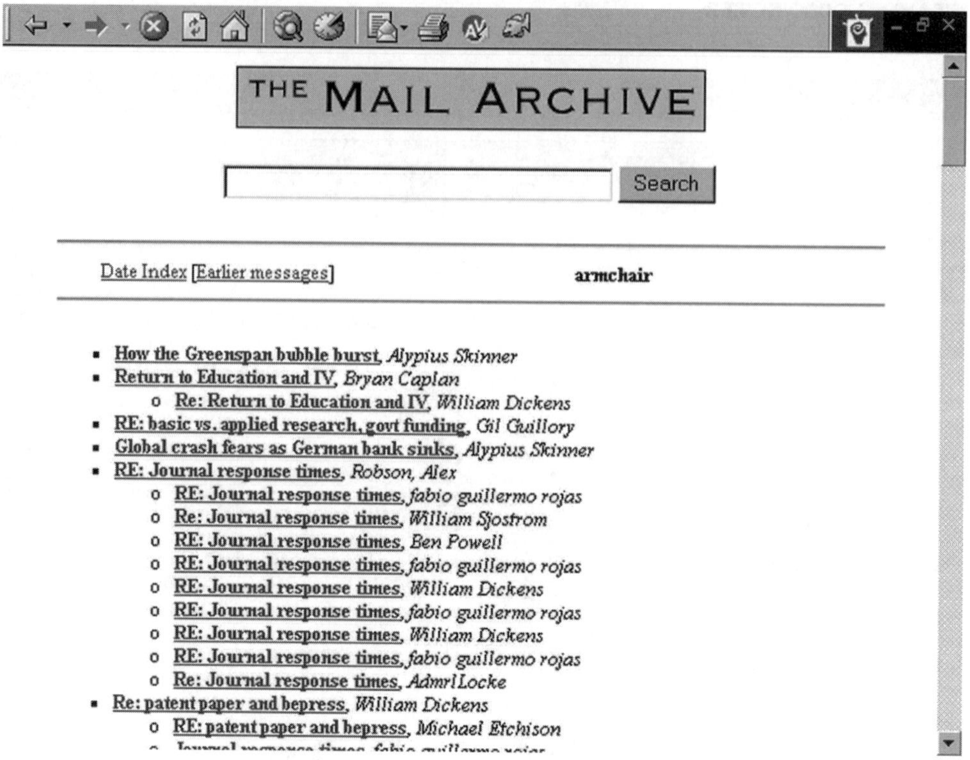

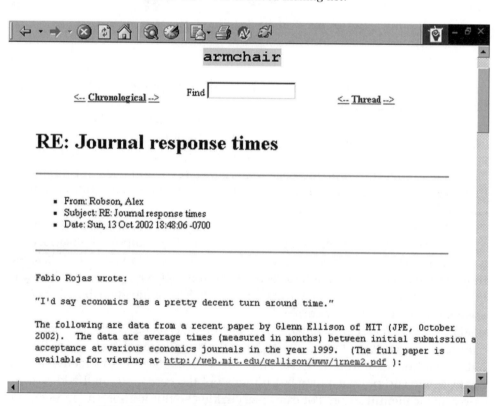

FIG. 4.8. An archived mailing list.

FIG. 4.9. An example of mailing list correspondence.

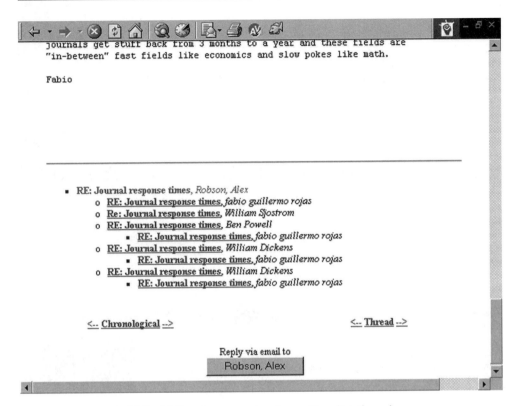

FIG. 4.10.   An example of a mailing list thread.

type in "www.anu.edu.au," I find the home page of Australian National University in Canberra, Australia, where the author turns out to be a faculty member in the School of Economics. Using the staff directory, I can easily find his office and telephone number. But we're getting ahead of ourselves—there's more on finding people in chapter 5.

EScribe

This site, www.escribe.com, is another handy one for searching mailing list archives, to find conversations on certain topics or locate individuals. *EScribe* has two great features that make it a good choice for researchers. First, it's deliberately low frills, so that Internet users with slow modems will have no trouble accessing the site or its archives. In fact, EScribe removes HTML content before archiving messages. Second, its search function offers effective choices to locate specific content.

At its Web site, EScribe offers a search box, and a category listing (Fig. 4.11). But to use the search, you must know the name of the list you're seeking. Instead, try the category list, as that's fairly broad. Those results display mailing lists archived under the category you've selected, as well as related ones. For example, selecting the "Internet" category finds about 50 lists, but scroll down and the re-

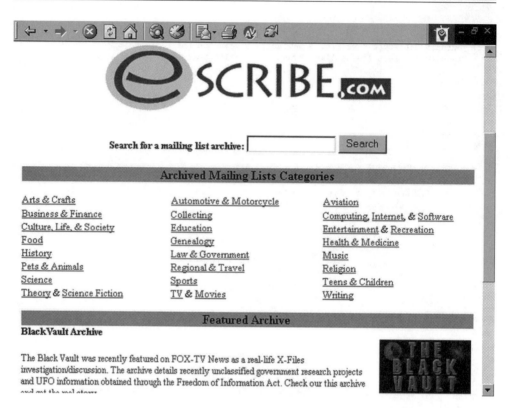

FIG. 4.11.   Searching mailing list archives at eScribe.com.

sults also include related lists, under the category headings of business, education, computing, and software (Fig. 4.12). Among the results is a link to the
archived messages from ow-defuct PAML, a Publicly Accessible Mailing List database. Click on that entry to see the messages, which are organized by date, then
subject line and author (Fig. 4.13). Clicking on the subject line displays the actual
message. As you view the message, there's another option to see other messages
the same author has written—although only within or addressed to that
particular mailing list.

At the same results screen, EScribe lets you search the text of archived mailing
list messages. Searching with the keyword "internet," EScribe looks through text
and subject headings to return 18 matches. What's nice is that it also indicates
how many messages it has searched, in this case 4,498, giving some idea of the
size of this particular database (Fig. 4.14).

EScribe does have a few disadvantages. First, its database is small; the only
lists archived are public lists, and among those, only the ones listowners have offered. Another more frustrating thing about EScribe is the advertising on the site.
You'll have to scroll down every screen to pass up the advertising to view results.
To make matters worse, there are numerous pop-up and pop-under ads, but a
good ad filter program can remedy that.

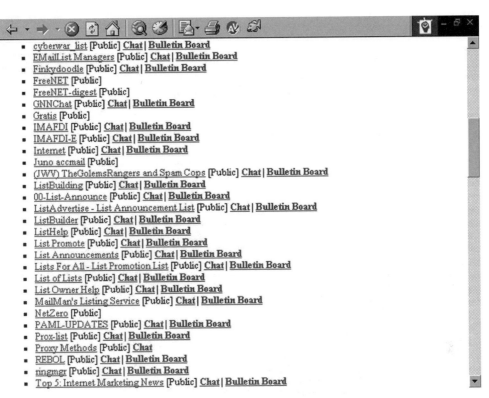

- cyberwar_list [Public] **Chat** | **Bulletin Board**
- EMailList Managers [Public] **Chat** | **Bulletin Board**
- Finkydoodle [Public] **Chat** | **Bulletin Board**
- FreeNET [Public]
- FreeNET-digest [Public]
- GNNChat [Public] **Chat** | **Bulletin Board**
- Gratis [Public]
- IMAFDI [Public] **Chat** | **Bulletin Board**
- IMAFDI-E [Public] **Chat** | **Bulletin Board**
- Internet [Public] **Chat** | **Bulletin Board**
- Juno accmail [Public]
- (JWV) TheGolemsRangers and Spam Cops [Public] **Chat** | **Bulletin Board**
- ListBuilding [Public] **Chat** | **Bulletin Board**
- 00-List-Announce [Public] **Chat** | **Bulletin Board**
- ListAdvertise - List Announcement List [Public] **Chat** | **Bulletin Board**
- ListBuilder [Public] **Chat** | **Bulletin Board**
- ListHelp [Public] **Chat** | **Bulletin Board**
- List Promote [Public] **Chat** | **Bulletin Board**
- List Announcements [Public] **Chat** | **Bulletin Board**
- Lists For All - List Promotion List [Public] **Chat** | **Bulletin Board**
- List of Lists [Public] **Chat** | **Bulletin Board**
- List Owner Help [Public] **Chat** | **Bulletin Board**
- MailMan's Listing Service [Public] **Chat** | **Bulletin Board**
- NetZero [Public]
- PAML-UPDATES [Public] **Chat** | **Bulletin Board**
- Prox-list [Public] **Chat** | **Bulletin Board**
- Proxy Methods [Public] **Chat**
- REBOL [Public] **Chat** | **Bulletin Board**
- ringmgr [Public] **Chat** | **Bulletin Board**
- Top 5: Internet Marketing News [Public] **Chat** | **Bulletin Board**

FIG. 4.12.   A roster of archived mailing lists.

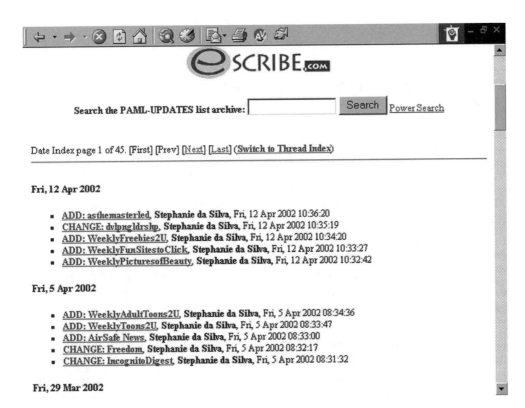

eSCRIBE.com

Search the PAML-UPDATES list archive: [_____]   Search   Power Search

Date Index page 1 of 45. [First] [Prev] [Next] [Last] (**Switch to Thread Index**)

Fri, 12 Apr 2002

- ADD: asthemasterled, **Stephanie da Silva**, Fri, 12 Apr 2002 10:36:20
- CHANGE: dvlpngldrshp, **Stephanie da Silva**, Fri, 12 Apr 2002 10:35:19
- ADD: WeeklyFreebies2U, **Stephanie da Silva**, Fri, 12 Apr 2002 10:34:20
- ADD: WeeklyFunSitestoClick, **Stephanie da Silva**, Fri, 12 Apr 2002 10:33:27
- ADD: WeeklyPicturesofBeauty, **Stephanie da Silva**, Fri, 12 Apr 2002 10:32:42

Fri, 5 Apr 2002

- ADD: WeeklyAdultToons2U, **Stephanie da Silva**, Fri, 5 Apr 2002 08:34:36
- ADD: WeeklyToons2U, **Stephanie da Silva**, Fri, 5 Apr 2002 08:33:47
- ADD: AirSafe News, **Stephanie da Silva**, Fri, 5 Apr 2002 08:33:00
- CHANGE: Freedom, **Stephanie da Silva**, Fri, 5 Apr 2002 08:32:17
- CHANGE: IncognitoDigest, **Stephanie da Silva**, Fri, 5 Apr 2002 08:31:32

Fri, 29 Mar 2002

FIG. 4.13.   Detail of an archived mailing list.

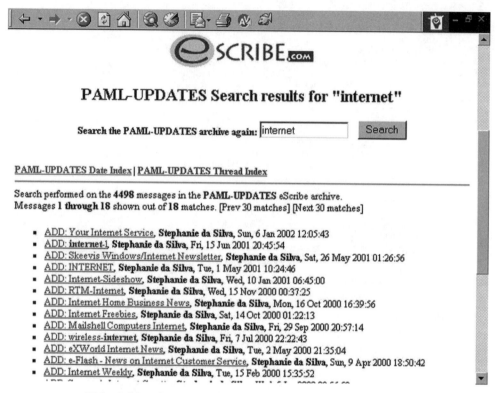

FIG. 4.14. Searching the text of an archived mailing list.

FINDING NEWSGROUPS AND ARCHIVES

Google Groups

Among the many changes to *Google's* popular search engine, http://groups.google.com, is the addition of Usenet discussion groups and their archives. This is the place to begin to search for current and archived newsgroups. Although some search engines have added an option for targeting newsgroups, they represent only a fraction of what Google has.

At the main Google Groups page, you can search for newsgroups by Usenet hierarchy, that is "alt" for alternative groups; "biz" for business-related groups; "soc" for social issues and so on. Alternately, you can view an alphabetical listing of newsgroups by clicking on the link at the bottom of the page, although this works best if you already know the name of the newsgroup you seek.

Your best choice is to type a category into the search box. A search for "journalism" returned 12 newsgroups related to that search and included in the results messages or posts from those groups (Fig. 4.15). Use the links at the top of the results screen if you want to see messages posted to one particular group. Otherwise, just beneath that on the page is a list of messages, that contain the word journalism either in the text, subject heading or newsgroup name. Clicking on

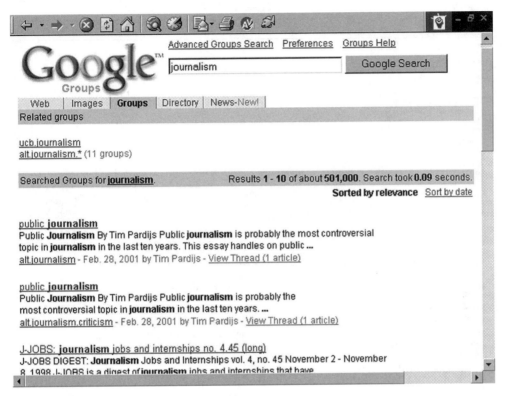

FIG. 4.15.   A search of Google Groups for journalism newsgroups.

any of those message headings will display the text of the message, including header information: the date it was posted, the newsgroup(s) to which it was posted, and the sender's name or screen name. In this example, a participant poses a question about the viability of a journalism education to the "alt.journalism.freelance" newsgroup (Fig. 4.16). If I click on the author's name, I can see other messages he has posted to Google Groups. If I click on his e-mail address, a mail form opens.

Just to the right of the author's name is a link to the complete thread, which indicates there are a total of four messages related to his query—his original message and three responses. Clicking on that link opens a split screen; to the right is the original message. You can scroll down to see the responses or use the menu at the left side to select a particular author. Clicking on any of those screen names takes you to that individual's response (Fig. 4.17).

Google's greatest feature is its archive of messages, a real treasure trove. Usenet messages were once kept on a site known as Deja, which has since been taken over by Google.[6] Before then, Deja had accumulated an archive of some 500 million messages dating back to 1995 and offered a clumsy search from its Web site. In its final days, the site was highly commercialized. Skimming news-

---

[6]Michelle Delio, "Google Buys Deja Archive," *Wired* (12 February 2001), www.wired.com . At this writing, Google was in a transition period while Deja archives were being reformatted.

FIG. 4.16.   An example of a newsgroup message or post.

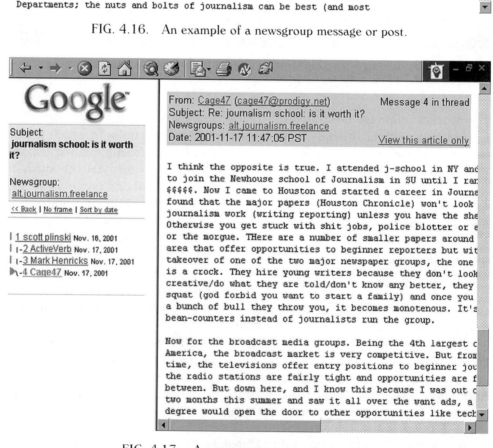

FIG. 4.17.   A response to a newsgroup post.

groups meant subjecting yourself to no end of advertisements, and search results invariably included the home pages of many hucksters. In true dot-com fashion, the transition from Deja to Google was abrupt, as some users discovered mid-post.[7] But the new and much-improved archive now boasts more than 800 million Usenet messages, archived back to 1981.

At the Google Groups main page, link to "Advanced Groups Search" a hyperlink to the right side of the search box. This is a much more efficient way to search through newsgroups, as it allows you to apply Boolean logic (see chap. 2, When Seconds Count) to your search parameters. Here, you have several options to narrow a search using any combination of: keyword, specific newsgroup or hierarchy, posting subject, date, author's name, and e-mail address (Fig. 4.18). Here is what each of those do:

All   In the "all" box, type in the words that must appear in the subject heading or text of the message or messages you seek, allowing a space between each word. The all search is the equivalent of the *and* Boolean search. For example, if you type journalism news technology, Google understands that as a request to find messages containing all three of those words.

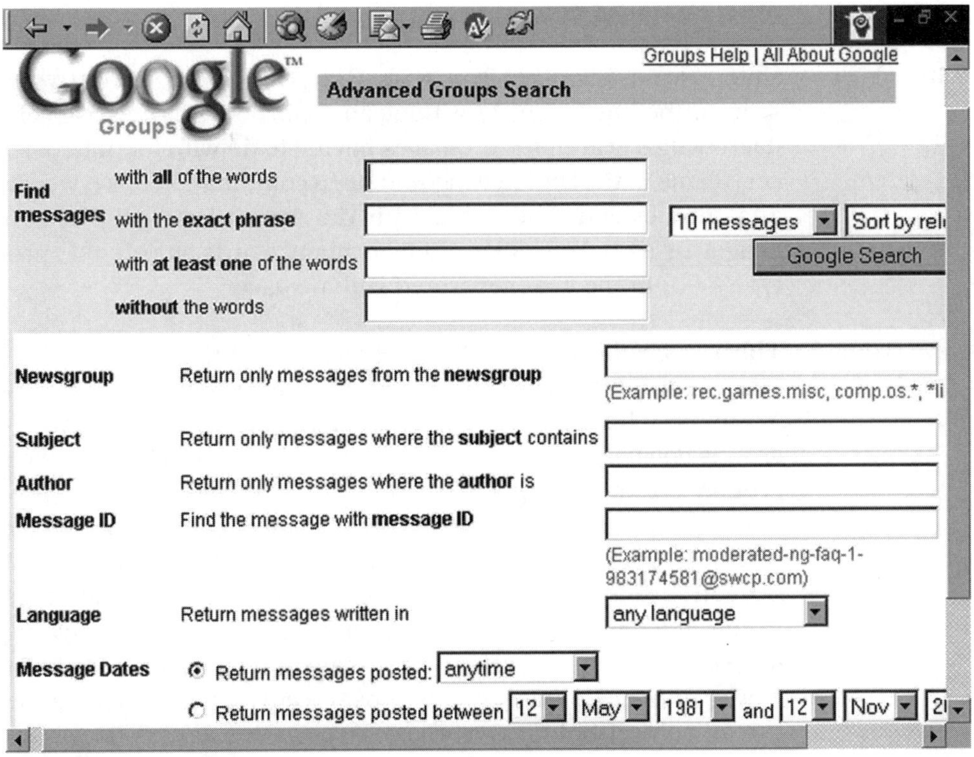

FIG. 4.18. Google Groups advanced search.

---

[7]Ibid.

Exact phrase   Similar to enclosing a phrase with quotation marks or paren-
                theses, this request tells Google to find messages that contain a
                phrase exactly as you've submitted it. For example, typing **In-
                ternational Cricket Council** tells Google to find messages in
                which that organization is cited. A note here: Remember that
                newsgroup postings are generally informal, so you may want to
                try variations on search terms such as *ICC*, the acronym for the
                aforementioned sports organization. Keep in mind that au-
                thors often adopt a kind of shorthand to save keystrokes, so ac-
                ronyms and abbreviations, even in proper names, are not
                uncommon.

At Least One   This is an "or" search, or perhaps better described as an "any"
                search. Type in your keywords, allowing a single space between
                them and Google will search for messages that contain instances
                of those words or combinations of them. Typing **rugby dublin**
                nets messages that contain either the word "rugby," "dublin," or
                both. This widens your search. As the advanced search does not
                support wild cards or partial word searches, you may need to en-
                ter several forms of your keyword in this box, for example, **com-
                pute computer computing**.

Without   Enter terms here that you wish Google to exclude from your
                search, the equivalent of a Boolean "and not" search. To begin
                narrowing a search for messages having to do with football (soc-
                cer) teams in the United Kingdom, try a combination of keywords
                and then exclude messages with the words National Football
                League or NFL. You can exclude as many words as you like, just
                type them in the box, separated with a space.

Newsgroup   This search allows you to find messages that belong to a particu-
                lar newsgroup or hierarchy. To find out what's included in a hier-
                archy, go back to Google Groups' main page (http://
                groups.google.com) and enter a subject keyword in the "search
                groups" box or click on a hyperlink in the "browse groups" list be-
                low that. You'll get a list of newsgroups related to that topic. Under
                "biz" for example, you'll find lists called biz.ecommerce and
                biz.entrepreneurs. Return to the advanced search page and type
                in that information in the newsgroup box. For instance, typing
                biz.entrepreneurs returns messages posted to just that
                newsgroup, beginning with the most recent posting. Click on the
                thread subject link to view the message. This search does sup-
                port the wild card, so if you want to find messages related to all
                business groups, type **biz.*** in the newsgroup box—of course,
                that returned more than 2 million messages, so you might want

to think of ways to narrow your search. The wild card can only be used as a suffix, thus you can only put it at the end of your search term, not at the beginning.

The newsgroup search remains a bit clunky, particularly if you try using a keyword here instead of a list name. For example, typing **cooking** in this box will return messages posted to the rec.outdoors.camping (recreation/outdoors/camping) and rec.food.preserving (recreation/food/preserving) groups. Why? Either the word cooking appears in a message or because cooking is related to recreation, Google assumes you're interested. You'll have better luck if you use the hierarchical name of the group rather than using a subject search.

Subject   Here's where you can enter a subject to find newsgroups related to a particular topic. Type **cooking** here and you'll get messages from all archived newsgroups in which the subject heading is cooking, or cooking appears in the text.

Author   To find messages posed by a particular individual (author), use this search request. Type in the author's first and last name (in that order) to find messages posted (and signed) with exactly that name. For variations, submit a portion of the name. Typing **anna** resulted in messages from a range of newsgroups posted by "anna morris," "anna b.," "lee and anna," and so on. Typing **conrad** resulted in messages written by "peter conrad," "conrad drake" and someone posting as simply "conrad," for example. Here, you can also enter an e-mail address rather than a proper name.

Message ID   This search allows you to find specific messages by an identifying protocol. This is handy if you have the message in its original format; the message ID appears in the header information as a jumble of letters, numbers and other symbols. Then, you can plug in that ID to trace the message to its original thread, to see what responses were given, for example, or to what a specific author responded.

Language   Use this option to find messages written in one or any of 25 languages. The default is *any*, but this will return pages in languages you may not be able to read, or your browser may not be capable of displaying. To minimize your results, change this to a language that both you and your browser can interpret.

Dates   Google's Advanced Search will also let you target messages by their posting dates. The default is "anytime," but from the same pull-down menu, you can select messages posted in the last 24 hours, week, month, three months, six months or year. Just below that is an option to target specific dates or date range. This is an effective way to minimize your search results.

SafeSearch   Here, users are given two options, no filtering and "SafeSearch" filtering, which will exclude many adult or explicit sites from your groups search results. What you select here is less important than what you select at Google's preferences page (http://groups.google.com/preferences). Moderate filtering is the default even if you select "do not filter" at the Google Groups Search page—unless you change your settings on the preferences page by indicating you want stricter filtering or no filtering at all. At that same page, you can adjust other settings, such as the number of results you want to see per page, and in what language you want them to appear. At the bottom or top of the screen, click on "save preferences" so your computer uses those settings every time you conduct a Google Groups search.

To Keep in Mind

In addition to capricious shorthand, there are a few more caveats to keep in mind when searching newsgroups. For example, when people respond to postings by clicking on the "reply" button, the subject line automatically appears in the "regarding" line. Rarely do people change the subject line, even when the thread of the conversation departs from its original topic. That means that although a subject search may turn up a message that has "search engine" as its heading, the text may be about something else entirely.

For maximum results, use a combination of Google's options to further limit your search of newsgroups. For example, you might specify a newsgroup (alt.journalism.freelance) then use the "without the words" option at the top of the search page to exclude messages that contain certain words or messages from specific authors. A shown in Fig. 4.19, to find comments regarding the contested results of the 2000 presidential election, I've requested a search of messages posted to a journalism group (alt.journalism) that contain the words "election" and the last names of the two major candidates, "Bush" and "Gore." I've added the word "Florida," because that is where the results were ultimately contested. I've excluded my own e-mail address so that my messages won't appear and because I'm interested in immediate reaction, specified a date range, November 7 through November 30. Once I see the results, I decide to resort them by date, rather than relevance (Fig. 4.20). The first three posts were posted to the newsgroup talk.politics.misc, not the group I specified on the search page. This is because the messages were crossposted, or duplicated, to alt.journalism—that becomes clear if you open the message by clicking on the subject line.

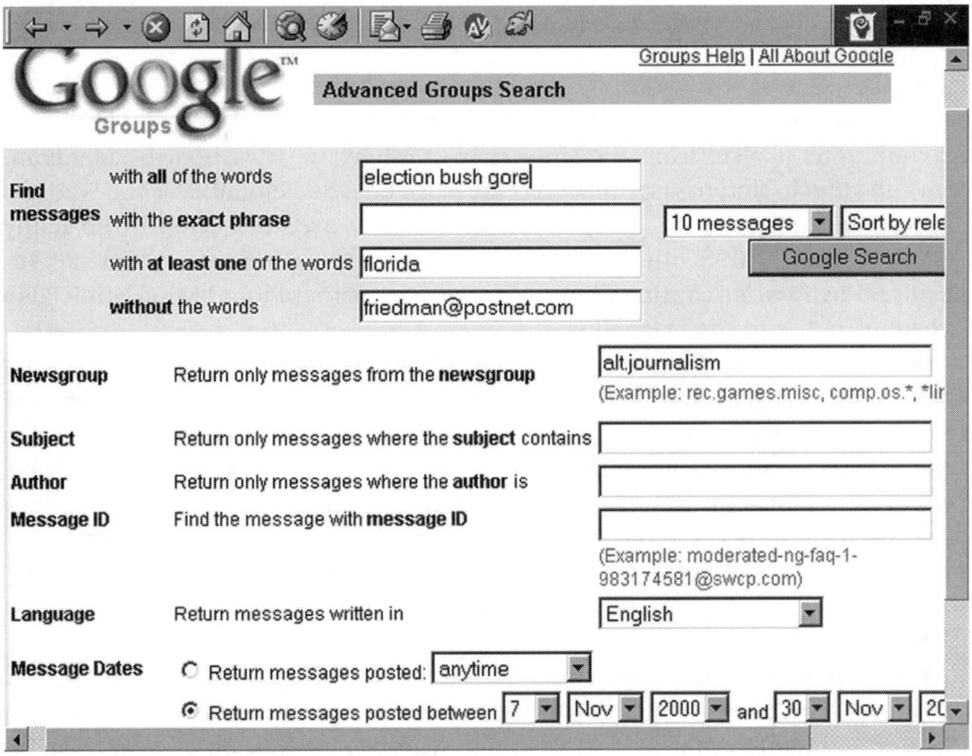

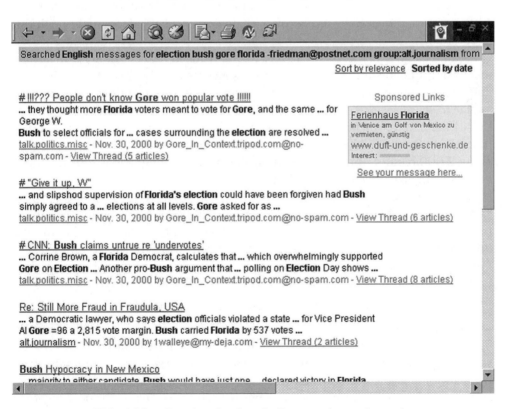

FIG. 4.19. Searching newsgroups using Google Groups advanced search.

FIG. 4.20. Results of a Google Groups advanced search.

BoardReader

An ambitious project from the University of Michigan, www.boardreader.com, this site aims to find newsgroups and message boards held all over the Web, including the "invisible" or "deep" Web, that murky area neglected by so many search engines. Unlike other sites, this is not an active database or host site. Instead, *BoardReader* captures messages and stores them for viewing, while also providing a link to the original site.

BoardReader has both a simple and advanced search. A keyword search combs through the subject lines, author's name, message text, host site, and threads of hundreds of thousands of newsgroup or bulletin board posts. At the results screen, you can organize your results in several ways: by date (most recent first, or oldest first), by relevance (how many times your keyword or phrase appears), by number of replies, or alphabetical by host site—including universities and not for profit organizations around the world. The "arrange results by" function still had a few bugs when I tried it, but showed promise as a way to speed research.

The advanced search works to refine your search criteria. By supporting wild cards and a bit of Boolean logic, users can really target content. By enclosing a phrase in quotation marks, BoardReader searches for that phrase exactly as it appears. Here, you can also specify whether you want the search engine to find any or all of your search words. The advanced search also allows users familiar with newsgroup hierarchy to narrow by category and subcategory, although this is optional.

As an example, I've used BoardReader's advanced search to target messages discussing Manchester United, the British soccer team. I begin by typing the team name in quotation marks, then use the optional criteria to narrow—directing the engine to search sports-related groups and further, those devoted to soccer. I get more than 20,000 results. A second search, using the same criteria, but changing "soccer" to "football," because that's what the sport is called in England, nets about 2,000 results—quite a reduction. This time, the engine has looked among groups or boards devoted to football.

A third attempt narrows the search considerably. This time, I want to see messages related to Manchester United from any and all groups, and then among those, only messages that mention former team captain David Beckham's endorsement deals. A bulletin board or newsgroup will give me some idea how much he stands to earn, and how soccer fans feel about the issue of sponsorship. So now the search string looks like this (Fig. 4.21):

"manchester united" beck* endorse*

The reason I've used wild cards is that Beckham is also known by the nickname "Becks" and I want messages that include either moniker. Further, messages might contain either the word "endorse," "endorsed," or "endorsement;" I want any of those. I check the box on the advanced search page for "all the words" so the engine knows I want only those pages where these words appear together. Now we've reduced the search results to 25 from the original 20,000 (Fig. 4.22).

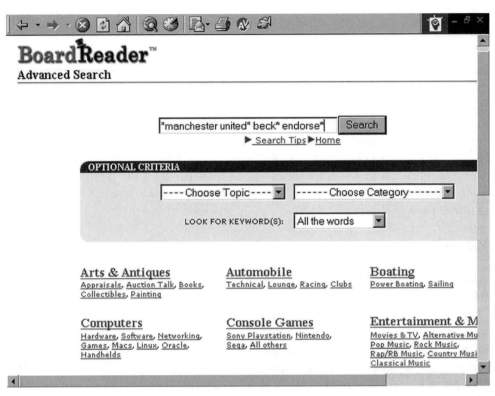

FIG. 4.21. An advanced search of newsgroup messages at BoardReader.

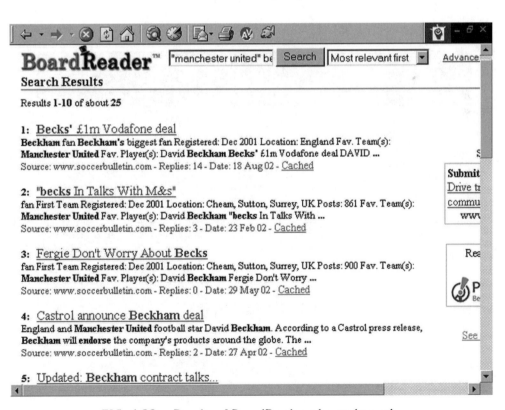

FIG. 4.22. Results of BoardReader advanced search.

At the top of the results list is a message, actually a reprinted newspaper article, announcing Beckham's recent endorsement agreement with Vodafone, the team's sponsor. According to BoardReader, this post had 14 replies and was originally posted at the site, www.soccerbulletin.com. Clicking on the subject line takes you to the original Web site where you can look for more recent activity. Click on "cached" to see the thread. There, you can also see which forum on the Soccer Bulletin site the message was posted to, the author's name or screen name and location—or at least the location designated by the user—don't count on those to be accurate. Scroll down to see the replies to the original post (Fig. 4.23).

Yahoo Groups

Yahoo (http://groups.yahoo.com), like most of the major search engines and ISPs, now supports online groups. But because each "sponsor" wants to be exclusive, its database of searchable archives are usually limited to its own groups. In other words, you cannot search Yahoo Groups at the AOL site. AOL, on the other hand, offers communities, but only those they deem acceptable. You won't find any of the alternative (".alt") groups there. Thus, while Yahoo hosts quite a few groups and is listed here because it's a good site for locating resources and people, its cache of postings doesn't even begin to compare with Google.

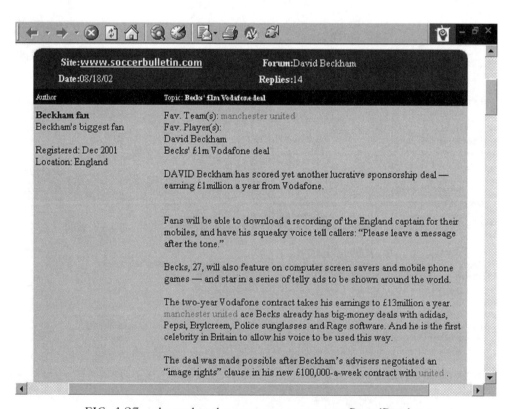

FIG. 4.23.　An archived newsgroup message at BoardReader.

At the Yahoo Groups main page (Fig. 4.24), you can search newsgroups by name, category, or keyword. Here, I searched for journalism-related groups, and Yahoo returned more than 500 results (Fig. 4.25). The results indicate which newsgroups are intended for members, such as those related to a college course, and which are open to everyone.

When you locate a group you'd like to participate in, you are required to establish a Yahoo Groups account. If you already use a Yahoo e-mail account, you can join using that information. Then, you can opt to have posts delivered to your e-mail address individually or in digest form. Alternately, you can read posts at the Yahoo site, a good choice if you don't want newsgroup posts cluttering up your mailbox.

Among the results of my search for journalism-related groups one called Scholastic Journalism. It is dedicated to journalism education, has 108 members, and is open to interested participants. Clicking on the name of that newsgroup provides me with a description of the list, as well as other details: that it was founded July 8, 1998 and posts are made in English, that it is unmoderated and the content is archived. The search results indicate there are more than one thousand messages posted already to the group, and at this screen I can view the most recent ones or search past messages. As you can tell from the subject lines, some are related to journalism and some are not, a typical problem with newsgroups and in particular, unmoderated ones.

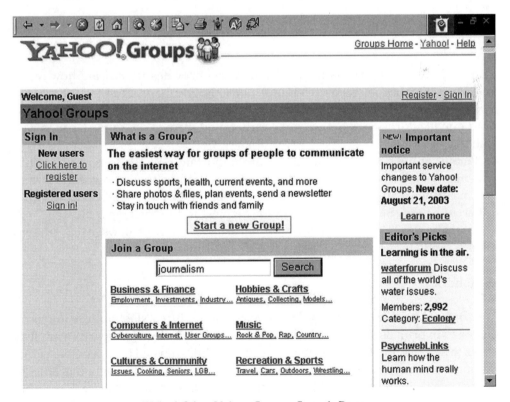

FIG. 4.24.   Yahoo Groups Search Page.

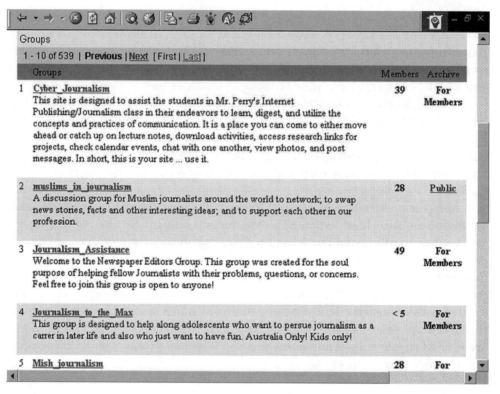

FIG. 4.25.   Results of a Yahoo Groups search for journalism newsgroups.

A helpful feature here is the calendar Yahoo provides to indicate how many messages have been posted each month since the group was founded. This helps you judge the volume of mail, and decide whether you want messages delivered to your e-mail address or whether you'd rather read them at the Yahoo Groups Web site (Fig. 4.26).

Finally, at the bottom of the screen are important e-mail addresses, for sub-scribing, unsubscribing, posting messages or reaching the list owner. It is very important to distinguish among the addresses, since each is associated with a different action. Sending a subscription request to the "posting a message" ad-dress may result in your request being broadcast to all newsgroup readers (which tends to make people angry) or an error message.

Slashdot

If it's information technology you're after, *Slashdot*, http://slashdot.org (often re-ferred to in print as simply "/.") provides an archive of message boards as well as links to a number of IT-related newsletters. Slashdot, owned by Open Source De-velopment Network, refers to itself as "news for nerds" and as such, has links to numerous technology related sites. At the main site, current messages are found under category headings on the left of the screen; click on the link to "read more"

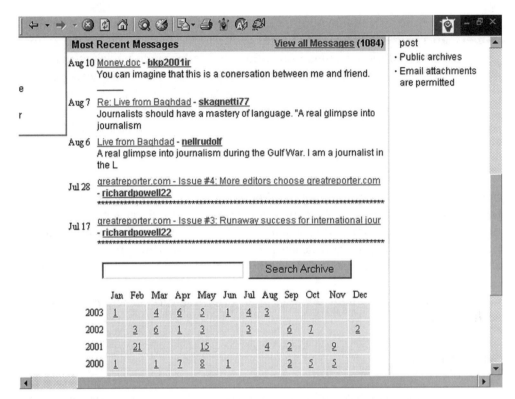

FIG. 4.26.   Details of a Yahoo Group dedicated to journalism education.

or on the number of comments to display the original message and responses. To the right, Slashdot arranges queries for technical assistance posted by and for subscribers. Clicking on those displays the question and the responses. Also at Slashdot's main page is a hyperlink tab to IT-related newsletters and subscription information.

A similar and helpful site is *Geocrawler* (www.geocrawler.com), a searchable archive of mailings lists related to the Open Source movement since 1985.

Finding Newsletters and Archives

As I've already suggested, the best way to find a newsletter is to be direct. Are you interested in reading the newsletter of a specific organization, for example? If so, your best bet is to go directly to their Web site and look for a newsletter link. That's likely to be where you can also find back issues of newsletters. Your knowledge of domain names, as explained in chapter 2, should help you locate the proper site.

Another way to find newsletters is by conducting an advanced Internet search, as described in chapter 2. For example, using AltaVista or Google's advanced search, you might try using the keywords "newsletter" and (as in "AND," the Boolean operator) the topic of the publication, or name of the sponsoring organization. A search using AltaVista's advanced option for **newsletter AND "American Lung Association"** led me to the home page of the organization, which included a link to publications and an e-mail form to begin receiving the "Weekly Breather" electronic newsletter. This technique worked well because the organization's Web site was not www.ala.org as I might have guessed, but rather it is www.lungusa.org.

Finding Web Logs

Web logs are fairly easy to locate, because bloggers tend to be a fraternal order, and their sites often feature links to other web logs. In other words, when you've found one blogger, you've found them all. That's not quite true, but you've certainly located quite a few of their friends, colleagues, and rivals. As an example, blogger Glenn Reynolds, a college law professor, provides links from his Web site, www.InstaPundit.com, to more than 100 other bloggers, in addition to online news sites.

To get started, you might use one of several blog directories. A few are described next.

Waypath

Waypath (www.waypath.com) is a great source for locating blog entries by keywords, and finding out what bloggers are saying about current news through a URL search. The site uses a robotic spider to crawl Web log update lists several times daily, so its database is fairly current. Based on your keyword, Waypath applies relational software to determine the "meaning" or context of the blog entries and determine which ones match your query. It's not always on target, but taking advantage of Boolean queries will help refine your search. Results include links to blogs, excerpts from blog entries, responses, and sites that have linked to a blog. Waypath also provides an option to further your search including (+) or excluding it (-) specific blogs.

Besides using a keyword search, you can find out what bloggers are saying about a current news story with a URL search. Select "URL" from the drop-down menu, then enter the Web site address for a particular news item. For example, entering the URL for an August 2003 news story on the CNN site about candidates for a possible California governor's race resulted in 236 distinct blogs. The first is from a blog called "Random Acts of Kindness" (Fig. 4.27).

Technorati

This site (www.technorati.com) works much the same as Waypath, though I find its results a bit cluttered. To its credit, *Technorati* allows Boolean queries, so for example, a search for "jack berger" (in quotation marks) finds blog entries commenting on the addition of this character to a popular television show. Among the results are the names of related blogs, excerpts and ratings. Enter the URL of a

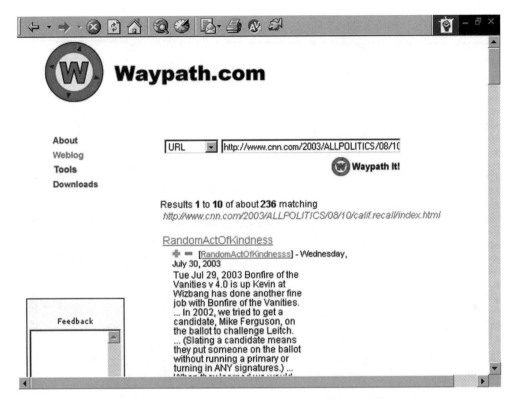

FIG. 4.27.   A Web log or blog search by URL at Waypath.

particular blog, and Technorati shows you sites or blogs that have linked to it. You can use this function in another way; enter the URL of a news story and find out which bloggers have linked to it with commentary.

Globe of Blogs

The *Globe of Blogs* site allows you to search among more than 6,000 blogs in several ways; www.globeofblogs.com. You can browse by topic and title, then use the "find" option from your browser's "edit" pull-down menu to zero in on a particular keyword. Because bloggers tend to forge links with one another often based on common interests or location (termed *webrings*), Globe of Blogs also allows searches by name, gender, birthday, and location, and age; there are no blogs here written by children under 14 years of age (Fig. 4.28).

The Pepys Project

An ambitious project named for Samuel Pepys, http://pepys.akacooties.com, whose diaries recount major events in 17th century London including the Plague of 1655, this site catalogs blogs by geographic location. There are some 800 links to U.S.-based blogs that are further broken down by state. The Web site also of-

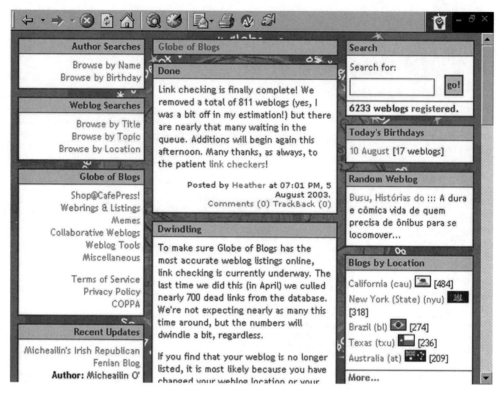

FIG. 4.28.   Globe of Blogs.

fers a search, located at the bottom of the page. Use keywords or titles to locate specific blogs.

Open Weblog Directory

As with many blogger directories, this one, www.weblogs.nu/directory, relies on authors to submit their sites for inclusion. Here, you can scroll through a list of recently added sites, or at the bottom of the page, search by keyword. As you search, think not just about how something might be categorized, but about words that might appear either in the blog's description or content.

Blog Critics

This site, www.blogcritics.org, is a compilation of blogs dedicated to critique of the arts: music, literature, film, and more. You can link to selected blogs which are organized under headlines and excerpts, or use the search function on the left side of the page to locate a blog by title, name, or keyword. Also in the left-side column is a lengthy roster of blogs.

The Blogdex Project

Not so much a directory as a listing of the Web's most popular topics or links, this MIT Media Laboratory project, http://blogdex.media.mit.edu, demonstrates what most of 10,000 blogs are talking about on a given day. For example, on November 5, 2002, election day in the U.S., among the most talked-about stories was a report that Florida's election machines had malfunctioned. Blogdex provided a link to the story's originating site (www.drudgereport.com), and to sites that had commented on and linked to it.

You can also search for blogs using an advanced search in either AltaVista or Google. On AltaVista, a search using the phrase **blog OR blogger AND politics** located more than 200,000 sites. You could easily narrow a search like that by including keywords having to do with a particular event or issue. Better yet, you could use a link search (see syntax searches in chap. 3) to find sites linked to a particular blog.

Finding blog archives is simple. Because blogs are time-stamped entries, nearly every site includes chronological archives; just look for the link. The better ones also offer subject searches.

To Post or Not to Post?

Once you've subscribed to a mailing list or find yourself reading the posts from newsgroups and web logs, you are under no obligation to participate in the discussion. In other words, if you are more comfortable eavesdropping or *lurking* as it is often referred to, that's fine. You are not doing anything wrong or illegal. Remember though, that participants in a mailing list can find out who the other subscribers are, so your inactivity does not conceal your identity.

It's always a good idea to read newsgroup or listserv messages and blogs for a few visits anyway, before you enter the discussion. That way, you'll be able to get a feel for the tone of the group and what kind of people populate it. If a list or group has a "FAQ" link (frequently answered question), you can find out what questions have been asked and answered already and thus avoid taking up participants' time with those same queries.

Equally important is that you note the differences in mailing addresses associated with listservs. When you subscribe, you'll receive a confirmation through e-mail, including directions for sending commands (e.g., unsubscribe, suspend, and so on) and for posting messages. These are usually two separate addresses and you ought not to confuse the two—list participants are a patient bunch, but this is something that gets under their skin.

A Word About 'Netiquette'

Although we think of the Internet as a kind of untamed land, it is not without rules of network etiquette, or *netiquette*, and mailing list subscribers are particularly fond of decorum. For example, advertising products or services in a newsgroup or listserv is frowned on, as is sending spam or junk mail. When messages are crossposted, that is, sent to more than one group or list, the author will usu-ally begin with an apology as in, "Excuse the crosspost."

Without the aid of body language or intonation to provide the message recipient with context, electronic mail has to provide the reader with nuances in other ways. Here's how:

- Typing a message using all uppercase letters suggests to the reader that you are shouting. This is generally discouraged, unless of course you are angry and want everyone to know. Likewise, using lowercase letters exclusively, al-though perfectly acceptable for e-mails between friends, is inappropriate in a forum where protocol is expected.

- Because electronic mail is considered a more casual form of correspon-dence than traditional letter-writing, acronyms are permissible. You may soon come across some of the most common: *IMO* (in my opinion) or *IMHO* (in my humble opinion), *TIA* (thanks in advance), *FYI* (for your information), *BTW* (by the way) and *FWIW* (for what it's worth), are just a few examples.

- The use of *emoticons,* icons and symbols to denote feelings, is also ac-ceptable, though less so on mailing lists where subscribers try to maintain a professional "appearance." Tip your head to the left so your ear is almost touching your shoulder, and look at the following emoticons and what they de-note. These are simple, but some computer users have also come up with elab-orate symbols to add distinction to their electronic correspondence.

> ;-) a wink and a smile (made with semi-colon, dash then right parentheses)
>
> :-0 shock or surprise (colon, dash, a zero)
>
> :-) happiness (colon, dash, right parentheses)
>
> :-/ ambivalence (colon, dash, slash)

Right to Privacy?

By now it should be clear that if you can read other people's e-mails, posted to newsgroups and lists, they can read yours too. There's no real guarantee of pri-vacy when you post something to the Web, and although programmers work dili-gently on encryption devices, hackers are every bit as industrious. Newspapers carry stories about their handiwork: stolen social security numbers, identity theft, harassment, and so forth.

Furthermore, employers freely tap the hard drives of their workers to check for abuses of work time, and current law upholds their right to do so.[8] In 2000, in a notorious case of male braggadocio, a London lawyer copied an explicit note sent to him by a girlfriend and e-mailed it to friends. After that the note was cop-ied and forwarded, and copied and forwarded again.[9] The sender, humiliated, hounded by the press and other curiosity seekers, finally went into hiding.[10]

---

[8]Michael J. McCarthy, "You Assumed 'Erase' Wiped Out That Rant Against the Boss? Nope," *Wall Street Journal* (7 March 2000), A1.

[9]Robert Uhlig and David Sapsted, "E-Mail Victim Flees Tangled Web of Betrayal," *London Tele-graph* (16 December 2000), 1; Sandra Barwick and Richard Alleyne, "Laddish Lawyers Turn to the Net for Sleazy Gossip," *London Telegraph* (16 December 2000), 7.

[10]Robert Uhlig, "Salacious E-Mail Returns to Haunt Sender," *LondonTelegraph* (16 December 2000), 7.

The government has admitted to inadvertently capturing private citizens' e-mails as part of a e-mail tapping program. *Carnivore,* a program used by the Federal Bureau of Investigation to intercept and collect e-mail similar to the way a telephone wiretap works, was intended to pick up communication between targets of an April 2000 counterterrorism investigation. Among the results however, were e-mails from many "noncovered" individuals.[11]

Whereas most e-mail ends up at its destination, some messages go astray. In the last year, I've received five e-mails intended for someone else. Two were friendly notes, two were business-oriented and one was quite personal.

Newsgroups are public forums, subject to scrutiny by anyone with computer access. But users can opt not to have their messages archived. Type "x-no-archive:yes" in either the heading or first line of your message before you post it. However, you cannot retract messages once they are posted. Your messages are available to others for viewing during a brief period, then deleted to make room for new posts. Mailing list messages are generally archived and available to subscribers too.

In a perfect online world, the information sent and received through our computers would be private, like written letters or personal phone calls. The creator of the Internet, Tim Berners-Lee, writes that a consensual privacy policy is part of "the greatest prerequisite for a weblike society: trust."[12] But even he admits privacy issues continue to be a concern for users. Because we tend to communicate informally by e-mail, we let our guard down and forget we might be overheard. It's prudent to avoid saying anything in messages you post to newsgroups, mailing lists, blogs, or your regular e-mail that you wouldn't want repeated and traced to you. As you'll see in chapter 5, even the most mundane information can be used to compile personal information about its author.

TIPS FOR SMART SEARCHES

- Use any combination of newsgroups, web logs, newsletters, and mailing lists to establish an online beat and stay current with new sites and changes in technology, and to find solutions to problems.
- To find sources use a direct approach whenever possible such as going straight to an organization's Web site to find newsletter archives. Otherwise, choose from a "list of lists" or use advanced search techniques to find what you seek.
- Mailing lists are owned by the people who set them up or the institutions that provide server space for the messages. Few owners want their lists to fail, so they take measures to attract a steady stream of interested participants who

---

[11]John Schwartz, "Bin Laden Inquiry was Hindered By F.B.I. E-mail Tapping," *New York Times* (29 April 2002), A12.

[12]Tim Berners-Lee, *Weaving the Web* (New York: HarperCollins, 1999), 126. The author favors public key cryptography, "a scheme for encoding information so no one can read it unless he or she has the key to decode it. How we can use it directly affects what we can do socially. With this tool, we can have completely confidential conversations at a distance—vouch for the authenticity of messages, check their integrity and hold their authors accountable."

keep the discussion lively, productive, and on track. Newsgroups are more volatile, here today and gone tomorrow, or gone as soon as the discussion wanes.

- As mailing lists discourage anonymity, requiring that every participant be identified, the conversations tend to be more productive and respectful. Although exchanges are not always amiable, there's less flaming among mailing list subscribers. The anonymity that characterizes newsgroups however, encourages knee-jerk responses to topics and does little to deter flaming or harassment of others. Should things get out of hand, it is usually left up to the people trading angry or nuisance messages to resolve the dispute or abandon the group for another.

- Mailing list subscribers are enthusiastic and serious about their topics, and their messages reflect some degree of thoughtfulness and experience. Mailing lists tend to attract professionals, whereas newsgroups attract anyone with an opinion.

- Mailing list messages are easier to check for credibility. Messages typically include the e-mail address of not only the list and list owner but also of the author of the post, and may also offer other contact information. Newsgroup contributors might not be identified by anything more than initials or a screen name.

- The text of mailing list messages tends to be more substantive than those of newsgroups. I find the navigation required to view newsgroup messages cumbersome, and it's even more frustrating when that message is nothing more than a single line, and not at all thoughtful (one message headlined "search engines help" and responding to a previous post, read simply "huh?").

- Read lists, newsgroups and blogs for a few days to discern the tone, unwritten rules and interests, before posting your message.

- To protect your privacy, opt not to allow your newsgroup messages to be archived.

- Take care when posting messages to a public forum; don't write anything you wouldn't want others to know.

5

Finding Out About People

From time to time, politicians and privacy advocates make a public demonstration of proving just how easy it is to gather personal information about private citizens using the Internet. For example, during his 2000 campaign for the U.S. Senate, Democratic candidate Ed Bernstein of Nevada convened a news conference to announce that if elected, he would be an advocate for privacy rights and support federal legislation making it illegal to buy or sell social security numbers. He offered a 17-page report detailing property he owned, former addresses and the names and phone numbers of his neighbors, all culled from the Internet.[1]

But if Bernstein intended to shock, he picked the wrong audience. Reporters in attendance routinely use the same kinds of public records to locate people and information—marriage records, assessors' records, voter registration lists, and such—records that are available to anyone in printed form or online. Gathering such information was routine long before the Internet was popularized; now it's just more convenient. The migration of public records to the Internet was prompted by agencies interested in cutting down on paperwork and reducing demands on their staffs.[2] Now, users can avoid many of the barriers posed by "traditional" research. For example, whereas an agency's or library's operating hours might have been restrictive, the Internet is a 24-hour virtual service counter—a real boon for journalists and other researchers.

Repeated warnings about identity theft[3] and increasing annoyance with junk mail[4] already have many people declining to provide personal data when promp-

---

[1]Jane Ann Morrison, "Bernstein Rips Ease of Net Invasion," *Las Vegas Review-Journal* (19 July 2000), 1.

[2]See for example, Amy Harmon, "As Public Records Go Online, Some Say They're Too Public," *New York Times* (24 August 2001), A1; Katie Hafner, "California Stops Selling Personal Data," *New York Times* (13 December 2001), D9.

[3]See for example, Adam Cohen, "Internet Insecurity," *Time* (2 July 2001), 45; Robert O'Harrow Jr., "Identity Thieves Thrive in Information Age," *Washington Post* (31 May 2001), A1.

[4]See for example, Saul Hansell, "Big Web Sites To Track Steps of Their Users," *New York Times* (16 August 1998), A1.

ted by a Web site. And in a Pew Research study done just after the September 11, 2001 terrorist attacks, 70% of Americans said they were opposed to government monitoring of e-mail communications.[5] When ISPs and Internet portals sell access to users' telephone numbers, postal, and e-mail addresses[6] or when they show no reservations at law enforcement officials' requests for subscribers' personal data,[7] Internet users are rightly outraged. Government regularly debates restrictions to prevent computer privacy invasions[8]—but new laws solve only part of the problem.

Far more shocking than what's available from public records is the amount of personal data people voluntarily place online for others to see. The number and variation of home pages attests to the eagerness of the public to share personal interests without too much concern over who's viewing the information or how it might eventually be used or abused. As one example, I came upon a university professor's Web site that included a scanned image of his pregnant wife's ultrasound. Although he only intended to share his family's joy over the impending birth, the documentation on the ultrasound disclosed more: his wife's full name and birthdate, her doctor's name, and admitting hospital; that's useful data for someone engaged in identity theft. I am constantly surprised at the amount of data parents are willing to post online regarding their children, such as names and photographs, particularly because we've learned that children are the Web's most vulnerable users.[9] Federal law requires Web sites that might be visited by children under 13 years of age to comply with Federal Trade Commission regulations, but that does not apply to unwitting parents who promote their children and their accomplishments to vast online audiences.[10]

What kind of information have you broadcast online? If you've ever sent an e-mail, shopped online, or registered at a Web site, you've left a trail of "digital detritus"[11] as one reporter called it. Last year, journalists assembled a profile of the suspect in a January 2001 mass killing by using, among other things, gift preferences the man had listed on Amazon.com.[12] *Wired News*, an online publication, uncovered and reported the same man's e-mails, posted to an online bulletin board.[13] In 2001, an investigator working a decades-old jet hijacking case found the vanished prime suspect after an Internet search turned up a newspaper arti-

---

[5]Michael Bartlett, "Americans Still Guard Telephone, E-Mail Privacy," *Washington Post* (19 September 2001), www.washingtonpost.com .

[6]Saul Hansell, "Seeking Profits, Internet Alters Privacy Policy," *New York Times* (11 April 2002), A1.

[7]"Colorado Police Look Into Possible JonBenet Lead On AOL," *CNN* (10 September 2001), www.cnn.com.

[8]John Schwartz, "Government is Wary of Tackling Online Privacy," *New York Times* (6 September 2001), C1; "Health Information Privacy Rules," *Internet Connection* 7:1 (January 2001), 6; Steve Lohr, "Privacy Group is Taking Issue with Microsoft," *New York Times* (25 July 2001), C1.

[9]John Schwartz, "Web Sites Found Lax in Protecting Child Privacy," *New York Times* (28 March 2001), A16.

[10]Mark LaRochelle, "Online Privacy Update: Enforcing COPPA," *Consumers' Research Magazine* 84 (September 2001), 43–44.

[11]Pamela LiCalzi O'Conner, "Tracking a Suspect on an Online Trail," *New York Times* (8 January 2001), C4. Also see, Doug Bedell, "Many Find It's Hard to Hide From Trackers in Cyberspace," *San Diego Union-Tribune* (2 December 2002), C1.

[12]O'Conner, "Tracking a Suspect on an Online Trail," *New York Times*.

[13]Michelle Delio, "Mucko: 'Thou Shalt Not Kill,'" *Wired*, (28 December 2000), www.wired.com .

cle written about the man's current work as a teacher and mentor.[14] As one technology executive has said, "If you're concerned about privacy, don't use the
Internet."[15]

So after all, this chapter serves as both a user's guide and a warning. Although
I'll direct you to some of the best methods for gathering information about people—using directories, search engines, databases, and above all, thinking creatively—you may be troubled by what's out there. After all, prying eyes may include
not only marketers but hackers,[16] stalkers,[17] government,[18] and employers.[19] You
might think about removing your personal information from these sites, or at
least become more careful about what kinds of private details you transmit
across the Internet.

USING ONLINE TELEPHONE AND E-MAIL DIRECTORIES

Perhaps the easiest and most obvious way to find someone is to use a phone directory. In fact, Americans spent some $5 billion on directory assistance in 1998,
according to a report in the *Christian Science Monitor*,[20] and a request for a single telephone number might cost an individual one dollar or more. When Verizon
Communications employees went on strike in the fall of 2000, making it near impossible to get through to the company's 411 directory assistance, many customers turned to free online directory services.[21]

The earliest sites offered the same information you would find in a typical
phone directory, but many have expanded to include features that traditional directory assistance services do not offer. Those features include e-mail and reverse directories (routinely used by reporters to locate sources), maps, area
codes, and even local weather. Multiple listings, for which most directory assistance services usually charge extra, cost nothing on these sites. White page (residential) listings for all 50 states are online, as are residential listings for many
countries outside the U.S. If an individual has an unlisted number however, you
won't find it by using telephone directory Web sites. Mobile phone registries are
beginning to accumulate on the Web, to help find cellular phone numbers and
contact information for some wireless customers.

---

[14]C. J. Chivers, "Traced on Internet, Teacher is Charged in '71 Jet Hijacking," *New York Times* (11
September 2001), A1.

[15]Bill Husted, "Web Marketers Push Envelope of Privacy, with Your Help," *Atlanta Journal-Constitution* (22 September 2002), Q1.

[16]Steven Levy and Brad Stone, "Hunting the Hackers," *Newsweek* (21 February 2000), 38.

[17]Andrea Rock, "Stalkers Online," *Ladies' Home Journal* (March 2000), 60.

[18]See for example, Helen Dewar, "Senate Passes Homeland Security Bill," *Washington Post* (20 November 2002); A1 and George Anastasia, "Big Brother and the Bookie," *Mother Jones* (January/Feb-
ruary 2002), 63.

[19]See for example, Dana Hawkins and Margaret Mannix, "Privacy is Under Siege at Work, at Home
and Online," *US News and World Report* (2 October 2000), 62; Ted Bridis and Glenn R. Simpson,
"Judges' Ire Stirs Debate on Web Monitoring," *Wall Street Journal* (9 August 2001), B9.

[20]Kelly Hearn, "Hold the Phone!" *Christian Science Monitor* (8 May 2000), www.csmonitor.com .

[21]Christian Berg, "Verizon Help Line Stressed," *The (Allentown, Pa) Morning Call* (10 August
2000), www.mcall.com . For example, AT&T reported a 10 percent increase in calls for directory assistance; Switchboard.com reported a 20 percent increase.

Unlike the white or yellow pages, there is no central registry for e-mail addresses, so if you don't find an address on one site, try another. How do these sites compile their listings? Many stock their databases with addresses collected from newsgroup postings. If you have ever posted a message on an electronic bulletin board, there's a good chance your e-mail address is included in a searchable database. Also included are the addresses of individuals who have volunteered the information to the registry, sometimes a condition of using the site. ISPs occasionally sell their subscriber lists;[22] this might be a good time to ask your service provider if they do so.

Some ISPs court customers by pledging not to sell their personal information, and try to bar nonmembers from accessing their directories; AOL is one example. But whereas ISPs might control access to their subscriber lists, they cannot control the individual members. If johndoe@aol.com decides to register with Infospace.com, a searchable telephone and e-mail address database, his address becomes available to others. Incidentally, AOL offers an e-mail finder on its site that does not include the addresses of AOL customers.

Some of the sites mentioned here offer e-mail "domain searches" or reverse e-mail searches. Rather than searching by individual name or address, you can enter a domain name only, such as "aol.com" (or on some pages "@aol.com") and the database returns several hundred AOL customer addresses. You can also use a domain search to find employees at a company. If an individual has registered with the site you are searching, click on their name among the results, usually a hyperlink, to gather additional information. Reporters use these sites to find individuals' maiden names, high schools, and professions this way, then build on a query by using additional search sites.

What follows is a list of sites and tips to help in searches for individuals or for collecting information about individuals. Most sites espouse privacy policies and certainly none are intended for nefarious purposes. Another note: The majority of the sites mentioned here are U.S.-oriented for a simple reason. The U.S. considers more records public information by law than any other country. For example, phone directories are available at most pay phones in America, but are harder to come by in other countries where privacy is more closely guarded. A quick reference guide to telephone and e-mail directories is included in Appendix A.

InfoSpace

InfoSpace, www.infospace.com, maintains a database of searchable phone directories, and they've done an admirable job by including directories from many countries other than the U.S. But that alone doesn't distinguish this site from other similar ones. Rather, InfoSpace has two features that make it a worthwhile people finder. First, it has a reverse lookup for phone numbers and e-mail addresses. That means if you only have an e-mail address or telephone

---

[22]Hansell, "Seeking Profits, Internet Alters Privacy Policy," *New York Times.*

number, you may be able to find out to whom these are registered. From the main page, click on "reverse lookup" under either the yellow pages or white pages heading. The next screen offers you four choices, but you have to scroll to see them all. Reverse lookup by phone number (residential or business), by area code, address, or e-mail.

The second feature, a domain search, is perhaps the more important one as this search type is becoming rare. This option can be used to find an individual when you only have an e-mail address, or to find e-mail users at a particular organization or affiliated with a certain ISP. To use the domain search, link to the reverse lookup under the white pages heading at the InfoSpace site. Then, scroll to the "Lookup Email" option and enter "@microsoft.com" (Fig. 5.1). This search returns a list of Microsoft employees who have either registered on the InfoSpace site or participated in an online forum from which their addresses have been culled (Fig. 5.2). Whereas some ISPs restrict access to their member directories (e.g., AOL), if their subscribers have registered on the InfoSpace site or taken part in certain online forums, you may have some luck finding them through this domain search. Although InfoSpace masks the actual e-mail address, it provides a hyperlink to an e-mail form. If the individual's name also appears as a hyperlink, clicking on it provides additional information provided by that user, such as education, work address, phone, and fax numbers.

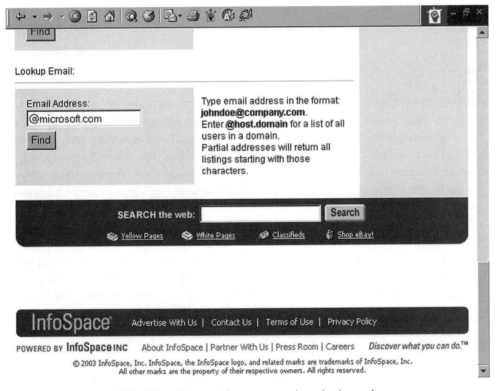

FIG. 5.1.   Using a domain search to find people.

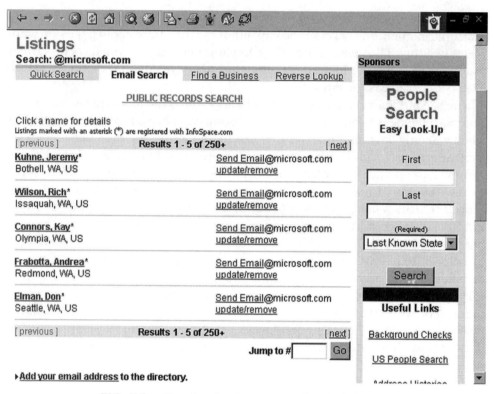

FIG. 5.2.   Results of a domain search at InfoSpace.

Bigfoot

This site, www.bigfoot.com, provides white pages and e-mail addresses for many domains. Like most, it includes e-mail addresses for users who have provided them, or whose ISPs have done so. The search is fairly straightforward, although you'll need to scroll down the left-hand column to find the form. By providing at least a last name, Bigfoot searches its database for matches. The less information you enter, the broader your search. The more information you provide, the more specific the results.

For a white pages search go to http://bigfoot.whitepages.com/person, where you can look up a person's address and phone number with as little information as a partial last name. Just above the search box, there are more options: a reverse lookup by phone number or address, an option to find area codes, zip codes, and international calling codes. Bigfoot used to offer a detailed search, but now provides links to a series of fee-based services.

Yahoo People Search

From the Yahoo People Search screen (http://people.yahoo.com), you've got three options: a residential telephone search, an e-mail search, and an alternate fee-based search of public documents (more on that later). The telephone search gives you pretty much what any other telephone directory site does. By clicking on the individual's name next to his or her phone listing, you then have an option to get a map to that person's home, or a list of businesses near the home. Other similar sites offer links to floral delivery services or greeting card services; these are advertisers who support the site.

Avoid the simple search and instead, click on Advanced Search; the link is on the e-mail search results screen, or go to http://email.people.yahoo.com/ py/psAdvSearch. Now you've got some options to narrow things down and this should help considerably. A simple search of my name netted 19 e-mail addresses in about 10 states. An advanced search lets you specify an individual's last known e-mail address, affiliation to a business or organization, and what kind of organization. This last item tells Yahoo to search particular domain names for the e-mail address. For example if you check "military," Yahoo goes in search of addresses in the ".mil" domain. If you check university/college, it searches for ".edu" addresses. Finally, you can request that Yahoo search variations on names, Bob for Robert, Dick or Rich for Richard and so on, by clicking on the "Smart Names" box. In Fig. 5.3, I've executed a search for Barbara Friedman, using smart names so "Barb" is returned as well as combinations such as "Barbara and Richard." Figure 5.4 shows the results. Then, by clicking on the names of the individuals listed, I'm provided with additional infor-

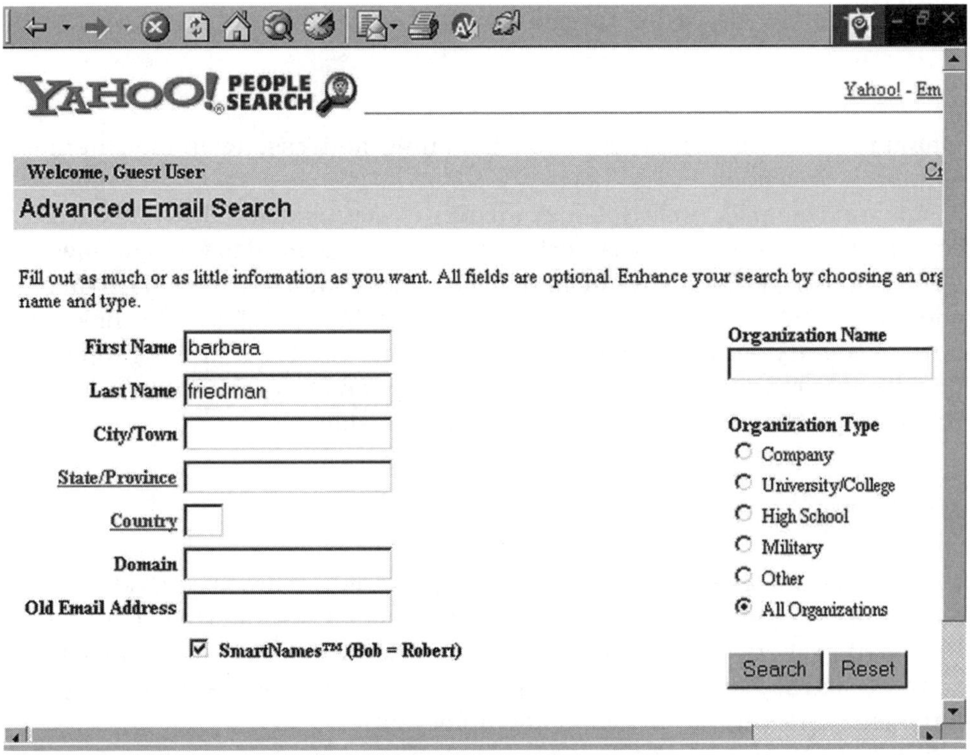

FIG. 5.3.   Yahoo advanced email search.

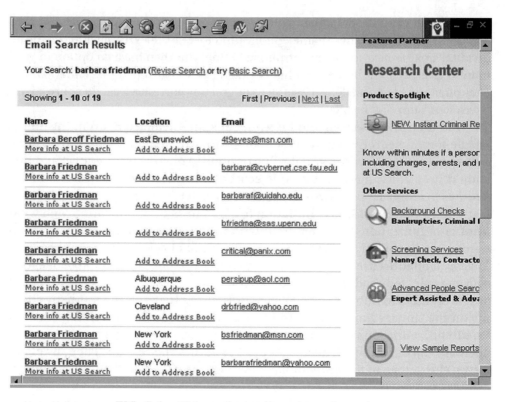

FIG. 5.4.   Yahoo advanced email search results.

mation, which may include a home mailing address, telephone number, employer, or school.

Yahoo's main page (www.yahoo.com) offers users links to Yahoo sites in other countries, but people search is worldwide so there's no need to wander. However, if you're looking for Web sites maintained in other countries, go to the main page and scroll to the bottom of the screen. Under "local Yahoo!s," click the link of the desired country. From the next page, change the "you are searching" option to that country and enter your search term and click on "search." Yahoo also has a yellow pages (http://yp.yahoo.com) for finding businesses.

WhoWhere?

Lycos offers this people-finding service, www.whowhere.lycos.com/AdvancedE. A celebrity search was a popular early feature of this site, offering biographical information about popular figures—the same information could be had with a conventional search engine or by using a specialized site like Arts and Entertainment's Biography site (www.biography.com).

But like Yahoo, WhoWhere offers an advanced e-mail search that gives you more options than just name and state for refining your search. However, only the e-mail addresses of registered users are included in this database, so if the person you're seeking hasn't provided that information to WhoWhere, you're not likely to find it. But if one is an enthusiastic hobbyist (say, a fan of *Star Trek*) and might share that with other like-minded people, this site could be helpful. Its advanced search lets you enter keywords: for a person's *interests* (might they have cited "Star Trek" in an online forum or on a web site?); *group* (if he was to identify himself as part of a community, what keywords would fit—Trekkie?); and *profile* (same idea here, which keyword or words can be used to describe the individual's hobby—television, perhaps?). Remember though, that this search interface only provides you with the e-mail addresses of individuals who have registered on the site, making this a real hit or miss exercise.

Mobile Phone Directories

Just as no directory of mobile or cellular phone numbers exists in the "real" world, there is no central database online. That will surely change since, according to many news reports, an ever-increasing number of people are dropping their land lines in favor of more affordable mobile phone services.

On the Web, there are several opt-in mobile phone directories, meaning listings include only those individuals who have registered on the sites. MobilephoneNo (www.mobilephoneno.com) includes listings in the U.S. and other countries, whereas Cellowpages (www.cellowpages.com) includes listings in Canada and the U.S. For mobile phone listings in the U.K., try Mobile118 (www.mobile118.co.uk). A New Zealand site offers mobile phone listings and other contact information at www.mobilepages.co.nz.

As with many people-finding services, you may have to visit more than one site to find what you're looking for.

Additional Phone Directories

Verizon's Super Pages	http://directory.superpages.com/people.jsp
BellSouth	www.realwhitepages.com/info.bls
Switchboard	http://switchboard.com
AT&T AnyWho	www.anywho.com/wp.html
Search.com	www.search.com/search?channel=10

Finding People Outside the U.S.

In the U.S., residential phone listings are pretty easy to find, but what if you want to find someone outside the country? Several Web sites offer an array of phone directories around the world, usually in the native language. But remember that many countries have strict laws prohibiting the distribution of residential phone listings and thus, many sites boasting international phone directories really only have business listings.

Try Infobel (www.infobel.com/teldir), which has links to 188 countries' e-mail and fax directories, white pages to find people, and yellow pages to find businesses. The interface is simple if you can avoid all the links to pay sites. For example, when I clicked on information for Indonesia Infobel displayed a search page, which I quickly recognized as a ubiquitous fee-based site. By scrolling down just a bit, I found the actual search interface for Infobel. This search also returns related advertiser information, such as hotels in the area you searched—another time-waster if you're looking for an individual.

Another good source for worldwide e-mail addresses is World E-mail (www.worldemail.com), although as with most e-mail searchers, this site only searches through addresses it has been provided, either by users or ISPs. Still, it claims to have 18 million addresses in its database. World pages (http://search.worldpages.com) also offers international e-mail addresses. From the main page, click on the "people listings" tab, then the link to "find an e-mail address." In addition, World Pages also offers business and people searches either in the U.S. or Canada. Lycos' Canada411 (www.canada411.com) has business and residential listings and postal codes for Canada. The site is bilingual, with instructions and information in English and French. British Telecom's site (www.bt.com) lets you search residential directories in the U.K. and allows you to search using a wild card if you lack full information or are unsure of spelling. This site allows you to include building and street name to narrow a business search; initials to narrow a people search.

Start Your (Search) Engines

When searching for an individual, a researcher's instinct may be to perform a simple search for his or her name. Like any search, it works best if you take advantage of advanced options to narrow it. To wit, I have received messages congratulating me for honors I wasn't awarded, books I didn't write, and degrees I didn't receive. Why? Because a simple Web search using a traditional search engine turns up many Barbara Friedmans, and too often, people don't go the extra step to distinguish one of us from the others.

Searches by name are most effective when combined with Boolean queries that allow you to search for a range of related information, such as Web sites that are linked to your subject somehow. Like developing techniques for finding information when a conventional search fails, people searches often require some creative thinking. At the Google Advanced Search site (www.google.com/advanced_search), type your subject's name in the "exact phrase" box, taking into account variations of a spelling, or whether the person you seek uses a middle initial or even a pen name. To avoid getting sites for same-named individuals, add a keyword that is likely to appear on a page related to your subject. For example, if you're searching for a university instructor, try adding words like "syllabus" or "faculty." If you know the department in which the professor teaches, you might use that to narrow your search. Don't forget to make other adjustments to your Google search, by specifying how many results you want to see per page, in what language the engine should search and whether you want it to search a particular domain—in this case, perhaps the ".edu" domain.

Similarly, AltaVista's advanced search (www.altavista.com/web/adv) allows you to construct a Boolean query to locate an individual or information about a person. Here, what I like is that you can use as long a search string as you like, in any order, adding or taking away items without having to concentrate on which box you're typing them into. For example, say I want to find pages about Microsoft CEO Bill Gates, specifically pages that provide his net worth and charitable work. I want to narrow the search by including keywords that I think appear on the page, such as his wife's name. In the "Search with this Boolean expression," I could type this string:

"Bill Gates" AND Microsoft AND "net worth" AND charity

If I was dissatisfied with those results, I could add on, by typing:

OR "Melinda Gates" AND domain:org

The same kind of query could easily be used to find someone less prominent. Type the individual's name in quotation marks or parentheses (use lowercase to find more results), then add or exclude terms to narrow the search.

Finding People With Syntax Searches

Another way to find individuals is by using a syntax search, to locate their Web sites, pages about them or that might link to theirs. Some of them are described here; chapter 3 has a fuller accounting of how syntax searches work.

A "title" search may help you locate an individual's home page, because people often use their names as titles to their personal Web sites. At AltaVista's advanced search site, type **title:friedman** and you'll find home pages for a psychoanalyst, an economist, and a composer, among others. You could easily narrow this search by adding a first name or by adding keywords—think about your subject's profession or hobby, for example. Typing **title:friedman AND journ*** locates pages that include "friedman" in the title and variations of the word "journalism" somewhere in the site's text.

Use the "host" syntax to find Web sites about your subject hosted by a specific organization or by a specific server. At AltaVista's advanced search, a search for my last name, joined with host:missouri.edu (**friedman AND host:missouri.edu**) turned up several sites and included a long mail thread (e-mail correspondence) among colleagues from several universities, conducted on the University of Missouri server. I could narrow this search by enclosing my full name in parentheses, but many college records include individuals' full names, including middle initials, and maiden names, so narrowing this way might exclude useful pages.

If your subject works for a particular company, try joining the name of the individual with the company's domain name. For example, typing **Gates AND host: microsoft.com** will find pages with Gates in the text and hosted by Microsoft, including Gates' speeches, biography and remarks to employees. Again, you can narrow to this search string by adding keywords that might appear on sites with the kind of information you seek. For example, typing **"george w. bush" AND host:whitehouse.gov AND terrorism** (see Fig. 5.5) results in 315 White House-hosted sites related to the president and terrorism (see Fig. 5.6).

To sites that might have information related to your subject, but not necessarily be sanctioned by them, try the "URL" syntax search. For example, using AltaVista to search for **URL:georgewbush** locates parody sites, jokes, "Bushisms" (amusing quotes), and profiles that use the president's name in the Web address. Remember not to leave spaces when you execute this search between the syntax and search word or phrase, and leave out punctuation and spaces within proper names.

The "link" and "anchor" syntax searches also help you locate sites that are related to your subject. The anchor search finds pages with specific words within the text of a hyperlink. For example, typing **anchor:georgewbush** locates pages where the president's name appears as a hyperlink. For a less prominent individual, results help suggest in what context the subject is being considered. Typing **link:whitehouse.gov** locates sites that link to the official White House site.

The link search is most effective after you've located your subject's Web page, and want to know with whom they associate, or if you want to construct a circle of professional or personal interests. For example, returning to the title search described in this section, I copied economist David D. Friedman's Web address (www.daviddfriedman.com) and performed a link search (see Fig. 5.7). The results showed the home page of an individual who cites Friedman as his "intellec-

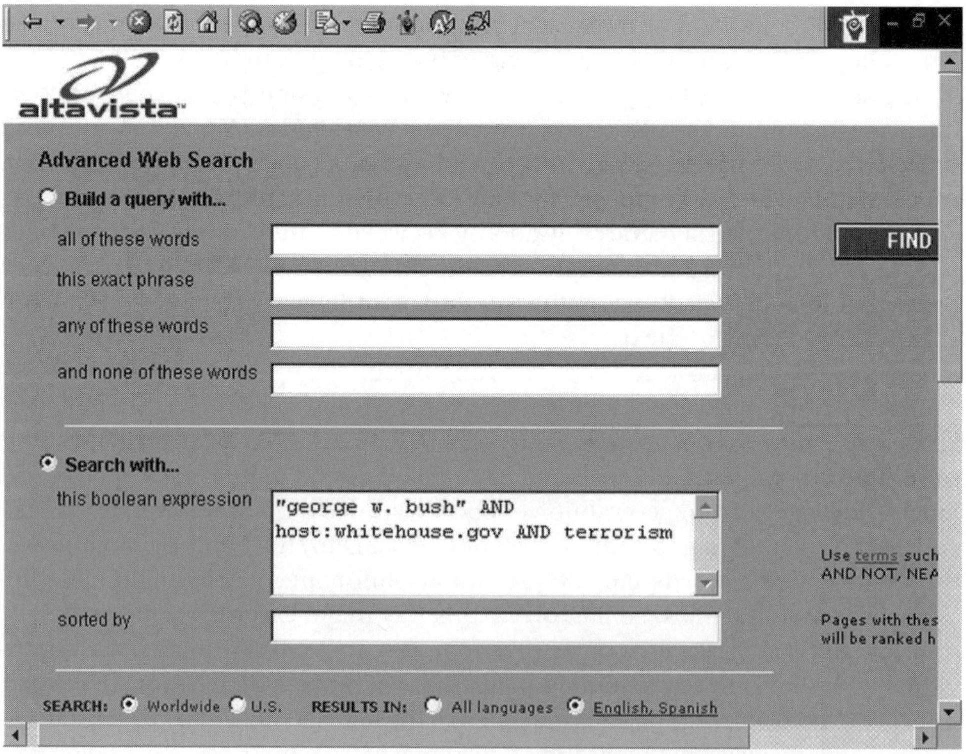

FIG. 5.5.   Search for people by host on AltaVista.

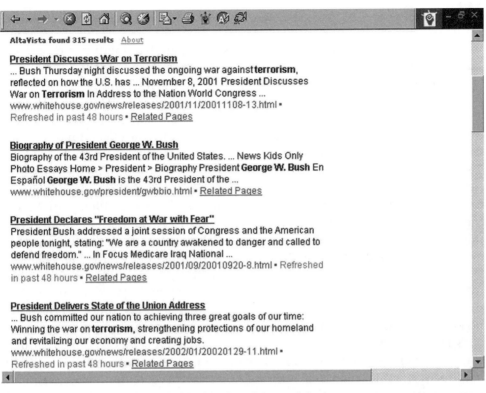

FIG. 5.6. Results of a search by host.

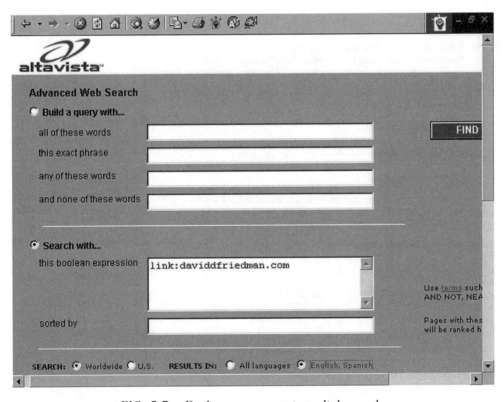

FIG. 5.7. Finding a person using a link search.

tual hero" and links back to the economist's site; an Ayn Rand tribute site that includes a link to Friedman's work on objectivism; an amateur site with links to "webspaces concerned with freedom" including his (see Fig. 5.8).

One site among the results puzzles me though, a "Culinary History Timeline" site. When I open it, I see no obvious connection to Friedman's site and using the "find" menu does not locate his name on the page. But by viewing the source code—the programming language used to create the Web page—(in Explorer, select "view" and then "source" from the pull-down menu), and then using the "search" option to find his name, I see that his site is indeed included as a link (see Fig. 5.9). The URL of his Web site appears as hidden or meta content, enclosed in brackets. Looking at the text just to the right of the brackets tells me that his Web site appears on the cooking page as a link to "Cariadoc's Miscellany." Now, if I return to the cooking site, find that hypertext and click on the link I end up at one of Friedman's personal pages, a cookbook inspired by his association with the Society for Creative Anachronism. At the bottom of that page are a street address, phone number, e-mail address, links to additional pages, and a link back to his original Web site (www.daviddfriedman.com). So, with a few keystrokes, we've gathered professional information about Friedman (links to his published work and how his work fits into the work of others), some of his hobbies (cooking, poetry and historical recreation), and perhaps a home address—that could then be entered into a reverse lookup to confirm a

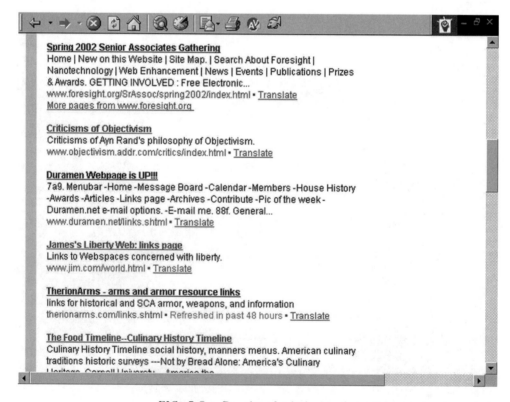

FIG. 5.8.   Results of a link search.

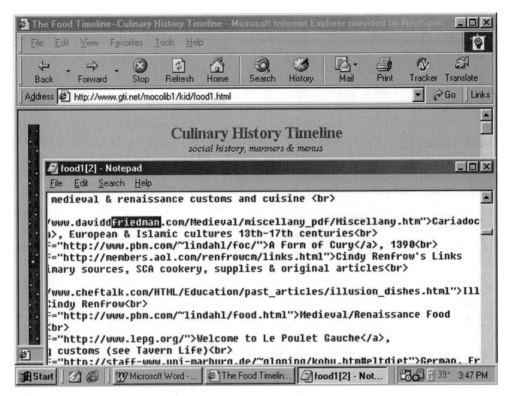

FIG. 5.9.   Viewing a Web site's source code to trace a link.

home phone number, and maybe, the name of a spouse or partner living at the same address.

Finding People Through Web Pages

As the previous section demonstrates, personal Web pages are a great way to find people, or to find personal and professional information about someone. There are three ways to locate those pages: using a syntax search, searching the registry of a Web page host, or of an online community registry. I favor them in that order, for reasons I'll explain here.

When people create home pages, they are often inclined to provide their URLs to the major search engines so that the maximum number of people may find their sites. Although the URL will not show up immediately in an engine's database, a Boolean search yields the most targeted results. For example, using a host search on AltaVista advanced search, such as **friedman AND host:hometown.aol.com**, I get 68 results. These sites have "friedman" either in the name or text of an AOL hometown page (see Fig. 5.10). If I want to search additional Web site hosts, I can add to the search string. An example is **friedman AND host:hometown.aol.com AND host:geocities.yahoo.com AND host:angelfire.com**.

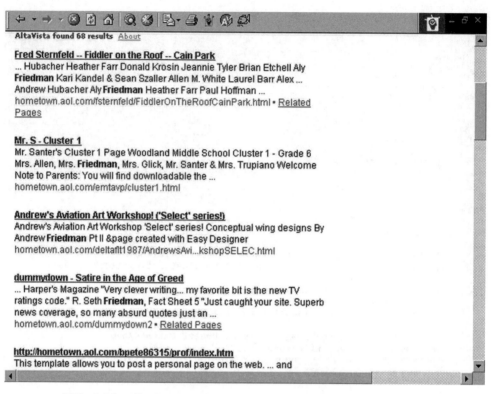

FIG. 5.10.   Finding people using a syntax search for home pages.

An alternate choice for finding personal Web pages is to go directly to the site of the Web page host. For example, at AOL (http://hometown.aol.com), you can search member pages by keywords or phrases, screen names, or categories. At Yahoo Geocities (http://us.geocities.yahoo.com/search/option), an advanced option lets you search the member pages directory using Boolean logic.

In addition to these options, you can try an online community registry, although the results with these sites tend to include a fair amount of advertisements and pornographic sites. An example of a registry is WhoWhere. At the main page (www.whowhere.lycos.com), link to "Advanced Email Search" from the left column. Then, click on the "homepages" link under "more people searches," then "online communities" under the "browse by category" heading. Now, you have a list of online communities and Web page hosts that are included in the WhoWhere database, but only if users have registered their Web sites with Lycos (see Fig. 5.11). You can search by keyword, phrase or name. Whereas WhoWhere appears to offer the option of narrowing a a search by host, it does not; results include all registered sites.

CNET's Search.com (www.search.com) offers a home page search too, and does allow the user to target specific Web site hosts or domains. At the Search.com site, click on the "quicklink" for "people." At the next prompt, you're provided with groups of sites from which to search. At the group "Home Pages," click on the link

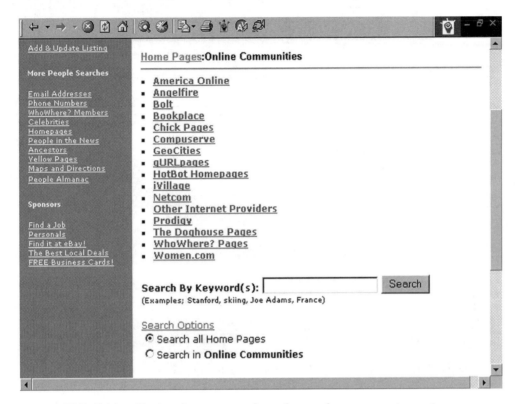

FIG. 5.11.   Finding home pages through an online community registry.

to "customize." Now, you can select among several hosts. A search for the name "friedman" among sites hosted by AOL Hometown results in about 200 sites with that name in either the title, text or member name. Returning to the search page, select "all hosts" and the results are organized by host, including GeoCities, Angelfire and Tripod. Under each group of results, clicking on the link for "see all matching results at" will take you to the host Web page (e.g., www.geocities.com) and a longer list of matches.

The number of sites you can use to determine who's behind a screen name or domain and host are dwindling, even as the ones offering to sell domains increase.[23] But let's say I want to find out which of the many Barbara Friedmans use or "own" the Web address known as www.barbarafriedman.com. At the WHOIS site (www.networksolutions.com/en-us/whois/index.jhtml), type in either a screen name if you know it, or domain and host name (e.g., barbarafriedman.com as in Fig. 5.12). In this case, I find out that the domain is registered to a Barbara Friedman in Austin, Texas, and how to contact her (see Fig. 5.13). Scroll further and WHOIS also provides me with the name and contact information for the Web site administrator and technical support.

---

[23]Steven J. Vaughan-Nichols, "Master of Your Web Domain," *Washington Post* (28 July 2002), H7.

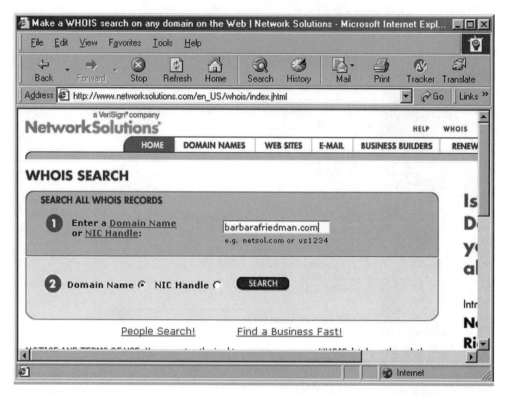

FIG. 5.12.   Using a WHOIS search to find out who's behind a Web site.

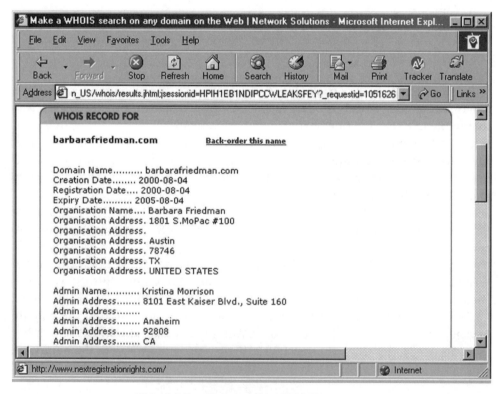

FIG. 5.13.   Results of a WHOIS search.

Alternatively, if you enter an e-mail address on WHOIS, @getcreative, you'll get a list of subscribers with that e-mail suffix. Note that if you leave out the domain, ".com," ".org," and so on, you'll get more listings. Names are arranged alphabetically, with identifying numbers following in parentheses. Click on that hyperlink for contact information.

Whereas one organization used to register domain names, now multiple agencies do. That means that one domain name search may not be enough. However, a new Web site called Better-WhoIs (www.better-whois.com) queries multiple registries at once. Enter a URL at the prompt, and search results will tell you if the site is registered and if so, to whom (you'll have to scroll down to see that information). Search results also indicate what particular registry or registries returned the appropriate information.

For European sites, try the RIPE Network Coordinating Center site, at www.ripe.net/perl/whois. There's a link to an advanced search as well, with a range of query support tools and an IP or Internet Protocol address lookup.

If you know someone's screen name, there are a few sites that might help you uncover that individual's identity. One site is ICQ's people search (http://web.icq.com), but the database is limited to people who use ICQ's (as in "I seek you") peer-to-peer or file-sharing network. Another site that might produce results is Sam Spade (www.samspade.org/t), a not-for-profit site that provides a range of search tools. Domain searches are also available at eAmnesia (http://eamnesia.com/index.jsp), where you can enter an entire or partial URL.

Using Newsgroups to Find out About People

Right now, there are thousands of newsgroups on the Web, and each time someone posts a message to one, it gets archived in a searchable database.[24] What those messages reveal might astound you. For example, a newly elected state representative was forced to resign after local, then national media revealed he had written hundreds of newsgroup postings advocating the killing of police officers.[25] Hundreds of lawsuits have been filed alleging libel and defamation based on messages posted to newsgroups, usually charging an individual with damaging a company's reputation or manipulating stock prices.[26] These are dramatic examples, yet even the most innocuous comments can be examined for clues about your preferences, location, hobbies, career, income, relationships, living situation, your family, and more.

Chapter 4 laid the groundwork for finding people through their online "conversations," but to further illustrate the point I took an e-mail address at random

---

[24]That is, unless you use an "opt-out" command to keep your messages from being archived, as described in chapter 4.

[25]"Lawmaker Reveals Criminal Past—After Election," *St. Louis Post-Dispatch* (11 January 2001), A5.

[26]See for example, "Online Anonymity Faces Legal Challenges," *USA Today* (30 November 2000), www.usatoday.com; Aaron Elstein, "AOL Sides with Anonymous Posters," *Wall Street Journal* Interactive Edition (5 March 2001); Gregg Wirth, "Tearing Down the Internet's Anonymous Posters," TheStreet.com (22 September 1998), www/the street.com .

from an individual who had contributed to a popular newsgroup centered on cooking and dining out. Then I entered the address into the author search on Google Groups (http://groups.google.com). From a dozen messages posted by her to a variety of newsgroups, I learned the following:

- Her name and age.
- The name and age of her husband.
- She lives in New Braunfels, TX.
- She moved from Houston, TX in 1994.
- She and her husband were married in 1989.
- Their rehearsal dinner was held at The Swingin' Door, a barbecue restaurant in Richmond, TX.
- They have two children, boys aged 3 months and 3 years (at the time of her post).
- In 1997, she longed for a romantic vacation as she and her husband were having trouble finding time for themselves.
- She enjoys cooking seafood and eating at seafood restaurants.
- Her favorite restaurant in Houston is Fajita Flats, on Fondren Avenue between Richmond and Westheimer Avenues. Her favorite waiter there is named Javier.

I'm sure the author never intended for that information to become public knowledge and perhaps she wouldn't think any of it harmful. Most of her messages were friendly responses to newsgroup inquiries, such as a recommendation for the best seafood restaurant in San Antonio. But as you've already seen, even the most innocent remarks can be used to create a profile of an individual, or pinpoint that individual's location. For example, advertisers can use the information to identify preferences and habits to target services and products accordingly—delivered nowadays in the form of banner or pop-up ads as you work online.

Once you've got some basic details about a person (e.g., an e-mail address), you can build on it by visiting other sites or using the syntax searches described already to find more related information. Here's what I went on to learn about my random subject:

- Her maiden name.
- Her home address and phone number.
- The names, address and phone numbers of her neighbors.
- The location of her home and directions to her front door.
- The name of her oldest son and his hobbies.
- The name and nature of her family's business.

Searching for individuals by perusing the content of online forums can be highly productive for the researcher, but discomfiting for the subject. Remember that you can exclude your posts from newsgroups archives by including the "x-no-archive:yes" command, as described in chapter 4.

OTHER WAYS TO FIND PEOPLE

By School

For many Americans, high school represents a significant life experience. Thus, alumni associations or similar organizations that allow and encourage people to relive those years, are great people-finding sources. For example, Classmates.com (www.classmates.com), a kind of virtual high school reunion, offers an advanced search by name. Search either by an individual's current name or name at graduation and choose "exact spelling." Or, you can search using a partial name, selecting the option "starts with." Alternately, you can search an entire graduating class, provided you know from what school your subject graduated. Class lists are incomplete, as individuals must register to be included. You won't be able to obtain any e-mail addresses unless you become a member, for about $30 and even then only links to an e-mail form as specific addresses are masked.

However, if you can look past the site's advertisement clutter, click the tab at the top of the screen and go to the site's message boards and search by topic or name. Users often include their e-mail addresses in the text. Additionally, clicking on the sender's name in the message header launches an e-mail form, although it won't show you the address. You could also post a message looking for an individual, or news of someone. You can't be inconspicuous on this site, as it "advertises" the date and time of your every visit as a banner on the site.

Other "class reunion" sites have appeared online, including www.alumni.net and www.gradfinder.com. These have far fewer entries than Classmates, and their search engines are not yet as efficient. For example, Gradfinders alphabetizes by current names, rather than name at graduation. They both require users to register to view personal information, but don't charge a fee. AlumniNet has databases for many high schools outside the U.S., whereas Classmates.com includes only U.S., Canadian, and overseas American schools.

To find alumni, you could go directly to the home page of their graduating institution. Some of those maintain searchable databases of alumni, including e-mail addresses and other current contact information. They may also publish their alumni magazines online, allowing you to search content for the name of the individual you seek. You might be able to gather information from alumni announcements, which include marriages, births, deaths, and employment notices. One example of such a Web site is the MIT Sloan School Alumni Directory, online at http://mitsloan.mit.edu/alum/alumdir.html.

Other Academics

If you're looking for someone who works for or is currently enrolled at a university, chances are you'll find information about them online. One site, Campus Phonebook (www.uiuc.edu/cgi-bin/ph), a project of the University of Illinois Urbana–Champaign, provides links to many university directories. Another collection of links to some 3,000 universities in and outside the U.S. is available at www.mit.edu:8001/people/cdemello/univ.html; it is searchable by name or geographic location. Yet another list resides at a Washington University site, www.cellbio.wustl.edu/school.htm.

If those searches are unproductive, or you want to know more, try using a search engine to locate the institution's official or main Web site. At AltaVista's advanced search, type the institution's name in lowercase, enclosed by parentheses. Or type in the browser's address box the name of or acronym for the institution, followed by ".edu." For example, try "www.msu.edu" for Michigan State University. Then scan the page for a link to an e-mail and phone directory, commonplace for many university sites. Often you can find address, phone, fax, and e-mail for an individual even if you only have a last name. And in many cases, you'll also be provided with a link to that individual's Web site, if they maintain one on the university server.

Alternately, you could use a search engine's "host" search as described in chapter 3 and available on AltaVista's advanced search. When you know the domain used by the academic institution, type your subject's name in parentheses and use the "host" anchor. Here's an example:

(barbara friedman) and host:missouri.edu

In this case, you'll be led to any sites I maintain on the University of Missouri's server. Using the "link" anchor, also described in chapter 3, you'll find out if other sites are linked to mine and that way, might discover who my friends or colleagues are. You can use the same method, substituting the "text" anchor for the host or link anchor to find out if I'm mentioned on other pages.

Military Personnel

In fall 2000, Russian military planes flew over the U.S. aircraft carrier Kitty Hawk, snapped photographs, then sent them with a taunting e-mail to the crew. Even as the military debated whether the incident represented a genuine threat, they had to wonder—how did the Russians know where to send the material? From the official U.S.S. Kitty Hawk Web site, which provided explicit instructions on how to e-mail the captain and crew.[27]

In fact, the military is relying more than ever on e-mail, to maintain enlisted members' morale and on Web sites, to keep family back home informed.[28] Note however, that war or other military actions result in many services being suspended. For example, the U.S. Army maintains a site with contact information for active duty personnel at www.erec.army.mil/wwl, but since the September 11, 2001 terrorist attacks, has restricted its search function to military personnel only.

---

[27]Thom Shanker, "How Much To Tell: A Balancing Act at Military Sites," *New York Times* (16 August 2001), D9.

[28]Nancy Beth Jackson, "To the Navy Ranks, Add Webmaster," *New York Times* (16 August 2001), D1.

Mailing information for some active duty personnel can be found at the DefenseLINK Web site (www.defenselink.mil/faq/pis/PC04MLTR.html). The site has instructions for sending requests (via snail mail) to obtain mailing addresses for the U.S. Navy, Army, Marine Corps, and Air Force. To find out whether an individual has ever served in the military, DefenseLINK has instructions for requesting a soldiers and sailors certificate; the cost is $5.20 (www.defenselink.mil/faq/pis/PC09SLDR.html).

The Department of Defense Network Information Center is online at www.nic.mil/dodnic. That site can be used to locate Department of Defense personnel by entering a name at the search prompt. Results include full name, mailing address, e-mail address, phone and fax numbers and NIC handle (that can then be entered at the WHOIS site—mentioned earlier in this chapter—for more information).

Less reliable than ".mil" sites but still worth a try for finding military personnel are popular ".com" sites. GISearch (www.gisearch.com) provides links to past and (fewer) current members of all branches of the military who have registered at the site. You'll also have to register to use the service. The best results are obtained if you know something about the individual's duty station. GISearch offers an advanced option for searching by name (www.gisearch.com/info/asearch). Another Web site, Military USA, is useful for searching out veterans (www.militaryusa.com), and offers a service number database, and reunion information. There's even a site for "military brats" (www.militarybrats.com), providing bulletin boards for locating people, and links to related alumni organizations.

Classmates.com (www.classmates.com) also maintains a database of military personnel. From the main page, select "browse military" from the left column. At each screen, you're asked to narrow your search. For example, start with "United States Merchant Marines," then select "vessels, boats, and ships," then "Canadian submarines," then the submarine by name. Like the list of college alumni, the military list includes only those individuals who have registered with the site.

Another site for military personnel is maintained by the *Army Times* at www.militarycity.com, which allows users to search the active U.S. Department of Defense personnel database or find retired military personnel. On the left side of the main page, click on "people finder." To find active members, a fee is required. For retired personnel, search by name, rank, military branch, specialty, or additional options. Alternately, use the message board to locate an individual. The site also archives and allows searches of four publications to 1994: *Army Times, Navy Times, Air Force Times,* and *Marine Corps Times,* often useful sources for finding people. The availability of the people finder at this site depends on the current political situation, that is, the service may be unavailable during a war or national crisis.

Professional Associations

Many people join clubs or professional associations related to their occupation or hobbies. The Society of Professional Journalists (www.spj.org), the National

Education Association (www.nea.org) and the National Rifle Association (www.nra.org) are just three of the thousands of professional organizations with an online presence. Many such groups also have searchable member directories. If you want to use a search engine to find one, use the "URL" or "domain" anchor to narrow your search. In this example, I've specified ".org" as many of these groups are not-for-profits:

(daughters of the american revolution) OR DAR AND domain:org

Once you've reached the site you can use your "edit" menu, then "find" to search for the keyword "members" or "directory."

Many such groups also maintain mailing lists. These lists may be closed to nonmembers, in which case you might consider joining, if only temporarily. If the list is open, subscribe and try to locate your subject this way. Assuming your search is not covert, you could post a message to the group asking for contact information. Use the subject line to state your purpose, as in "looking for Mr. Wright." That way, you'll avoid being overlooked, and you won't raise the hackles of list members who might resent the intrusion.

By Hobby

If your subject has a hobby or recreational pursuit, check a directory of newsgroups (http://groups.google.com) or mailing lists (such as CataList, www.lsoft.com) devoted to that topic. As mentioned at the beginning of this chapter, you can often search the databases of newsgroups. To find someone on a mailing list you'll have to subscribe, although you can do that temporarily. For more details on using newsgroups and mailing lists, see chapter 4.

If you're not sure of your subject's hobbies, you might find them through an online auction site, such as www.ebay.com. From the main page, link to "search" then "search by seller" or "search by bidder." You'll be able to view a list of items the individual has either bought or sold in the last 30 days.

By Business or Employer

You may be able to find an individual by mining the Web site of the business for which they work or worked. Business.com (www.business.com) allows you to search by name or ticker symbol. The site claims a database of about 400,000 listings in 25,000 categories. Avoid the "search the business Internet" option at the top of the page and instead, link to "find companies." Then search by business name or ticker symbol. A search for "Anheuser Busch" yielded a chart with the company's stock performance. Furthermore, the right side of the screen offers extras: a profile of the company, financial data and recent press releases. Granted, this information would likely appear in an annual report, but this is quicker, and it also provides minibiographies (including ages) and contact information for top executives.

If you know an individual's past employer or simply want to identify a former employee at a company you're interested in, start with Eliyon's Corporate Alumni

Directory (www.networking.eliyon.com), which claims to have information on nearly 16 million people. At the Web site, typing in a company name results in a list of former employees whose information has been culled from a variety of public records and online activity. Details may include a current e-mail address, current employer and company profile, title, location, board membership and affiliation, and education. This search also lists the Web sites from which some of the information originated, allowing the user to conduct further research.

Many "business search" sites are merely glorified yellow pages. When you search by name, you're often "rewarded" with an address and phone number and occasionally, the URL of the company's official Web site. You may have better luck using a traditional search engine like AltaVista. If you choose that option, when you find the Web site of the business you seek, look for a link that says something like "contact us," "about us," "directory," or "help." From there, you may find a link to a company directory, with e-mail addresses and other contact information.

InfoSpace (www.infospace.com) offers several searchable databases and their business search works well. Under the yellow pages heading, click on the link "find a business." The interface offers you the option to search for businesses by name or category. You can search by location, or use the option for a nationwide search, if you're not sure where the business is located. InfoSpace used to offer business profiles and credit reports free, but now charges a five dollar fee. That option appears as a link at the bottom of the business search page.

For businesses outside the U.S., try Paris-based Europages (www.europages.com). Like many business search sites, this is a portal to preselected sites, some 500,000 companies in 30 European countries. Europages has an annoying amount of pop-up ads, which you'll have to close before proceeding from the main site. Choose a language, then search for a business by product, service, or name. Alternately, scroll down and search by category. The information you'll find is similar to a yellow pages search: contact information often including e-mail addresses and Web site addresses.

Another site, www.freeality.com offers a list of hyperlinks to business directories from many countries, including Puerto Rico and Canada. At the main page, link to "find companies" on the left side of the screen. Then scroll down and link to "International directories."

By Profession

Is the individual you're searching part of a profession that requires licensing or certification? If so, you may be able to find contact information and employment history online.

For example, if the individual you're searching for is a practicing attorney, graduated from law school or sits on the faculty of a law school, try www.martindale.com/locator, a site maintained by the law firm of Martindale-Hubbell. You can search by name only or a combination of name, law school, specialty, and current location. If you want variations on a name, Pete and Peter, use the operator "or" (as in Pete or Peter) or a wild card (at this site, the wild card is an exclamation point, as in Pete!). Your search results include the firm with which the individual is associated (including address, phone and fax numbers), his or her position there, education, birthdate, specialties, and professional memberships. The site also links you to the firm's listing, which gives information about its work and associates.

Try also West's Legal Directory site (www.lawoffice.com), which allows you to search through a database of some 1,000,000 lawyers. The site is intended for consumers trying to find lawyers for hire so it emphasizes searching by practice area (specialty). But there are links to searches by name and firm name as well. The Institute of Continuing Legal Education has a list of links to lawyer directories, www.icle.org/lawlinks/gen/lawyers.htm#lawdir. If you know where your subject practices law, you could execute an advanced search on Google or AltaVista for that state and "state bar" or "bar association."

To find a doctor by name or specialty, consult the official site of the American Medical Association at www.ama-assn.org. The National Certification Corporation (www.nccnet.org) has links on its site to associations and certification boards for nurses, physicians, and other health care professionals.

If a pilot is certified, you can view that information at www.landings.com. Scroll to the bottom of the page and click on "search databases." At the same Web site, you can identify and locate aircraft owners.

The New York State Board of Education regulates professional practices through the Office of Professions. The OP site (www.op.nysed.gov) provides links to certification information, databases, and press releases. You might check board of education sites in the state your subject resides or works in, and look for links to a similar regulatory agency.

If you're looking for an employee of the U.S. federal government, try First Gov's employee directory, located at www.info.gov/phone.htm. The directory includes contact information for members of congress, cabinet agencies, and various commissions.

Individuals who serve on boards of directors can often be found at the 10K Wizard site, www.tenkwizard.com. Try a search by company name, then use the keyword option to specify "board of directors" or "executives." The results typically include a range of forms from the company's SEC filings, including spreadsheets and memos. By perusing the forms, you may find names, contact information, and more.

Is the individual an inventor who might hold a patent? Search the intellectual property database at www.delphion.com by name or invention. Advanced search (scroll to the bottom of the main page) allows users to search by patent number.

Crime, Law Enforcement

A limited amount of law enforcement data exists online and can be used to locate or find information about individuals. Many states are reluctant to put law enforcement information online, due to legitimate concerns about inaccuracies.

Perhaps the most controversial record now is the Sex Offenders Registry, prompted by a Senate Bill that requires convicted sex offenders to register with their communities for 10 years following release from custody, probation, or parole. The SOR has already been shown to contain numerous errors.[29] To post that online as public information risks labeling innocent people as felons and makes the government and federal agencies vulnerable to legal action. In fact, a U.S. judge ruled in 2001 that the state of New Jersey could not post its registry online.[30]

Yet, some records are available. One Web site, www.stopsexoffenders.com, maintains links to registries or information about registries in all 50 states and Canada, England, and Australia. The State of Montana recently launched its own site, http://svor2.doj.state.mt.us:8010/index.htm, where users can view the Sexual and Violent Offender Registry database. The site allows the user to search by name or more generally, to see where registered offenders in their city or county live. The site provides additional information about each registrant's crimes, as well as photos for noncompliant offenders and those offenders who have been designated at higher risk of committing repeat offenses.[31]

If the person you seek might be part of the current prison population, check that state's department of corrections site for a database search. For example, the New York State Department of Correctional Services Web site includes a link to an inmate population search (www.docs.state.ny.us). The state of Illinois has an inmate search online at www.idoc.state.il.us. The Federal inmate population can be searched online at www.bop.gov. To find a state's DOC site, use AltaVista's or Google's advanced search options; a Boolean query might look like this:

(state name) AND "Department of Correction*" AND search OR prison*

Family History

Tracing one's family history has long been a popular pursuit, but even more so because of the availability of records online. Many of the Web sites constructed for geneaological research offer public records searches. One example is the National Obituary Archive (www.arrangeonline.com), which compiles its database from U.S. funeral directors, the Social Security Administration and news sources. The site offers an advanced search by name, date or date range of death, and place of residence. The Ancestry.com site (www.ancestry.com), intended for amateur genealogists, offers a search interface for the Social Security Administration's death index. It also includes military records and other public documents. Although that information is available at public libraries or historical societies, this is a kind of one-stop genealogical site where databases

---

[29]Reese Dunklin, "About 700 Sex Offenders Do Not Appear To Live at the Addresses Listed on a St. Louis Registry," *St. Louis Post-Dispatch* (2 May 1999), A11.

[30]Charles Toutant, "U.S. Judge Enjoins Putting Offenders' Addresses Online," *New Jersey Law Journal* 166:11 (10 December 2001), 1–2.

[31]See "Web Site Locates Sex Offenders," *Billings Gazette* (12 January 2001), www.billingsgazette.com.

are conveniently gathered. The service is free although registration is required. Along those same lines, the USGenWeb Project site (www.usgenweb.com/index.html) endeavors to create Web sites for every county in every state in the U.S., with searchable databases of public documents. The WorldGenWeb Project (www.worldgenweb.org) is similar, providing links to sites maintained in countries around the world. Both Web sites are operated by not-for-profit organizations, serious about making genealogical records available to everyone on the globe, at least those with Internet access.

More Ways to Find Public Records

If you're wondering if the records you seek are even publicly available, you could stop at the U.S. government's own vital records site (www.pueblo.gsa.gov/cic_text/misc/vital-records/alphabet.htm). States are arranged alphabetically and each listing shows what records are available, where they can be obtained, and if there is a cost involved. Another site, Search Systems (www.searchsystems.net) provides links to public records databases in the 50 states, U.S. territories, some Canadian provinces, and a few additional countries (see Fig. 5.14). The emphasis is on free sites, although some links indicate fee-based services. Figure 5.15 shows partial results for a search of Texas-based records.

Fee-Based Services for Finding People

As more Web sites include personal ads and dating services in their content, so too do more people want to "check up on" potential sweethearts.[32] Employers, too, are often interested in gathering information about prospective employees beyond the standard resume.[33] There are numerous fee-based services willing to comb public records to find out if someone's been married, divorced, arrested, sued, jailed, or has filed for bankruptcy. In some cases (and for more money), a search service can locate financial records, including credit reports, to determine an individual's assets or net worth.

One of the most ubiquitous pay sites online is U.S. Search (www.ussearch.com), which allows you to search several databases for a range of information: to locate a person; determine whether they are alive or dead; find out if an individual has a lien or civil judgment against them; if a person or organization has filed for bankruptcy; and whether someone has a criminal record. The information available applies only to individuals at least 18 years of age; no juvenile records are included.

Planet Investigations (www.people-finder.tv) offers a people finder for about $8, and a professional or business finder for twenty-five dollars.

---

[32]See for example, Tom Zoellner, "Private Investigators Ease Cyber-Lovers' Minds," *Las Vegas Review-Journal* (6 August 1998), D3; Teresa Strasser, "Spying on Potential Mates Over the Net," *St. Louis Jewish Light* (24 January 2001), 11; Saul Hansell, "Yahoo Gains in Revenue, Aided by Online Dating Service," *New York Times* (11 April 2002), C8.

[33]Jeff Siegel, "Search Me," *American Way* (1 June 2001), 96.

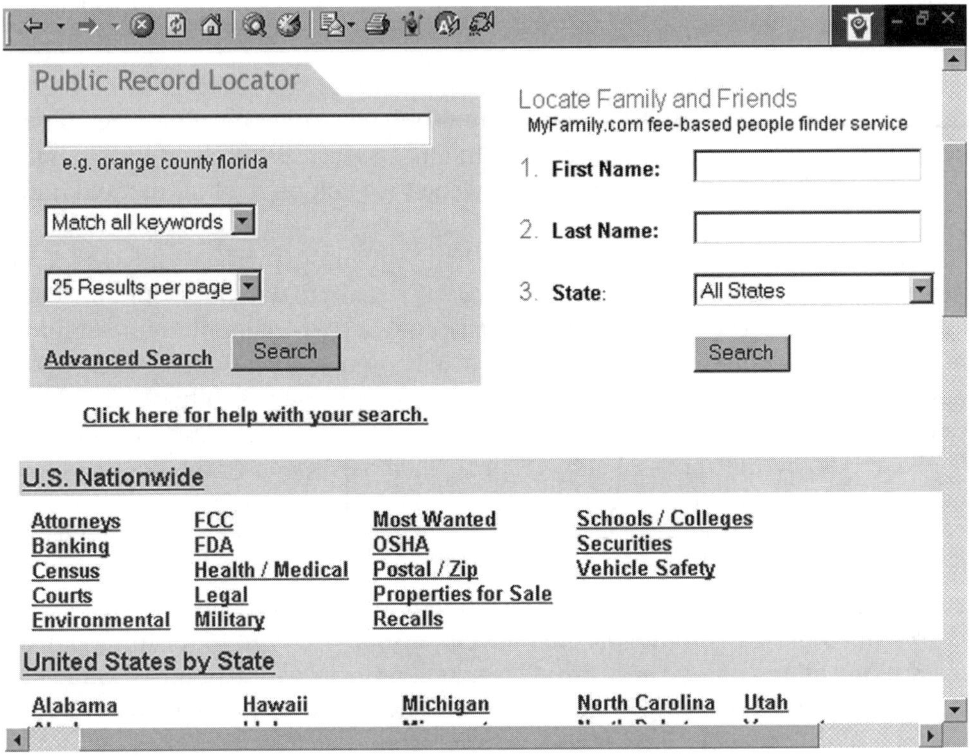

FIG. 5.14. Finding people through public records at Search Systems.

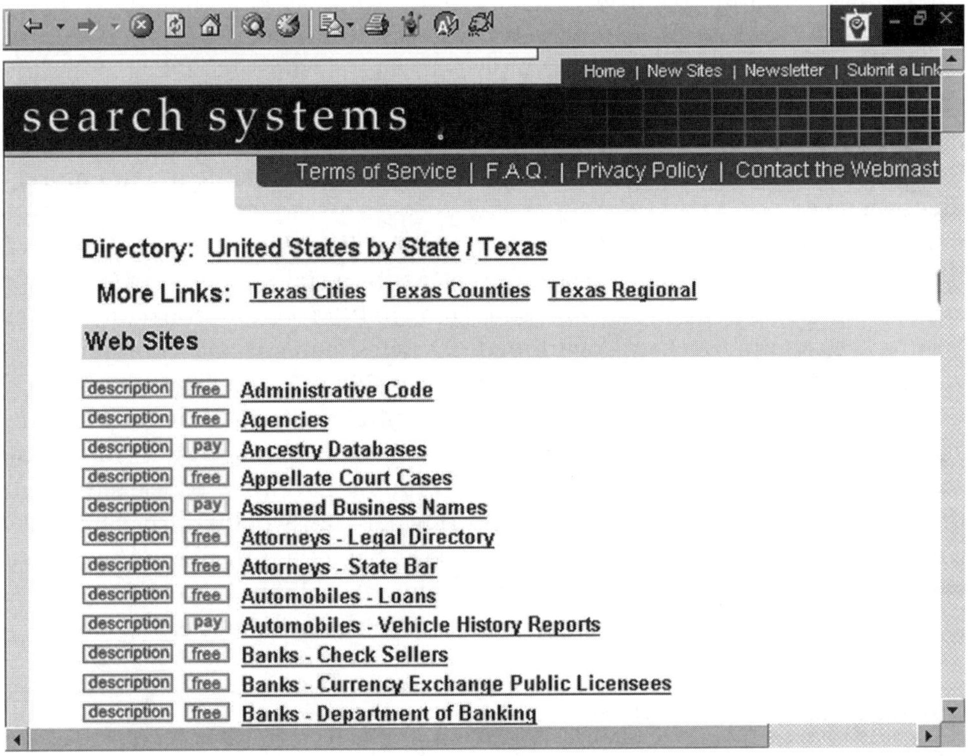

FIG. 5.15. Results of a public records search.

Another site, 555-1212 (www.555-1212.com/mindex.jsp), used to be one of the best phone and e-mail directory sites but has since become a fee-based search service. The new site emphasizes business services but does offer individuals 100 lookups for ten dollars. At the Web site, click on the link to "consumer products."

Popular among employers and private investigators is AutoTrackXP (www.autotrackxp.com), which searches a wide range of databases for subscribers. To use this service, you'll have to first provide personal and financial information, then wait up to 10 days for approval of your application, as some of the data is proprietary and not available to the general public. Another site, KnowX (www.knowx.com), has some free searches, but the most substantive ones are fee-based. An itemized price list by records database is located on the Web site; a business background check is twenty-five dollars, for example.

When you use a fee-based service, you're paying for more than just information. In fact, they all use public records, available to anyone willing to go to the appropriate office and ask for them (although a fee may be involved for copying). What you're paying for is the convenience of searching multiple records from many states on one site, and from the comfort of your home or office. In some cases, you're paying a local agent to physically go to a courthouse and search records for you. But before shelling out money for any of these services, I'd want to know exactly what records they search. Then, I'd cross-check that information with a site like Search Systems (www.searchsystems.net), which provides links to public records online. Is the "cyber snoop" charging you for records that you can access for free? If it's just phone and e-mail directories, those kinds of searches are easy to do yourself, as this chapter has already shown. Furthermore, if the site claims to search the FBI's National Crime Information Center (NCIC) records, you should probably avoid it altogether. It is a federal crime to buy or sell NCIC data, which is only available to law enforcement agencies.

In addition, the Drivers' Privacy Protection Act (DPPA), passed in 1994 after the highly publicized murder of a young actress by a stalker, restricts American states from disclosing a driver's personal information without consent. Certain groups are exempt, such as government agencies or insurance companies investigating claims, but I'd be wary of any service that offers to delve into driver's license records.[34] In April 2000, a New Hampshire family filed a federal lawsuit against an Internet information broker after their daughter was murdered by someone who obtained her social security number and work address through that service. As a result, the Supreme Court is debating whether private investigators or information brokers have any legal obligation to notify the people whose information they sell, and whether an individual can claim an invasion of privacy when their personal information is obtained without permission.[35]

---

[34]A driver's personal information would typically include name, address, telephone number, vehicle description, Social Security number, physical description and medical conditions. See for example, John W. Fountain, "License Revoked for Small-Town Nosy Parkers," *New York Times* (13 January 2001), A8.

[35]"Killing Prompts Suit Against Internet Brokers," *CNN* (29 December 2002), www.cnn.com .

TIPS FOR SMART SEARCHES

- Rather than a simple search using an individual's name, use an engine's advanced options to pair a name with a syntax search.
- Use the "title" syntax search to find your subject's Web page or pages.
- Use the "link" and "anchor" syntax search to find sites that are linked to your subject's page, or that include your subject's name as a hyperlink.
- Type proper names in lowercase to increase results, unless a search site specifies otherwise.
- For the most part search engines are not very sophisticated. That means they won't return variations on names, which can be a problem with some foreign names. In some countries, a married woman often takes the feminine form of her husband's last name. For example, when Russian Yuri Zlobin marries Natasha, she becomes Natasha Zlobina. Use the wild card option on an advanced search, or execute more than one search to find variations (as in zlobin*).
- When searching phone directories, do not abbreviate addresses, unless the site specifies otherwise. If you're not sure whether Main is a street or drive, type only "main." Alternately, you could perform multiple searches for "main street" and "main drive."
- Think creatively about other ways to find an individual: by profession, hobby, or school, for example.
- When you find information about an individual do not broadcast it to others.
- Before using a fee-based service, be sure you won't be charged to search records you could access online for free. Search Systems (www.searchsystems.net) has a useful listing of free and fee-based public records for comparison.

How to Protect Your Personal Information and Identity

As stated at the outset of this chapter, the information here works as both a guide to researchers and a warning to Internet users. It's not just marketers that we should be concerned about, nor should we rely solely on government to help us retain our privacy online. Users must take responsibility for what they post, and understand that even the most innocuous comments can be used for illicit purposes. Following are some simple ways to secure your personal information and identity online:

- Before you register at any Web site, check the privacy policy to determine what kind of information about its users a site might keep in its database. Look for a link on the site's home page to "privacy policy" or "notice." If the policy statement is not clear and you have questions, look for company contact information in the policy or at the site.
- Set up a "dummy" or alias e-mail address to provide each time a site asks you to register, or when you participate in newsgroups or other public forums. That can be done for free on a site such as www.hotmail.com or www.ya-

hoo.com. When you register, you can use an alias or a gender-neutral name or initial. Give your primary e-mail address only to family and friends.

• Avoid providing personal details in public forums, particularly informa-tion that might disclose your actual location. One woman I know gives the co-ordinates of the local police station rather than her home address. It's probably better not to adopt a signature line at all. Or, if you must sign a mes-sage, use your initials only.

• Check your personal home page for proprietary information. Do you re-ally need to include your home address, for example? And if you absolutely must brag about your children or grandchildren, try to do it without providing their e-mail addresses, names, nicknames, or ages.

• Consider removing your phone number from online directories. Even if your number is listed in your local phone book, removing it from these sites makes it more difficult for people to find you. To do that, you'll have to visit each site and locate a customer service or "opt out" link.

• Don't respond to e-mail if you don't recognize the sender. To do so only verifies yours as a working address; this is true for personal or junk mail. In-stead, use the filter or blocking function of your e-mail program to keep that sender's mail from getting through. Or, sign up with a spam-reporting service like SpamCop (http://spamcop.net) to determine the validity or origin of an e-mail, or report junk mail.

• If you receive harassing e-mail, report it immediately to the sender's ISP (in most cases, postmaster@ISPname). If the situation warrants, also contact the local police.

• Identity theft is a real problem online; don't provide your social security number, credit card number, or bank account information to anyone unless you're absolutely sure who is asking and how that information will be used.

• Take advantage of privacy software to encrypt or mask your IP and e-mail address and other personal information when you're online. Programs like Anonymizer (www.anonymizer.com) or Zero-Knowledge's Freedom WebSecure (www.freedom.net) cost anywhere from twenty to one hundred dol-lars a year, and the peace of mind is well worth the price.

Finding and Using Databases

Journalists and historians alike know that some of the best sources of information come from public records, documents that record things like vital statistics (birth, marriage, and death certificates); ways of life (e.g., census data, government reports on welfare and housing, economic indicators, or a consumer spending index); politics (voter registration records, papers of the presidents, senate hearings, congressional testimony); preoccupations (newspaper and magazine articles), and so on. In fact, one author writes that the best investigative journalists operate with a "documents state of mind,"[1] believing that for every project, records exist ... somewhere.

But many public records have remained essentially private, gathering dust in courthouses and libraries. That's where the Internet comes in. Perhaps the greatest strides made on the Internet concern data collection. All sorts of records: medical, financial, political, and others have made their way onto the Web, and the public appears eager for more. In the first month of going online, the California Assembly Web site was queried 23,000 times and more than 80,000 documents were retrieved from the site, for example.[2] For academic work, students and other researchers are enthusiastic and regular users of searchable databases with full-text articles,[3] such as Lexis-Nexis and Dow Jones Interactive.

The proliferation of data is a boon to news organizations that rely on government-maintained records, such as the FBI's Uniform Crime Report or the Federal Reserve's Home Mortgage Disclosure Act database. Access to information is criti-

[1]Steve Weinberg, *The Reporter's Handbook: An Investigator's Guide to Documents and Techniques (New York: St. Martin's Press, 1996)*, 5.

[2]Jo Anne Bourquard and Pam Greenberg, "Savvy Citizens," *State Legislatures* 22:3 (March 1996), 32.

[3]Peter Applebome, "Internet Makes Term Papers Hotter Property Than Ever," *New York Times* (8 June 1997), A1; Yin Zhang, "Scholarly Use of Internet-Based Electronic Resources," *Journal of the American Society for Information Science and Technology* 52:8 (June 2001), 628; Susan Davis Herring, "Faculty Acceptance of the World Wide Web for Student Research," *College and Research Libraries* 62:3 (May 2001), 251.

cal to reporters, after all, if they are to fulfill their responsibility to inform the public on important matters of the day. Now many federal agencies, long known for their inefficiency in providing information to citizens, have easy-to-search databases available online. News organizations regularly download raw data to analyze and write award-winning investigative reports.[4]

But what about the average person who's not interested in sifting through 20,000 loan applications to analyze lending patterns in his metropolitan area, or who can't afford access to the kinds of proprietary databases that news organizations use? What kind of data might be of use to this individual? Plenty. Individuals can use online data to: find employment, keep up with politicians, access federal services (e.g., those due veterans), track census data, manage finances, research neighborhoods and homes for sale, view social security records, listen to music, read books, news dispatches, and magazines, and more. The Internet Movie Database (www.imdb.com) and the Movie Review Query Engine (www.mrqe.com) are two popular collections of movie reviews and filmographies (see Fig. 6.1). A newspapers' online archive of past issues represents one kind of database, as do the people finders described in chapter 5.

Thus, a database is nothing more than an organized file or files of information or records. Previously, Internet-based files were retrieved by a tool called *Gopher*,

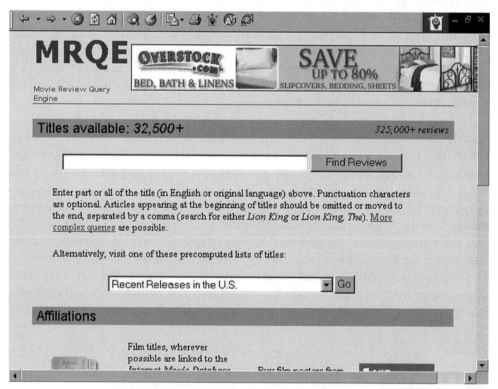

FIG. 6.1.   The Movie Review Query Engine is an example of an online database.

---

[4]Bruce Garrison, *Computer-Assisted Reporting* (Hillsdale, NJ: Lawrence Erlbaum Associates, 1995), 18–19. For the uses of computer-gathered data in reporting, also see Brant Houston, *Computer-Assisted Reporting: A Practical Guide* (New York: St. Martin's Press, 1996).

developed at the University of Minnesota in 1991, which allowed users to see menus of files on other computers. *FTP*, or file transfer protocol, was another way of transferring files from one computer to another. But now most data is accessible on Web sites as HTML documents, which makes it much easier for the average user to mine information.

In this chapter, I'll show you what kinds of raw data[5] and searchable databases are available online and some of the best ways to find them—collections of periodicals, research articles, records, reports, and so forth. If you're looking for data in a particular file format, I'll explain how to find that too. There are many file types, some requiring special software to *decompress* ("unzip"), open, or run. File types include graphical files (e.g., .jpg and .bmp), animation (.avi), and program files (.exe). Program files should never be launched before checking to be sure they are virus-free. Although there are many fee-based databases, this chapter concentrates primarily on free and low-cost sources. Chapter 7 offers tips for evaluating the information you find online for accuracy and reliability, a critical consideration.

Newspapers, Magazines and Journals

Perhaps the most common use of searchable databases is to locate archived newspaper, magazine or journal articles. For this kind of search, it's best to begin by going directly to the publication's Web site and look for a link to archived content. For example, at the *New York Times* Web site (www.nyt.com), there is a link to "archive" under the services heading. Clicking on that takes the user to a search box that can be used to locate content dating back to 1996. For seven days after publication, content can be viewed or downloaded for free online, but any content older than that costs $2.95, with the exception of reviews (e.g. books, movies), which are all free. At the *International Herald Tribune* site (www.iht.com), look for the "search" link at the top of the page, which allows users to search the previous week's content. A lesser-known link (www.iht.com/ihtsearch.php) provides a free search interface for content dating back to 1996. On the search results page, articles appear in order from most recent to oldest.

Some publications allow free access to archives for the most recent issue only. If a publication charges for access to archives or to download articles, look for an alternate, free source. For example, networking allows even the smallest public and private libraries to offer access to large, commercial databases. The subscription rates are usually prohibitive for an individual, but the databases can be used at the library, or in many cases, from home with a library card. The St. Louis County Library (www.slcl.lib.mo.us) offers patrons remote access from home to, among other databases: ProQuest, a collection of national newspapers; EBSCOhost, a range of general interest magazines and

---

[5]Raw data refers to the data in its original form. Some organizations allow their raw data to be downloaded and manipulated by others, who refashion it into a format that is more easily navigated or suits their audience's purposes better than the original or raw data. One example is an online newspaper that gathers test scores from numerous school districts and puts them together on their Web site, in a searchable, single database.

scholarly journals; and InfoTrac, which has magazine and newspaper articles dating back to 1980. The Kansas City Public Library (www.kcpl.lib.mo.us/resources) offers Kansas and Missouri residents access to *ERIC*, a database of 2,000 educational publications; *ECO*, an electronic collection of 3,000 scholarly journals dating from 1995, and more.

Many of these databases include archived articles from national newspapers—the same papers that charge for access to past articles on their Web sites. The *New York Times* and the *Washington Post* each charge $2.95 to download a single article at their sites, about what it costs to buy an entire copy of either newspaper. On the other hand, a public library card is usually free for residents, and costs only a nominal fee for those living outside the circulation area. Plus, you won't have to enter credit card information to search or read archived material through the library's database access.

University libraries may have still richer resources—I'm thinking particularly of premium database services like Lexis-Nexis and Dow-Jones Interactive (see Fig. 6.2). In the best case scenario, you can enter the library and use its resources without a student identification card. But usually, a valid identification number is required to log on to the databases. In that situation, it might be possible to gain temporary access to work on a particular project; approach the librarian and inquire. I know of several people who generously loan their student identification

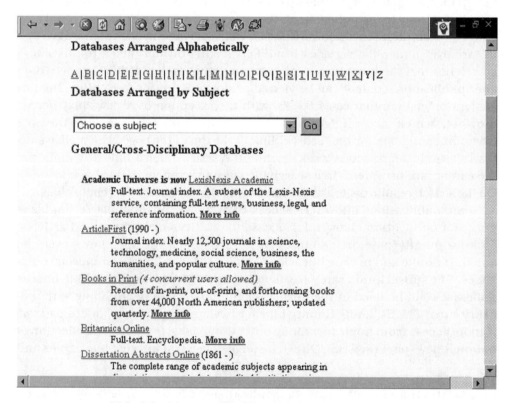

FIG. 6.2. A partial list of databases available on the
Washington University library Web site.

numbers to other researchers to access certain online databases from home. Of course, I'm not advocating you abuse the privilege, but as long as you're conducting legitimate research, there's little harm done.

If the libraries charge for printing out articles, see if the database offers the option of sending articles to your e-mail addresses; this is my preference. It's particularly helpful if I feel rushed at the library and want to peruse many articles. I send them to my home e-mail address so I can linger over them and decide with more certainty what's worth printing and keeping and what to discard. When you receive the articles through e-mail, you may also choose to save them on your computer, eliminating the need for (and expense of) printing altogether.

Using Search Engines to Find Data

What other kinds of information can you find online? "At first, too much,"[6] wrote Brant Houston, director of the National Institute of Computer-Assisted Reporting (NICAR). The volume of information may seem overwhelming. According to the Federal Database Finder, a published guide of accessible federal data,[7] the U.S. government produces some 10,000 databases and that number promises to increase. In 2000, *Wired News* reported "nearly every federal agency has begun releasing major new documents on the Web."[8] A quick visit to either FedWorld (www.fedworld.gov), a Web site maintained by the Department of Commerce, or FedWeb (www.fedweb.com), provides some idea of the amount of information produced by the government.

To begin a search for data, Houston suggests journalists categorize the data in two ways: *secondary sources*, such as newspapers or magazines and *primary sources*, such as raw data or government databases that cost little or nothing.[9] That approach is equally helpful to nonjournalists, because it forces the user to think about the source of the data. In other words, what organization or what kind of organization would be most likely to hold the information you seek? Is it a government report or some kind of government-generated data, for example? If so, go directly to the appropriate agency's Web site and look for a link to publications. You may be able to guess at the Web site address if you're not exactly sure what it is. The Department of Veterans Affairs is known as the "VA" and it's a federal agency, so you might try www.va.gov—and you'd be right. For a list of domains and country codes, see Appendix B.

In general, you should avoid a simple search, that is, using search engines to find data or databases by a single keyword. Even adding "database" to your subject keyword search is a better strategy (as in congressional bills database), but is still likely to return wide-ranging results.

A better approach is to apply some of the strategies described in chapter 2 to locate specific kinds of information using search engines' advanced options.

---

[6]Houston, *Computer-Assisted Reporting*, 106.
[7]Sharon Zarozny and Monica Horner, (Eds.), *The Federal Data Base Finder* (Potomac, MD: Information USA), 1984.
[8]"U.S. Agencies Stepping Up Web Access," *Wired* (1 March 2000), www.wired.com .
[9]Houston, *Computer-Assisted Reporting*, 106.

Choose keywords that describe your subject, paired with words related to it, or words that might appear on the kind of document or site you seek. For example, an AltaVista advanced search for the president's addresses to the press might look like this (see Fig. 6.3):

"press briefings" AND archive AND "white house" AND president

Topping the list of search results are two sites that just might fit the bill: an index of the current president's radio addresses, and an archive of all White House documents, including press briefings (see Fig. 6.4).

There's an easy way to narrow the search described above by using your familiarity with domain names. Adding **AND url:gov** indicates the search engine should return only those sites within the government domain hierarchy, for example. Alternately, you could add **AND host:whitehouse.gov** indicating you want only those sites hosted by the White House. Either approach would help you to quickly zero in on your subject.

Remember that you can use the Boolean connector, "and not" along with your keyword or phrase to exclude commercial sites (as in **"campaign finance" AND donors AND NOT url:com**). Also, you could specify a president's name, a date range or use a keyword to prioritize or sort your results. For example, if you want searchable databases or archives of presidential addresses that pertain to the economy to appear at the top of your search results, use AltaVista's ranking ("sorted by") function.

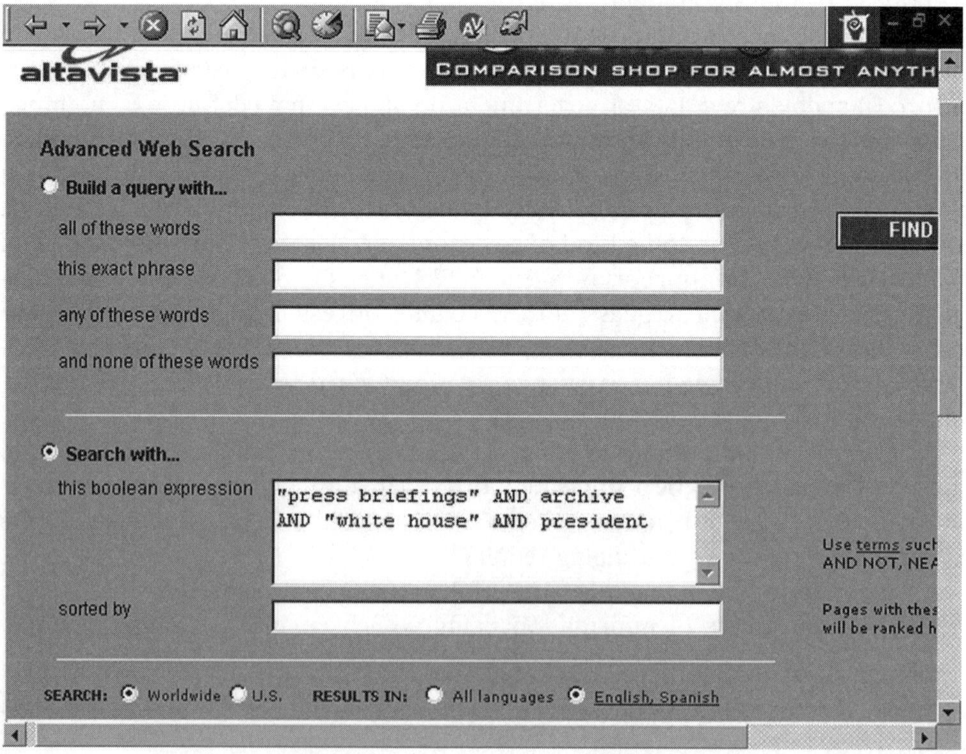

FIG. 6.3. Finding databases using an AltaVista advanced search.

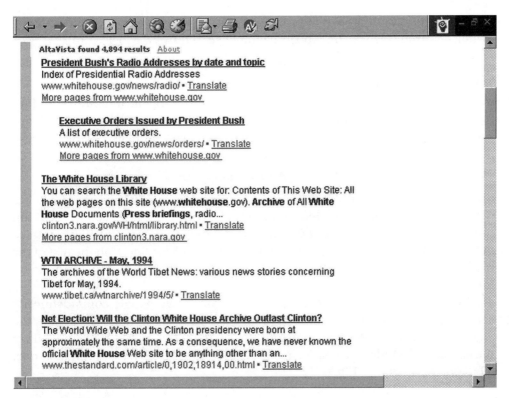

FIG. 6.4.   Results of an AltaVista advanced search for databases.

Search For Data By File Type

Much of the "invisible" Web, that portion of information search engines do not or cannot reach, is composed of searchable databases. One reason so much data remains "invisible" is because of its file format. Search engines typically look only for files with HTML content, since that's the language of the Web and also the kinds of pages searched by users most often. But quite a bit of data is written in other kinds of programming language—think about spreadsheets, images, and plain text, for example. Searching by file type then, is a great way to find that "invisible" data.

Many, but certainly not all, databases are created as *.pdf* files (Portable Document Format). To view and print a .pdf file requires Adobe Acrobat Reader, a free program users can download at a number of sites including Adobe's home page (www.adobe.com). If you don't have this plug-in program on your computer already, you'll be prompted with an offer to download it before a .pdf file can be displayed. Other popular formats are ".dbf," indicating a dBase data file; ".nsf," a Lotus Notes program; ".mdb," Microsoft Access Database Manager; ".xls," Excel spreadsheet program, and ".wdb" for Microsoft Works Database. For more file formats, see the list of helpful Web sites at the end of this chapter.

To find all data in a particular format—in this example, portable document format—search this way on Google's simple search (www.google.com):

data filetype:pdf

Take care not to leave spaces between the syntax (filetype) and format (pdf). Obviously, the results for this kind of search will be wide-ranging and numerous (see Fig. 6.5). But you can add a keyword or phrase to narrow your search. For a search of .pdf files titled or including the phrase "war on drugs" using Google, search this way:

"war on drugs" filetype:pdf

Now, you can see the results are more on target. Google has returned reports with the title or primary content related to the war on drugs (see Fig. 6.6). You must tell Google you want .pdf files by using the "filetype" syntax. Without it (as in "war on drugs" .pdf), Google will return sites that have ".pdf" in the text of the page, including links to .pdf files, while not necessarily the actual .pdf documents you seek.

Alternately, use Google's advanced search (www.google.com/advanced_ search) to specify file type, although the choices here are limited. By default, the engine searches for all file formats unless you tell it otherwise. You can instruct the engine to include or exclude one of the following file formats: .pdf, .ps, .doc, .xls, .ppt, and .rtf (see Fig. 6.7).

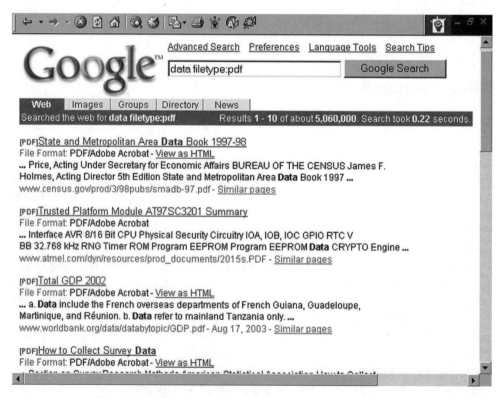

FIG. 6.5.   Results of a Google simple search by file type.

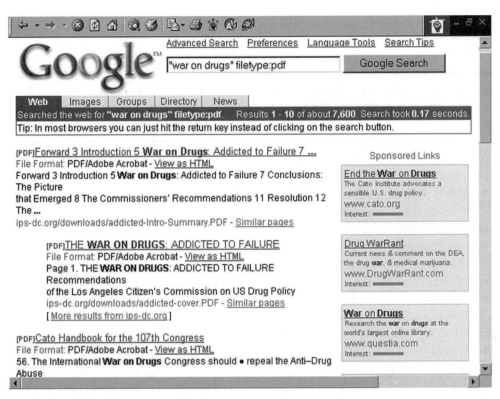

FIG. 6.6.   Targeting a search by phrase and file type.

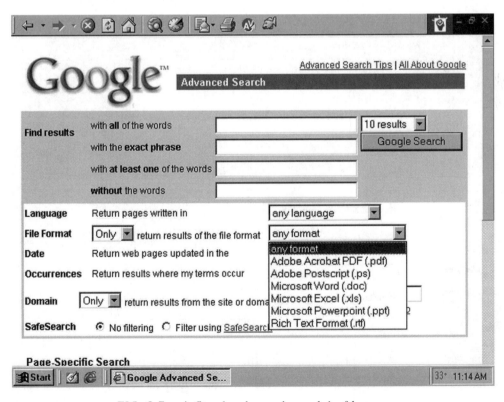

FIG. 6.7.   A Google advanced search by file type.

At AltaVista's advanced search page (www.altavista.com/web/adv), the choices are even fewer. At the bottom of the page, you can check the "file type" box to tell the engine to search for either HTML or .pdf files. Here, I've instructed AltaVista to do a title search for documents called "war on drugs" in portable document format (see Fig. 6.8). Also at AltaVista, you can use the "sorted by" option to prioritize your search results. For example, to the same search I might add "Colombia" to the "sort by" box to see documents related to the war on drugs in Colombia at the top of my search results.

MSN's Advanced Search (http://search.msn.com/advanced.asp) is another good resource for searches by file type. After typing in your keyword search (use the drop-down menu to apply Boolean logic), scroll down the page, where MSN offers two options for narrowing your search by file type. First, you can indicate what kind of file, or combination of files, you want to search among: HTML, Word, PowerPoint, Excel or .pdf. Second, you can refine your search by specifying what kinds of file type links the pages in your results should include; MSN calls this a search by page content. For example, you may be searching for an HTML document with a link to a .pdf file. There are 10 file types listed, as well as a box for typing in others; select as many as are appropriate for your search (see Fig. 6.9). The more you select, the fewer sites MSN will return for your search.

It should be clear then, that the best kind of file type search takes advantage of more than one search strategy to target information. For example, combine a host or domain search with a file type search to find specific kinds of pages or files.

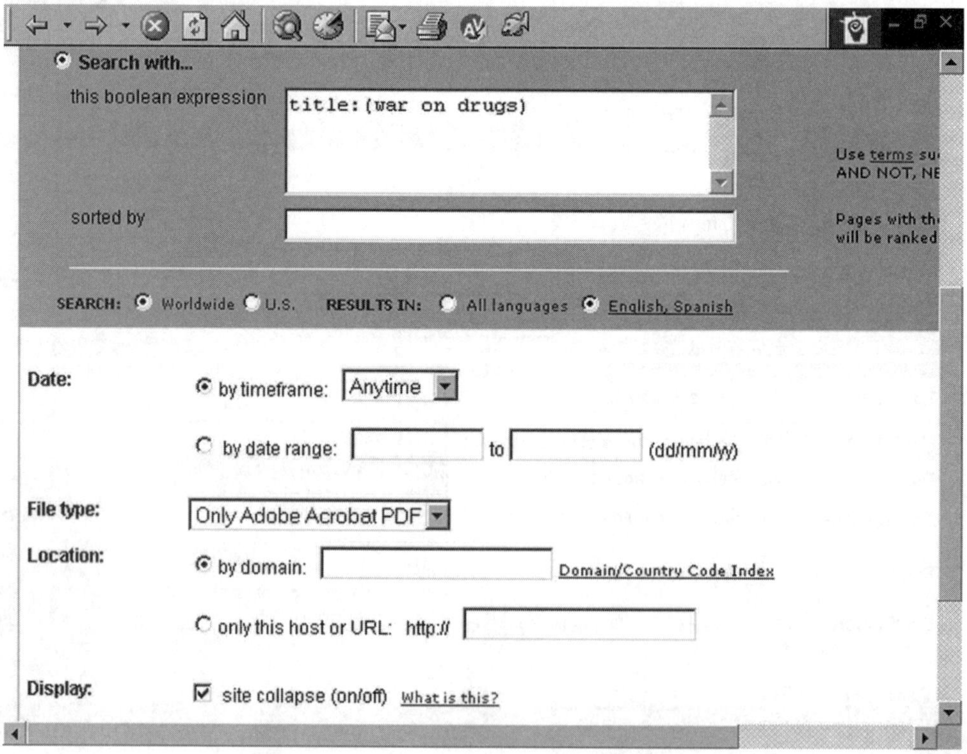

FIG. 6.8.   An AltaVista advanced search by file type.

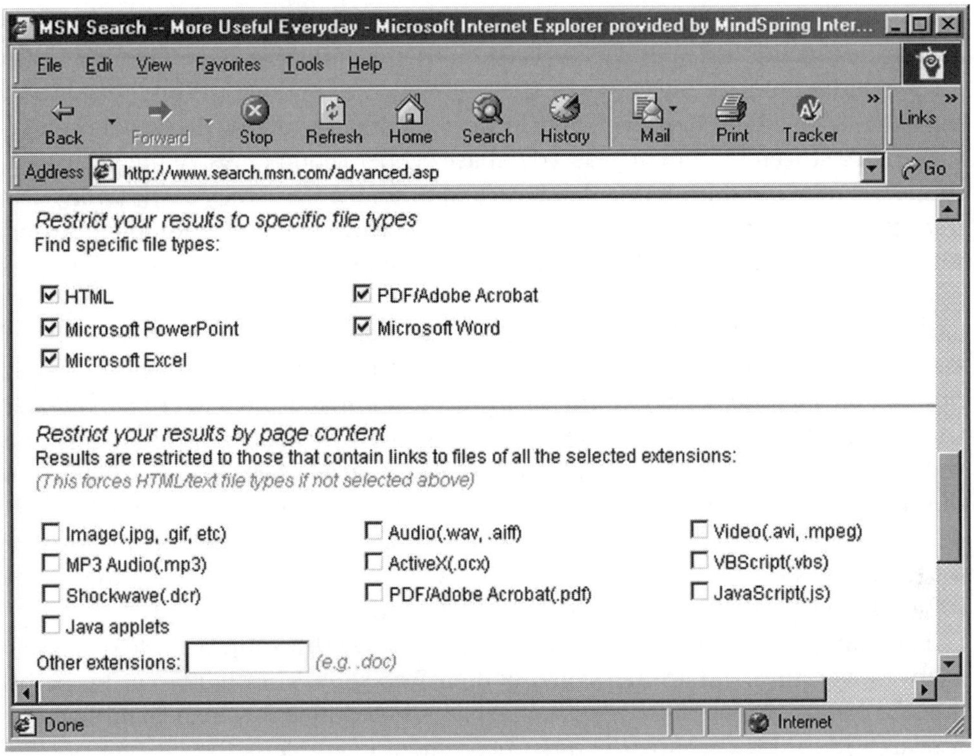

FIG. 6.9.   An MSN advanced search by file type.

Subject Guides: Let Someone Else do the Legwork

By using a keyword search, you are almost sure to turn up subject guides maintained by libraries, universities or individuals with an interest in that particular topic. These kinds of sites don't usually have the actual data, but instead are maintained as lists of hyperlinks, intended to lead the user to the original data sources. For example, an educator might compile on a Web site a list of the "best Web sites for historical research." Among those links might be the U.S. National Archives and Records Administration (www.archives.gov/index.html), where users can search genealogical and other kinds of data. Fans of the popular television series *Buffy the Vampire Slayer* have been known to assemble copious links to slayer related data including episode lists, dialogue, video clips, and cast biographies. At least one enterprising fan created an original database, tallying the death count for each episode of the show's seven seasons. These kinds of lists, of course, can range from amateurish to authoritative.

There are a number of Web sites that offer users collections of subject-specific resources. In fact, most of the major search engines offer subject directories that group resources by category. The Web Site Directory at Yahoo's main page is one such resource, as is Google Directory (www.google.com/dirhp). Topics are general: sports, travel, entertainment, science, and so forth.

One Web site gaining in popularity is Teoma (www.teoma.com), which divides search results into three categories: results, refine and resources. The latter category includes links to collections or sites developed by enthusiasts and "experts" (a term that is on some sites used quite loosely). At Teoma, among the "resources" returned in a search for "opera" was a database of opera companies. At the same time, in the "results" list was an aria database and Stanford University's OperaGlass, an information server with links to numerous databases including additional, related information servers. Teoma's suggested "refinements" were links to the Web sites of specific opera companies, such as the Lyric Opera of Chicago.

Thus, link-intensive Web sites save precious research time by rounding up and categorizing resources for you. And quite often, they include resources you would not find on your own. They're among the easiest kinds of sites to create, but also the most difficult to maintain. Many Web developers have neither the time for nor the interest in checking the viability of links regularly. They can quickly become outdated and lead the user nowhere. But if you note the URL on your browser screen as you link to other sites, you may be able to work your way back to the original, raw data. On a PC, you can use the CTRL + left arrow to move the cursor left to the next logical break in the URL to find the root of the address.

For academic research, a better choice might be the subject directories that many universities and libraries offer at their Web sites. They tend to be better organized and maintained than enthusiasts' lists, because they're assembled with research in mind. Perhaps the most prominent example is the Library of Congress (www.loc.gov). Link to the library's research tools for a list of full-text resources. Luckily for researchers, many libraries and research institutions have begun placing manuscript collections online, such as the University of North Carolina at Chapel Hill's Southern Historical Collection (www.lib.unc.edu/mss/shcgl.html) and London's Imperial War Museum (www.iwm.org.uk).

Presidential libraries too are valuable repositories of searchable databases. For example, the Truman Library in Independence, Missouri has an outstanding Web site with a wide range of resources and documents pertaining to Harry S. Truman's administration (www.trumanlibrary.org/index.html).The Internet Public Library (www.ipl.org) offers a reference collection categorized by subject area. Also, try Academic Info (www.academicinfo.net), a gateway site to academic resources arranged by discipline. AI also offers a monthly update through e-mail; look for the link at the main page.

And speaking of libraries, you might take advantage of any of the numerous books that serve as "databases of databases," typically arranged by subject.[10] But be circumspect, as Web sites come and go and such guides may quickly become obsolete. Check the publication date and favor the most recent books, or still

[10]One of the best is Nora Paul et al.'s *Great Scouts! Cyberguides for Subject Searching on the Web*, (Medford, NJ: Cyberage Books, 1999) which categorizes, describes, and evaluates sites. Similarly, Bruce Maxwell's *How to Access the Federal Government on the Internet* (Washington: Congressional Quarterly, 1999) organizes a wide range of government databases. See also Laura Andriot's *Internet Blue Pages: The Guide to Federal Government Web Sites* (Medford, NJ: Information Today, 1999); Chris Sherman and Gary Price, *The Invisible Web: Uncovering Sources Search Engines Can't See* (Medford, NJ: CyberAge Books, 2001); Mick O'Leary, *The Online 100* (Wilton, CT: Pemberton Press, 1995).

better, the ones whose authors maintain Web sites where updated information can be obtained. Another helpful source, available in many public and academic libraries, is the *National Directory to Public Record Vendors.*[11] This reference provides detailed information on a huge range of paid and free databases, including online databases.

Database Services

There are a number of not-for-profit services that offer datasets for little or no cost. The advantage is that these organizations have already negotiated for the information from government agencies, issued Freedom of Information requests where necessary and arranged the data into a format that can be read by a variety of programs. Some, like the National Institute of Computer-Assisted Reporting (www.nicar.org), only work with journalists and news organizations. Others, like Project Vote Smart (www.vote-smart.org) offer data free to everyone: candidates' voting records, campaign finance data, position statements, and evaluations. The U.S. Government Printing Office (GPO) produces federal government publications including congressional reports and federal forms (see Fig. 6.10). Users can download documents free at the GPO Web site (www.gpo.gov). The General Accounting Office, the investigative arm of Congress, offers documents to the public free at its Web site (www.gao.gov). Users can search by date a database of federal programs and analyses and congressional testimony.

One way to find searchable databases is to visit the Web sites of organizations that monitor specific issues or agencies, such as public interest or advocacy groups. For example, the Missouri Public Interest Research Group has a searchable database of "legislative scorecards" on its Web site, where users can search by state to see how U.S. congressional representatives voted on public interest issues (www.mopirg.org). At its Web site, the consumer advocacy group Public Citizen offers a searchable database of disciplinary action leveled at doctors in many of the 50 states (www.publiccitizen.org). Another organization, the Privacy Rights Clearinghouse (www.privacyrights.org) archives speeches, legislative testimony, and issue papers related to consumers' personal rights.

Peer-to-Peer File Sharing

Many computer users first heard of *peer-to-peer* (or *P2P*) software when the wildly popular music sharing site Napster came under fire from the Recording Industry Association of America. The RIAA accused Napster of massive copyright violations, by distributing software that allowed its users to freely swap MP3 music files across the Internet. In 1999, the RIAA sued on behalf of the recording companies and Napster was eventually shut down.[12] In the meantime, other file-sharing networks rushed to fill the void, and the momentum of P2P now seems

---

[11]Michael Sankey et al., *The National Directory to Public Record Vendors* (Tempe, AZ: BRB Publications, 2001).

[12]See for example David Segal, "Napster Looking for a Groove," *Washington Post* (26 July 2000), E1. Also see Brad King, "Kazaa Taunts Record Biz: Catch Us," *Wired* (25 September 2002), www.wired.com .

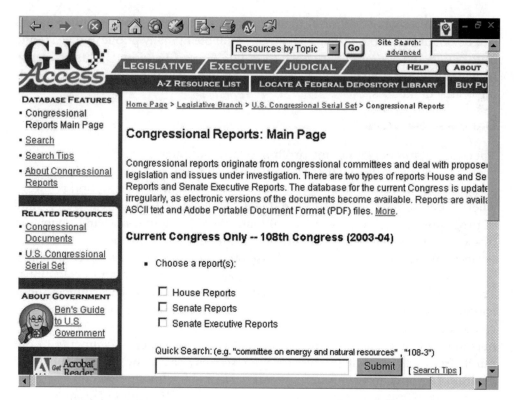

FIG. 6.10.   The Government Printing Office (GPO) database search.

unstoppable.[13] More recently, the RIAA escalated its anti-piracy campaign by filing thousands of subpoenas in 2003 against individuals who shared music files online, including college students, children and grandparents. Legal challenges (and outright nose-thumbing) to that campaign are equally fervent, but the legal disposition of file-swapping bears close watching.[14]

But swapping music files isn't all P2P services are good for. On the contrary, users can trade many other file formats. Morpheus, Kazaa, LimeWire, BearShare, and many other file-trading networks[15] allow users to download document files in addition to music and movies. For example, BearShare (www.bearshare.com) allows searches for applications, audio, images, music, movies, and videos or documents. A search on BearShare for documents using the keyword "constitution" turned up approximately 50 files in four formats: Word, text, .pdf and .html. Another search, this one for the file type ".pdf" turned up more than 1,400 documents in only a few seconds. Among the results were manuals, ebooks, and

---

[13]John Perry Barlow, "The Next Economy of Ideas," *Wired* (October 2000), 240.

[14]See, for example "File Swappers to RIAA: Download This!" *Washington Post* (6 July 2003), F7; Scott Morrison, "Recording Industry Follows Tracks to Online Music Sharers," *Financial Times* (4 August 2003), 6; Benny Evangelista, "Advice to Avoid Copyright Litigation," *San Francisco Chronicle* (28 July 2003), E1.

[15]"P2P Pages: Wired's Guide to Global File-Sharing," *Wired* (October 2000), 243–250.

charts. A subsequent search for ".dbf" netted files related to mailing lists and customer databases.

I've had some success finding data this way, but as you may guess, this strategy is still hit or miss. You'll need to know something about the data you seek, a file name or source, to identify it among the results, which are not arranged alphabetically but more typically by availability. And of course, the success rate depends on whether another user on the network has the files you seek and is willing to share them.

To use one of these file-sharing networks, you must download the software at the Web sites of the service or services you want to use. Most offer a version free of charge, or upgraded (and ad-free) versions for twenty dollars or more. Each has a slightly different interface but allows users to search by file name and file type using keywords or phrases.

Keeping up With the Data

Keeping up with the proliferation of data online is a Herculean task. In fact, you should relieve yourself of the idea that you can ever keep up with all of it. However, it is possible to divide the work into manageable tasks.

As I recommended previously in this volume, online researchers should establish a beat, to track data based on your areas of interest or concern. Bookmark the Web sites for the organizations or data you want to keep up with, and make a point to return regularly. That way, you'll be able to see what's been added or updated and what's been changed.

Also, sign up for e-mail alerts from those organizations likely to have the data you seek. For example, the Government Accounting Office will e-mail you whenever a new product or report is made available online. Joining data-related mailing lists is one of the best ways to find out about the launch of new resources and their highlights or shortcomings (for more on using mailing lists, see chap. 4).

You can make a point to search once a week or once a month for new Web site databases using keywords such as "database," "data," "information," or a combination of words. The Google search for "data filetype," described earlier in this chapter, is a good search to perform routinely. Sometimes new sites offer beta versions free of charge (temporarily) to test and refine their products. If you're willing to act as guinea pig, you may be able to access services that are otherwise cost prohibitive. Check BetaNews, a Web site that provides notice and evaluations of new and pending software releases (www.betanews.com). At the main page, a search of recent betas using the phrase "search engine" netted 33 related programs (see Fig. 6.11). Clicking on a program name opens a screen with technical data, ratings, description, and a link to download the software.

If you're willing to pay for it, try one of the new metabrowser services that allow you to create a "quilt" of Web pages. Quickbrowse (www.quickbrowse.com), for example, lets you construct one long, scrollable page of the Web sites you visit often. It's quite clever, saving you the task of navigating from one bookmarked site to another. At the Quickbrowse Web site, you can choose pages from a list of pre-

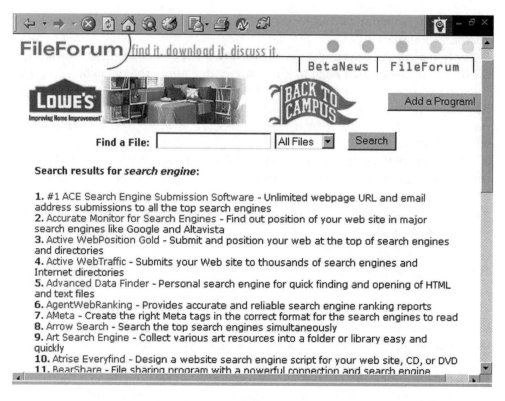

FIG. 6.11.   Keeping up with new software releases on BetaNews.

selected sites, or put together your own list. Then, bookmark the site and return to it for updates. You can even create multiple pages grouped by category. All links remain intact and if you're worried about speed, you can disable images so downloads work faster. A 14-day trial version is free, then the service costs approximately thirteen dollars for three months.[16]

Following is a sample of useful databases available online, grouped by category. For a more complete list see Appendix C. As mentioned earlier, there are entire books written on the subject of online databases and you should take advantage. In addition, several magazines including *Forbes, Yahoo Internet Life* and *Wired* publish annual "best of the Web" issues.

Media

- *Public Libraries, University Libraries*: The best, and the cheapest sources for portal access to large collection of searchable databases. If you

---

[16]See for example, Jim Regan, "Site Reviews" *Christian Science Monitor* (19 February 2001), www.csmonitor.com ; Walter S. Mossberg, "New 'Metabrowsers' Allow You to Create a Quilt of Web Pages," *Wall Street Journal* (18 May 2000), B1; Wendy Grossman, "Web Browsing, For Your Eyes Only," *London Telegraph* (21 September 2000), www.telegraph.co.uk .

don't hold a library card, get one. If you're not a college student, see a librarian about gaining short-term and possibly, remote access to the institution's research facility.

• *American Journalism Review* (www.ajr.org): A trade publication for journalists, the organization's Web site includes a searchable database or magazines, newspapers, television networks and affiliates, radio, wire services and media companies. Follow the links from the left side of the page.

• *British Journalism Review* (www.bjr.org.uk): Online version of this quarterly publication featuring analyses of news process and practice. Follow the links to Great Britain's major print media, some with searchable archives and some without.

• *Citeseer* (http://citeseer.nj.nec.com/cs): A digital library of scientific publications, this site offers a searchable database of papers, tutorials and other documents. Users can download in a number of formats, view comments, citations and e-mail the authors.

• *Dow-Jones Newswires* (www.dow-jones.com/index_finance.htm): This site offers real-time news from Dow-Jones and the Associated Press. Individuals can register for a two-week free trial (renewable after six months) and search archives dating back about a year. Subscribers to the Wall Street Journal Interactive Edition receive free access to the database, but must pay $2.95 to download full-text articles.

• *FindArticles.com* (www.findarticles.com): Free archive of articles from 300 journals, dating from 1998. The database is searchable by date or publication name.

• *Gigalaw* (www.gigalaw.com): If it's Internet-related law you're looking for, this site offers it in the form of news and opinion, produced by lawyers and law professors, as well as court documents. Users can search the content by keywords, phrase and Boolean expression.

• *The Internet Public Library* (www.ipl.org/div/news): The IPL site has links to online newspapers from around the world, searchable by title or region.

• *Kidon Media-Link* (www.kidon.com/media-link): This site offers links to news sources all over the world, including news agencies, print and broadcast news organizations and online news. Searchable by media, by title and/or location. The site offers it content in English, Spanish, French, German, Arabic, Russian, Chinese and Dutch.

• *LexisNexis* (www.lexisnexis.org): The gold standard of searchable databases, this is a gold mine for academic and legal research, but can also be pricey. Try gaining access through a public or university library first and if that fails, check the pay options at the LexisNexis site. Documents are grouped by category, which saves research time. Non-subscribers can view news headlines free, and pay $3 to download single documents; legal documents cost $9. A daily subscription ranges from $30 to $75, depending on the database you select.

• *NewsLink* (http://newslink.org): Links to newspapers, television and radio networks around the world. Searchable by city, state, continent or media type.

- *Newslook Magazine* (www.newslookmag.com): This ambitious site gathers news about Nepal from a wide range of sources, and provides link to the original text source. Updated daily, the site includes a Google search of its contents.
- *Northern Light* (www.northernlight.com): This database allows users to search for publications, articles and transcripts by keywords, phrases and title. A power search lets users narrow the search, by excluding sources, specifying language, date range and limiting subjects. Charges a fee of $1–5 to download full text of articles.
- *Radio Locator* (www.radio-locator.com): Database of radio station Web sites and audio streams from U.S. and around the world. Search by format, frequency, location or used advanced search to find stations by call letters or owner.
- *Rocketinfo* (www.rocketnews.com/index.html): Searchable by topic, this service retrieves articles posted within the previous five days from a wide range of news and information sources, including the *Manila Times, Atlanta Journal-Constitution, International Herald Tribune,* the major wire services and more. Offers an advanced search that allows user to exclude terms.

Government Sites

- *The Digital Daily* (www.irs.ustreas.gov): operated by the Internal Revenue Service, this site provides federal tax information including tax forms, tax filing information, statistics, publications and links to other government sites. Brace yourself for some goofy narrative, like the "news" headline "Teenager Tanya Taylor Tries to Tackle Taxation Training ... Interactively." Makes a journalist cringe.
- *FedWeb* (www.fedweb.com): Offers links to federal agencies, searchable blue pages and gateways to government-related information.
- *FedWorld* (www.fedworld.gov): Hosted by the Department of Commerce, FedWorld offers searchable databases of government jobs, Supreme Court decisions. Also offers links to government research publications and science and technology Web resources.
- *FirstGov* (www.firstgov.gov): Opened for business in September 2000, this site allows access to local, state and federal government agencies. This is intended to centralize on a single website all government information available on the Internet—very handy and easy to navigate. Information is searchable by topic, rather than agency. Search results will direct you to the appropriate authority.
- *Government Printing Office* (www.gpo.gov): This site has databases with the full-text of bills introduced in Congress, the Federal Register, the Congressional Record, Supreme Court decisions from 1937–1975, and much more. Simple and power searches are allowed, and the site offers lengthy descriptions of the databases and tips for searching them.
- *GovStats* (http://govinfo.kerr.orst.edu): A site maintained by Oregon State University and including databases of federal data on demographics, eco-

nomics, education and many related subjects. The data comes straight from the Census Bureau, National Center for Education Statistics and other organizations. Very easy to use, and you can receive notices of updates by subscribing to GOVINFO, a mailing list. Send an e-mail message to listserv@mail.orst.edu with the message in the body of the e-mail "subscribe govinfo firstname lastname."

• *Library of Congress* (http://lcweb.loc.gov): The next best thing to being there, this site offers text and images from current exhibitions and numerous databases. Among them, you can search the catalog or search a database of records related to American prisoners of war or soldiers missing in action during the Vietnam War. In addition, the site has bibliographies on many topics and links to online library catalogs around the world.

• *PACER* (http://pacer.psc.uscourts.gov): Electronic access to case and docket information for United States district, bankruptcy and appellate courts. Users must register and acquire a password, and then are charged either a per-minute fee (.60) for dial-up access or per-page fee (.07) for Web access.

• *Social Security Online* (www.ssa.gov): Here's where to find information on your social security benefits, Medicare, retirement benefits, disability benefits and more. It includes links to forms and information about numerous Social Security programs.

• *Taxing Times* (www.maxwell.com/tax): An electronic compendium of information related to the filing of income tax, including forms. This site is maintained by Maxwell Technologies in cooperation with the Internal Revenue Service. Most of the forms are in Adobe Portable Document Format (.pdf) and require Acrobat Reader.

• *Thomas Legislative Information* (http://thomas.loc.gov): Hosted by the Library of Congress, this site offers full text of legislation under consideration by Congress, public laws, the *Congressional Record*, roll call votes, Committee Reports and more. Searchable by keyword or sponsor, and advanced options for narrowing search.

Public Records

• *Docusearch* (www.docusearch.com): A kind of Web detective agency, this site offers a range of databases and links to state agencies. You'll find records on sex offenders, property ownership and court records, among others. Some of the searches are free, others cost as much as $250 although you don't pay unless you get results. In some cases, Docusearch staff may contact you by phone to verify your identity and you may be asked to justify your search if it requests sensitive information.

• *FindLaw* (www.findlaw.com): A Web site with links to an array of public legal records, including case law, law firm salaries, professional organizations, and a pretty good bulletin board system for advice regarding topics like immigration, bankruptcy, government and housing. You can find a lawyer or just read current legal news. Free for now.

- *KnowX* (www.knowx.com): At this site, you can search public records to determine if an individual or business has been involved in any court proceedings, liens, bankruptcies, divorce, and so forth. The site does not indicate how many states' records are represented in the database, but the information is U.S.-based. Depending on the search, the results may be free, or run from $3.95 to $15.
- *Search Systems* (www.searchsystems.net): Provides links to more than 1,500 public records online, with an emphasis on free. Simple and advanced search options available to locate information in the United States, Canada and other countries worldwide.

Medicine and Health

- *Cochrane Collaboration* (www.cochrane.org): Includes a database of reviews, which evaluate current medical research to help people make informed decisions about health care.
- *Health A to Z* (www.healthatoz.com): Searchable by topic, also offers recipe database and link to PubMed, a service of the National Library of Medicine with access to more than 12 million citations or full-text articles.
- *JAMA, Journal of the American Medical Association* (http://pubs.ama-assn.org): Non-AMA members can download articles from the journal for $9 apiece, or get 24-hour access to the archives for $30. Check your local library's database for free access to this publication.
- *National Women's Health Resource Center* (www.healthywomen.org): A site with news related to women's health, searchable by topic and a database of publications.
- *Searchpointe* (www.searchpointe.com): Allows you to check on doctors' (MDs and doctors of oseteopathy, DOs) credentials and find out if there are sanctions or disciplinary actions against them. The basic search for credentials is free, but a license and sanction report costs $9.95. A Health and Human Services site, http://defaulteddocs.dhhs.gov, lets you find out if a doctor has defaulted on a student loan. There is no fee for this service.

Business and not-for Profit

- *BPubs.com* (www.bpubs.com): A business publications search engine, this site allows users to search by keyword, category and sub-category a range of business-related articles, published online and traditional print media.
- *Fortune* (www.fortune.com): The Web site of this popular business magazine includes data from many of the magazine's infamous lists, such as the Fortune 500 and the Global Most Admired. Clicking on links takes the user to detailed company profiles. Searchable by company or executive name, or industry.
- *GuideStar* (www.guidestar.org): GuideStar is a national database of not-for-profit agencies, and their Web site offers a search of more than

850,000 organizations. Results include IRS Form 990s and other financial statements.

- *Hoover's Online* (www.hoovers.com/newscenter): At Hoover's news centers, users can search by keyword through a range of wire services, including: Associated Press, PR Newswire, Knight-Ridder Business News and Canada Newswire. Advanced search options are available by subscription.

- *Monster.com* (www.monster.com): The online career center offers users searchable database of sample resumes, interview tips and career advice.

- *Securities and Exchange Commission* (www.sec.gov): Offers users access to many searchable databases, including EDGAR, regulatory actions, publications, litigation releases and more.

- *Yahoo Commercial Directory* (http://dir.yahoo.com/Business_and_Economy): Yahoo's business and economy directory is a subject guide with links to business-related Web sites, including publications and business libraries. Most of the major search engines have similar directories, arranged by category.

Consumer Services

- *Better Business Bureau* (www.bbb.com): At this Web site, users can search for businesses by name, phone or Web address, to determine if complaints have been filed against it. At a companion site (www.give.org), the BBB offers a searchable database (Wise Giving Alliance) of charitable organizations, which returns evaluations and information on donor inquiries.

- *Center for Voting and Democracy* (www.fairvote.org): Articles and commentary on electoral reform and other politics-related issues. The site offers a Google search of its archived contents.

- *Consumer Product Safety Commission* (www.cpsc.gov): At this site, users can find out about product recalls and download CPSC annual reports. The site offers a simple and advanced search of its contents.

- *Consumer Reports* (www.consumerreports.org/main/home.jsp): Published by Consumers Union, this Web site offers a limited amount of content from *Consumer Reports*, a magazine that tests and evaluates mass-marketed products. Users can search contents by product category or read consumer advice, including reports on Internet shopping.

- *Election Resources* (http://electionresources.org): This site has links to election results from the U.S. and other countries, including a searchable database of U.S. presidential election results from 1789 to 2000.

- *Federal Citizen Information Center* (www.pueblo.gsa.gov): Formerly the Consumer Information Center, this Web site offers hundreds of publications at no cost. Search by topic or use the site map link to view a text version of contents.

- *Public Citizen* (www.publiccitizen.org): Founded by Ralph Nader, this organization seeks to shape public policy on behalf of consumers. Online resources include records of congressional votes and publications, which are available for download.

Polling and Surveys

- *Harris Interactive* (www.harrisinteractive.com): Known for the Harris Poll, this organization offers Web users poll results, as well as text of articles that refer to Harris Interactive data. The site has a search interface for archived contents.
- *Ipsos-Reid* (www.angusreid.com): A market research company that provides polls and news releases at its Web site. Also offers e-mail newsletters, including a weekly alert of newly-released polls and data.
- *Pew Internet and American Life Project* (www.pewinternet.org): An endeavor of the Pew Research Center for People and the Press, this project funds scholarly research addressing the impact of the Internet on society. The Web site offers many downloads, including current and past research, polls and statistics.
- *Scarborough Research* (www.scarborough.com): At the Web site, users can download newly released surveys and polls.

Peer-to-Peer Networking (P2P)

BearShare	www.bearshare.com
Grokster	www.grokster.com
Kaaza	www.kaaza.com
LimeWire	www.limewire.com
Toadnode	www.toadnode.com

File Formats

Ace Net	http://ace.net.nz/tech/TechFileFormat.html
The Beeline	http://bton.com/tb17/formats.html
Tech Tutorials	www.techtutorials.com/fileformats.shtml#d
WhatIs?com	http://whatis.techtarget.com/fileFormatA
Wotsit's Format	www.wotsit.org/search.asp?s=ALLFILES

The Future of Online Data

The breadth of information available to Internet users is indeed impressive, and gathering it is more convenient than ever, from faraway places and at all hours. Yet the nature of some online databases raises valid considerations about security and privacy. For example, a New York teacher was shocked to discover his neighbors' political contributions were available on a Web-accessible database developed by two former Federal Election Commission employees. "These lists could have a chilling effect on individuals' contributions, especially donations to unpopular candidates and parties," he told a reporter.[17] In a more serious incident, the *New York Times* reported in December 2000 that hackers

---

[17]Fred Bernstein, "An Online Peek at Your Politics," *New York Times* (4 October 2000), A31.

had obtained data on thousands of patients at the University of Washington's medical center, including social security numbers and medical procedures.[18] More recently, civil liberties groups have expressed concern over the government's increased surveillance powers, which includes the authority to read e-mails between private citizens.[19]

So, the migration of records to the Internet proceeds in fits and starts, as groups wrangle over the legalities of the online collection, storage and use of information.[20] When President George W. Bush signed the E-Government Act of 2002,[21] he promised federal agencies would work together to provide information to the public. But that same initiative could actually make it harder for citizens to use the Internet to find government documents, by allowing private companies to bid on printing jobs.[22] And concerns over national security have already led the Bush Administration to cut off Web access to numerous databases in the aftermath of the September 11, 2001 terrorist attacks.[23]

What does this mean to online researchers? It means that online data is unstable. Using a library's database to search for a newspaper article is an easy task once you understand how the search interface works, but learning to find and work with online data is an ongoing process. Searching the Internet for a particular kind of data one day might produce quite different results on another day. Searching by file type may unearth documents on the "hidden" Web, whereas using subject guides might lead you to just the kind of esoteric site you seek. For those reasons, savvy researchers keep up with new resources and continually refine their search techniques, using a combination of strategies to locate the best and most reliable information sources.

TIPS FOR SMART SEARCHES

- Begin a search for online data by focusing on the likely source and go directly to it whenever possible. For government documents, check the Web sites of the corresponding government agency, or watchdog organization.
- If you're looking for a news article, first check the publication's Web site. If they charge for access to their archives, note the citation and then use a free database to locate the particular article.

---

[18]"Hackers From Abroad Obtain Data on Washington Patients," *New York Times* (8 December 2000), A21.

[19]For example, Shannon McCaffrey, "Decision Widens U.S. Wiretap Power; Court Expands Authority to Eavesdrop on Citizens," *Milwaukee Journal Sentinel* (19 November 2002), 1A.

[20]See for example, Patti Waldmeir, "Database Legislation: Who Should Own the Raw Facts?," *Financial Times* (22 May 2002), 19; Conor O'Clery, "Poindexter Plan to Create U.S. Citizen Database Criticised," *Irish Times* (22 November 2002), 14; Warren Richey, "High Court to Decide Who Owns Newspaper Archives," *Christian Science Monitor* (27 March 2001), 2.

[21]E-Government Act of 2002, H.R. 2458, Public Law No. 107–347 (17 December 2002); "Bush Puts More 'E' in Government," *Wired* (17 December 2002), www.wired.com .

[22]For more, see Brian Krebs, "E-Gov Law Sets Up Clash Over White House Outsourcing Plan," Washington Post (17 December 2002), www.washingtonpost.com.

[23]See for example, Jonathan Riskind, "Shielding Records: Government Continues Rush to More Secrecy," *Columbus Dispatch* (9 September 2002), 7A; OMBWatch, a not-for-profit group that monitors the White House Office of Management and Budget, also tracks access to government information post-September 11 at its Web site, www.ombwatch.org.

- For subject guides, identify the university or institution that specializes in the subject you're researching and check its Web site for searchable databases.
- Take advantage of public libraries' remote access to large commercial databases such as Lexis-Nexis and Dow Jones Interactive.
- When using databases in the library, look for an e-mail option to send the articles you find to your home or office address. That saves research time and money, as some libraries charge a fee to print out articles or limit the duration of an online session.
- Temporary access might be granted to researchers who want to use private libraries' resources; ask the librarian or archivist.
- Use databases that indicate clearly the source of the data provided. You'll want to know if the data is in its original form or if it has been evaluated, analyzed, or somehow manipulated.
- Before you pay a fee for any data, determine exactly what you're paying for: access, breadth of records, format? Would you do better to visit the particular agency involved to get the records? Are the same records available through a public database (e.g., at the library) free of charge?
- Use a combination of search techniques to find online data. Searching by file format helps locate "invisible Web" resources.
- Search and use online data responsibly; do not reprint or publish it without permission.

Evaluating
the Information You Find

A college professor of mine began class each semester by regaling students with his long, colorful career in the news business. He recalled his work as a young correspondent during the Spanish-American War, and described what it was like to charge San Juan Hill at dawn as part of Teddy Roosevelt's Light Brigade. The professor went on, waxing nostalgic about his colleagues: Edward R. Murrow, Ernie Pyle, and Ernest Hemingway.

The professor's account was complete fiction, of course, intended to test his students' knowledge of history. True, he was a grizzled veteran, but could not possibly have been a correspondent in a war that began in 1898. The "Light Brigade" was a British cavalry unit in the Crimean War some thirty years earlier; it was Teddy Roosevelt's "Rough Riders" who fought on San Juan Hill. Furthermore, the professor's supposed colleagues were known for their work as correspondents during World War II.

Nevertheless, many students took the professor at his word. Even those who suspected tomfoolery were willing to give him the benefit of the doubt. And why not? Everything about him appeared credible. He was a prolific author and distinguished faculty member, a recognized authority on journalism history. Without the requisite knowledge of history, students were either too ignorant or intimidated to challenge his claims.

Eventually, the students' naiveté was revealed and the professor went about the business of teaching journalism. But the most important lesson had already been taught—that no matter how credible something (or someone) might appear, gullibility has no place in newsgathering. Journalists are trained to check and re-check information. In fact, some organizations employ full-time factcheckers to maintain the integrity of their news products. As the admonition goes, if your mother says she loves you, get confirmation.

Now that the Internet has become a standard tool for newsgathering, journalists are finding they must continue to rely on "low tech" safeguards. "Using the computer does not alter traditional concerns about accuracy, fairness, privacy, plagiarism, or other ethical issues. But using the computer to gather and analyze information can put reporters and editors on unfamiliar ground,"[1] wrote Bob Steele and Wendell Cochran in *ASNE Bulletin*. Thus, many news organizations insist that e-mails be authenticated, bulletin board messages verified, and most data is considered suspect until proven otherwise.

For other online researchers, concerns about credibility are just as important as they are for news organizations. Whereas there are many sophisticated kinds of software available to help the average user filter out offensive sites, no such product exists to screen out unreliable sites. In this chapter, I provide you with guidelines to check the integrity of online information, including data from Web sites and e-mail communications.

To Err is ... to be Expected

It would be unrealistic to expect every Web site to be well-researched and well-reasoned. Recent events tells us few sites are invulnerable to hackers, who can tweak things so that critical errors go undetected, or wreak vandalism on a grand scale.[2] The Securities and Exchange Commission (SEC) reports that fraud online is so widespread, users should assume every investment opportunity is bogus until proven otherwise.[3] And yet, few people take time to verify the information they find. "Those who might benefit most from verifying online information, because they may lack experience that helps to discern valid from bogus material, are doing so the least,"[4] wrote researchers in a 2000 study of users' perceptions of Internet credibility.

Sometimes the errors found in online data are negligible; they can often even be amusing. For example, after a clerk entered incorrect data on a travel agency Web site, a British family purchased tickets to fly to the U.S. for £15 apiece, approximately £450 less than usual. When they discovered the fare, they immediately called other family members and friends who also booked flights at the bargain price.[5]

Other kinds of mistakes, however, can prevent consumers from making informed decisions or provide researchers with inaccurate source materials. Students who rely solely on the Internet for academic research often find material riddled with bias and inaccuracies.[6] Data errors or inaccuracies can disrupt or

---

[1]Bob Steele and Wendell Cochran, "Computer-Assisted Reporting Challenges Traditional Newsgathering Safeguards," *ASNE Bulletin* (January 1995), www.asne.org.

[2]See for example, David Noack, "Hack Attack Sends Chills Through News Web Sites," *Editor and Publisher* (19 September 1998), 14.

[3]Lynn Brenner, "Online Investment Scams," *Parade* (16 July 2000), 8.

[4]Andrew J. Flanigan and Miriam J. Metzger, "Perceptions of Internet Information Credibility," *Journalism and Mass Communication Quarterly* 77:3 (Autumn 2000), 531.

[5]Rebecca Allison, "Travel Website's Mistake Nets Family £15 Flights to Florida," *London Guardian* (28 August 2002), 6.

[6]See for example, Laura Sessions Stepp, "Point. Click. Think?" *Washington Post* (16 July 2002), C1.

endanger lives, particularly now that so many Americans rely on the Internet as a primary source of information about health, finance, and politics.[7] Consider the following:

- In 2000, police auditors found an 86 percent error rate among data held on the Police National Computer, a British database of criminal records. That represented a 34 percent increase in the error rate found in an earlier, 1997 audit. Auditors said that 85% of the overall error rate was composed of "major errors ... those that could potentially lead to serious consequences."[8]
- A study published in the journal of the American Academy of Pediatrics in June 1998 reported that universities were publishing medical information online that was filled with errors and outdated theories. The mistakes went largely undetected because they were sponsored by traditional sources of medical information, such as practitioners, research institutions, and university medical centers.[9]
- Financial and health advice offered on Web sites is often misleading and inaccurate, according to a global survey of 460 Web sites and 13 groups by the watchdog group, Consumers International.[10]
- In November 2002, several "hugely inaccurate" stock quotes appeared on some news and financial services' Web sites, the fault of the company that distributes the data. General Electric, which closed at $27.10 on November 29, was quoted at $919.[11]
- In a 1998 study, of the *Arkansas Democrat Gazette's* Web site, a researcher discovered serious errors among its archived issues. Inaccurate material that was never printed still made its way to electronic archives, an important record for historical research. "Misunderstood technology, misguided assumptions, poor planning and plain inattention all play roles in dirtying newspapers' electronic archives. And the situation is worse than you probably think," wrote Bruce Oakley.[12]

Many of the mistakes in online data are probably the result of clerical error. Data entry ranks as one of the most tedious (and notoriously low-paid) jobs available and the potential for mistakes is high. But even a seemingly minor error can have major consequences. "The bigger the database, the likelier it is that errors have crept in and metastasized throughout the system,"[13] one software consultant has said. Errors involving numbers often hard to catch and can throw off an

---

[7]"Counting on the Internet," Pew Internet and American Life Project study, December 29, 2002.

[8]Mike Simons, "Errors Rife in Police Data File," *Computer Weekly* (27 April 2000), 1.

[9]H. Juhling McClung et al., "The Internet as a Source for Current Patient Information," *Pediatrics* 101:6 (June 1998), 2.

[10]Susan Schwartz, "Watchdog Sees Pitfalls to Advice Web Sites," *South China Morning Post* (5 November 2002), 5.

[11]Jennifer Bayot, "Errors in Some Web Stock Lists," *New York Times* (2 December 2002), C2. See also Simon Kennedy, "Errors Pop Up in First U.K. Financial Services Database," *Compliance Reporter* (16 December 2002), 1.

[12]Bruce William Oakley, "How Accurate are Your Archives?" *Columbia Journalism Review* 36:6 (March-April 1998), 13.

[13]Erik Thomsen, "It's an Uncertain World," *Intelligent Enterprise* (December 1998), 22.

entire set of data. In a 1992 election, a candidate for a state office in Missouri supposedly recruited her young son to enter voter returns on her Web site. Reporters relied on this official campaign site only to learn later that in his haste the boy had made numerous errors.

Credibility at a Glance

To evaluate Web sites, you can begin by making a general check of the site's contents. Does it seem reliable? Some sites are obviously bogus. *The Onion*, a satirical newspaper carries headlines and stories that few people would take seriously, such as "United States Toughens Image with Umlauts"[14] (see Fig. 7.1). But with most sites or data, just trusting your gut isn't enough.

Another quick measure of a Web site's credibility is to look at the domain. Many journalists apply a hierarchy of trust when judging the credibility of a site.[15] It's actually not all that different from the standards applied to traditional information sources. For example, government information is considered the most reliable, probably because there are copious checks of (and restrictions on) the contents of federal .gov sites, and of the individuals who develop and maintain them. The Web sites of U.S. Senators, for example, must meet with restrictions set forth by the Secretary of the Senate, and are monitored for compliance by the Senate Webmaster. Military sites also rank high on the trust scale, for the same reason.

Following ".gov" and ".mil" sites, university sites are among the most trusted. Academia is a fiercely competitive profession. Research that includes questionable or inaccurate data is challenged quickly and loudly. The contents of peer-reviewed journals are representative of the best research in a particular field. Keep in mind however, when using ".edu" sites that they can also be the personal pages of students and staff members. In that case, the credibility of a site's content diminishes.

Not-for-profit groups or special interest groups, indicated by ".org" or ".net" domains, publish quite a bit of data online. Identification is usually made clear on the site, along with contact information. Of course, these organizations have an agenda, and usually that's immediately clear.

Commercial or ".com" sites are thought to be the least trustworthy. They're not necessarily "bad," but they require more careful consideration. A personal Web page has no authority or oversight to vouch for the content, for example. An individual's Web page can often be identified by the URL, which may contain a personal name, a tilde ($\sim$) or percentage sign. If the name of a commercial ISP or Web hosting service appears in the URL, it may be a personal Web page (as in www.barbarafriedman.aol.com).

---

[14]"United States Toughens Image with Umlauts," *The Onion* (29 April 1997), www.theonion.com.

[15]Few journalists stop there, however. Most news organizations require their reporters to verify Web-based information by at least one other means.

FIG. 7.1.   Web site for The Onion, a satirical newspaper.

Digital Literacy: Checking the Data

Domain names are a quick way to judge a site's level of credibility in general, but certainly the evaluation shouldn't end there. To gauge the integrity of a site, users should consider these items: accuracy, authority, currency, agenda, and audience. The next section looks at each topic in detail:

Accuracy

Accuracy is one indicator of quality and suggests the author or host feels a degree of responsibility for the image or content that's put forth. Although a typographical error or two isn't grounds to dismiss an entire site, an abundance of mistakes makes me think the Web site author was careless and has likely made other mistakes in content. Impossible facts are also a giveaway that a site is either bogus or carelessly put together.

- Likewise, if the site uses text or graphics without giving credit, that suggests the author has not bothered himself with fairness or accuracy—might additional content be plagiarized? Scholarly literature is often characterized by footnote or endnote documentation of sources; check the site's content for attribution.

- Does the site contain any statistical data? Are charts and graphs clearly labeled? The source of the data should be apparent. Look not just for a citation of the original source, but also an explanation of the method used to gather the data.
- Can the information be verified with nondigital or traditional sources? This is an important step that is often overlooked, although it's one of the quickest ways to spot inaccurate information.
- If you come across research you believe is plagiarized, you can apply any one of several software programs to substantiate or refute your suspicions. For example, Essay Verification Engine (www.canexus.com/eve) compares the material in question to Web sites, looking for copied passages. A trial version is offered on the EVE Web site, and the software can be purchased for $19.99. A similar service is offered at Plagiarism.org (www.plagiarism.org), and by WordCheck Systems (www.wordchecksystems.com). Although many of these programs were originally marketed to teachers concerned with plagiarized and Web-purchased student papers, they are also used by publishers and other researchers concerned with copyright infringement.

Authority

Checking the authority of a Web site allows you to identify an individual or organization that claims responsibility for its content. Does the author have the proper credentials to speak authoritatively on this particular subject? Is it hosted by a reputable organization?

- Ask, who wrote this page? An authoritative site clearly indicates who or what organization sponsors or maintains it. Start by looking for names or logos. For example, check the URL for identifying information: www.harvard.edu suggests this is a site at Harvard University. If it's not immediately clear, truncate the URL to get back to the publisher or host.
- Also check for information describing the purpose of the organization, either on the site or a linked page. Look for a link called "about us," or copyright information.
- If you need to contact the organization for verification, does the site provide a postal address, fax, and phone number? Is the organization listed in the (hard copy) phone pages or a professional directory? If the organization represented is a not-for-profit, they must file an annual Form 990 with the Internal Revenue Service. You should be able to locate those records online to confirm and clarify information on the Web site; try GuideStar (www.guidestar.org) or The Foundation Center (http://fdncenter.org/funders/grantsmart/index.html).
- You can also check the source code for meta tags, information that does not appear on the site. On your browser tool bar, select "view" then "source."

Scroll through the coding and see if there are meta tags that list contact or other relevant information.

- Can you establish who actually composed the information on the site? If an individual, can you ascertain that person's qualifications? If the material is not original, is it cited so that you can trace it back to the original author?

- If you're using a Web site guide or subject directory, what do you know about the person or organization that assembled it? At About (www.about.com), guides are screened and trained to provide Internet users with subject-specific links and content.

- Use search engines to evaluate organizations and Web site authors; what other kinds of sites are they affiliated with?

- Check the authority of a site by seeing what types of sites it links to, and what kinds of sites link to it. Use the "link" syntax search, as described in chapter 3.

- A seal of approval or trustmark can indicate the veracity of a Web site, although the absence of one does not necessarily mean a site is suspect. If a site does have a seal or trustmark, is it from a reputable organization? Is there a way to determine what standards have been applied, such as a link to the granting organization? Perhaps because online health and medical information has come under fire for being inaccurate and even dangerous, the American Accreditation Health Care Commission recently began granting seals of approval to sites it deemed worthy. Web site owners must apply for accreditation and meet certain minimum standards.[16] Similarly, TRUSTe offers its insignia, and the Better Business Bureau offers a "reliability seal" to sites that safeguard the personal data of their users.[17] Both organizations perform spot checks and revoke their seals for noncompliance (see Fig. 7.2). Unfortunately, there's no one source to help you identify the range and origin of online trustmarks. Personal seals of approval, given by one Web page designer to another, don't count for much as there are no minimum requirements to help you understand the credibility of a site.

- If you're not sure who's behind a site, enter the URL at a domain lookup site, such as WHOIS (www.networksolutions.com/en_us/whois/index.jhtml) or Better-WhoIs (www.better-whois.com).

- Don't rely on counters that tabulate how many people have visited a site, those are not an indication of credibility. Counters keep track of how many times a site is visited, but not how the site is used during or after. Furthermore, they are too easily manipulated to be used in evaluating a site. A popular site isn't necessarily a credible site, and vice versa.

Currency

News generally depends on timeliness for its relevance. After a mere 24 hours, a newspaper is "old," more likely to end up as fish wrap than required reading. On

---

[16]See for example, Charlene Laino, "Health Sites Granted Seal of Approval," *MSNBC* (12 December 2002), www.MSNBC.com.

[17]Jeremy Quittner, "Should You Pay For a Privacy Seal of Approval?" *Business Week* (27 April 1999), www.businessweek.com.

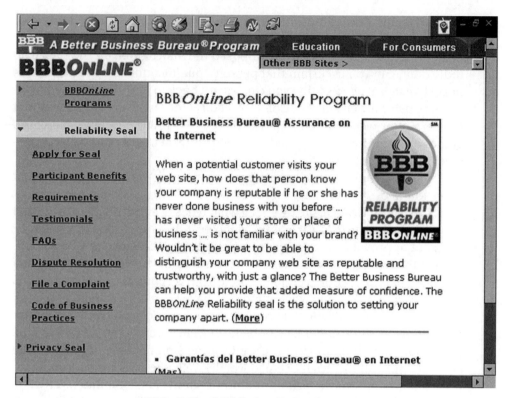

FIG. 7.2.   BBBOnline Reliability seal.

the Web though, information has a longer shelf life: a Web site developer might lose interest in maintaining a site, yet leave it intact; a company may fold but its Web presence remains; a school project is posted then abandoned. For these reasons alone, you should always check the currency of the information you find online. I am reluctant to use any information I find online if it cannot be verified in regard to when it was posted and updated.

- Look for dates on the page or in the source code to determine when the page was written and posted on the Web.
- Also look for a date indicating when the page was last revised. That might appear on the site or in search engine results. AltaVista indicates in its search results whether a page has been refreshed within the last 48 hours (see Fig. 7.3).
- If you want to find out just what changes were made to a page, Google may have a cached or stored (previous) version of a Web site. Look for a link to "cached" in search results (see Fig. 7.4). Another way to check an earlier version of a page is to use the Internet Archive's Wayback Machine (www.archive.org). Enter a URL at the site and you'll be provided with links to earlier snapshots of the site, often with links intact.

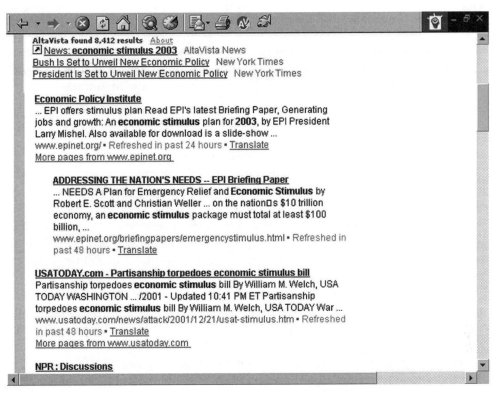

FIG. 7.3. AltaVista search results indicate whether a site has been recently updated.

FIG. 7.4. Google search results may include a cached version of a Web site.

- You might be able to judge something about currency or timeliness from the site's subject matter—is it "old news" for example, or a time-sensitive topic?
- Broken links are an indication that a site is not being maintained.

Agenda

In journalism, the term *objectivity* refers to an approach to news that is "detached, unprejudiced, unopinionated, uninvolved, unbiased, omniscient and infallible,"[18] wrote John Merrill, a journalism scholar and professor. Objective reporters maintain an emotional distance from their work and balance their writing in a way that does not suggest they have been swayed by personal feelings toward either a subject or source, using verification and attribution. While many practitioners, including Merrill, argue that objectivity is an impossible goal, it remains a principle of journalism.

Authors of Web content feel no such compulsion to remain objective. In fact, an appealing feature of the Web is that it offers personal ideas and opinions a public forum. Take for example, the site Sucks500.com (www.sucks500.com), a forum where Internet users can complain about Microsoft, corporate America, bad credit, and many other sore subjects. Or the many Web logs (blogs) whose authors comment on and critique news coverage of current events. Free and candid speech flourish online.

But the Web is also characterized by a lack of accountability. There's nothing wrong about espousing an opinion online; evidence of bias is not intended to make you doubt a site, but rather understand its purpose. If you're using the Internet for research, you'll want to determine whether an author is motivated by a personal or professional agenda so that you can place the information into a wider context.

- Ask first, are biases clearly stated? At its Web site, the National Center for Public Policy Research (www.nationalcenter.org) describes itself as a "nonpartisan, conservative, free market foundation." That, paired with the site's content, suggests a distinct bias (see Fig. 7.5).
- Is there advertising on the Web site, and if so, is it separated from the information content? Does the content suggest there is a reciprocal agreement with an advertiser?
- Does the Web site provide links to information that might challenge or contradict its own? Or do links only direct the user to the original page?

Audience

Determining the purpose of, and intended audience for, a Web site helps you contextualize the information it offers. A site about Civil War history designed for elementary school students may be of little use to college students.

---

[18]Everette E. Dennis and John C. Merrill, *Media Debates: Issues in Mass Communications* (New York: Longman Publishing, 1991), 110.

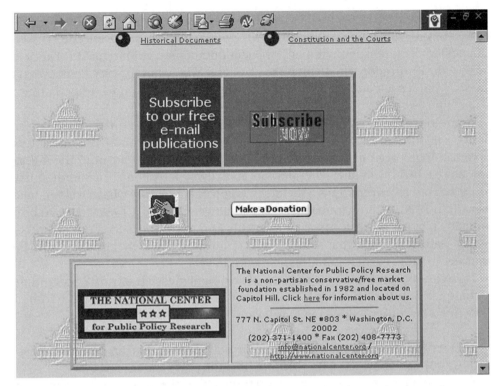

FIG. 7.5.   The National Center for Public Policy Research agenda is stated on its
Web site.

- How is the site being presented, as if to a subject expert, hobbyist, or student?
- Ask, why was this site created? To sell something? To inform? To persuade?
- Find a link to information about the sponsor or author of the site, which often states the purpose or mission of the organization.
- What is not being said on the Web site that ought to be; what information has been left out?

Evaluating E-Mail

In his book, *Next*,[19] Michael Lewis tells the story of a legal expert who soars to popularity on Askme.com, a knowledge exchange Web site. In response to hundreds of e-mail queries, "Marcus" offered advice on topics ranging such as Miranda rights, legal appeals, sentencing, and more. Soon, he was ranked in the top 10 of some 150 experts in AskMe.com's criminal division, many of whom were lawyers. Until he confessed, Marcus' clients had no idea that he was really a 15-year-old boy, not a 25-year-old lawyer, as he'd claimed in his online profile. Had he not told them, they might never have known they were duped by a teenager who earned his legal "education" by watching television.

_____

[19]Michael Lewis, *Next: The Future Just Happened* (New York: W. W. Norton & Company, 2001).

As one writer put it, "A rose is a rose by any other name and on the Internet, the rose can go by any name it chooses."[20] One of the Internet's charms is that users can post information anonymously or pseudonomously, as Marcus did. That's an important feature for whistleblowers or people who want to voice controversial views.[21] But it's a troublesome one for researchers, who want to verify that individuals posting information online are who they say they are.

Some journalists have taken to conducting interviews via e-mail, or trolling for sources in online chat rooms or on mailing lists and newsgroups. But many news organizations prohibit reporters from quoting e-mail content until the author can be reached by an alternate method, usually by telephone. The method isn't foolproof but gives reporters a means to confirm and clarify what's written in an e-mail. In 1996, veteran journalist Pierre Salinger claimed a TWA flight had been shot down by a U.S. Navy missile. FBI agents found that the "secret document" on which Salinger based that allegation was an e-mail widely circulated on the Internet months earlier and already discredited.[22]

How can you determine the veracity of an e-mail message or post? Some of the techniques outlined in chapter 5 about finding people are helpful. In addition, here are a few other guidelines to follow:

- Does the author include contact information other than an e-mail address? Can it be confirmed with a phone book or professional directory?
- Can you locate or determine something about the author by his e-mail address? For example, johndoe@rutgers.edu suggests this is a student, staff, or faculty member of Rutgers University in New Jersey. Check the university Web site to determine the individual's affiliation or expertise.
- Conduct a Web search of author names to see with what organizations they are affiliated.
- Use a reverse e-mail search, such as InfoSpace (www.infospace.com) to identify an author who is using a obvious pseudonymous screen name.
- If you receive an e-mail message with a claim or appeal that you suspect is bogus, check one of the many sites that investigates Internet hoaxes. Some examples are Hoaxbusters (http://hoaxbusters.ciac.org), Urban Legend Zeitgeist (www.urbanlegends.com/ulz), and Symantec's Security Response page (www.symantec.com/avcenter/hoax.html; see Fig. 7.6).
- Was the e-mail written and posted recently? Be wary of outdated e-mail, as the author may have changed his affiliation or clarified his position since composing the original message.
- Was the message sent or posted by the original author or has it been forwarded by others? Forwarded messages can be easily edited, altering the original meaning.

---

[20]Wendy Leibowitz, "On-Line Anonymity: Myth and Reality," *New York Law Journal* (27 April 1999), 5.

[21]See for example, Tanya Schevitz, "Mom's Web Site Accuses Professors of Bias; Students Complain in Anonymous Posts," *San Francisco Chronicle* (28 November 2002), A27; "The Spin On Seattle: What People Are Saying About the WTO," *Ottawa Citizen* (2 December 1999), A17.

[22]Dan Barry, "FBI Questions Salinger About Crash Claims," *New York Times* (10 November 1996), A44; "Missile Document Rubbish," *London Telegraph* (11 November 1996), 23.

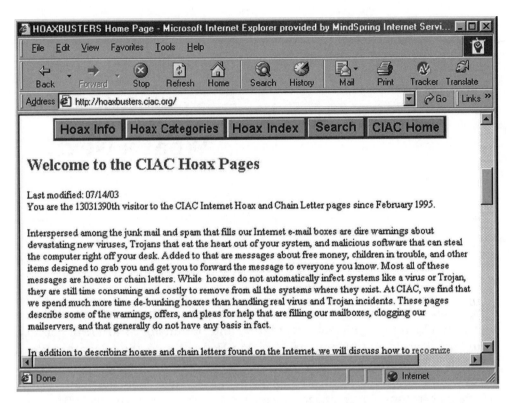

FIG. 7.6.   Hoaxbusters, a site dedicated to investigating Internet hoaxes.

American households have made the Internet a common source for information, and have high expectations that the quality and quantity of online information will continue to improve.[23] This will surely occur, but in the meantime we
should approach online research with a healthy dose of skepticism, and take a
systematic approach when determining the credibility of Web content.

---

[23]"Counting on the Internet," Pew Internet and American Life Project study, December 29, 2002.

What's Next?

The introduction of new technologies to American society has historically been met with a blend of cynicism, trepidation and optimism. In the 19th century, *New York Herald* founder James Gordon Bennett said the telegraph would usher in great "revolutions and changes,"[1] whereas others suggested telegraph wires would "induce cholera, stunt growth, or even rejuvenate the dead."[2] Early television was thought a menace, at least by its competitors. But by 1951, its effect on the social and economic habits of the nation was said to be "unparalleled since the advent of the automobile."[3]

The Internet had its share of detractors, too. Popular author Michael Crichton suggested in 1994 that the Internet, as a more efficient source of information, would cause the demise of newspapers, books, and magazines.[4] A Clinton Administration policy paper on high-tech communications was called "a blueprint for corporate domination"[5] by one commentator. Internet addiction became the new pathology and three 1995 films, paranoid thrillers all, offered deadly scenarios for the Information Age.[6] More recently, the September 11, 2001 terrorist attacks on America exacerbated suspicions that emerging technologies could be used to harm us.

Still, optimists insisted from the start that the Internet could be a source for social good, that it offered myriad "exciting activities"[7] and endless possibilities.

---

[1]Isaac Clarke Pray, *Memoirs of James Gordon Bennett and His Times* (New York: Stringer and Townsend, 1855), 364.

[2]Paulette D. Kilmer, "A Wake-Up Call for Zombies: The Telegraph as Wayward Spark," *American Journalism* 17:4 (Fall 2000), 94.

[3]Jack Gould, "TV Transforming U.S. Social Scene; Challenges Film," *New York Times* (24 June 1951), A1.

[4]Michael Crichton, "Mediasaurus: Bye-bye to the Times and the Networks," *New Perspectives Quarterly* 11:3 (Summer 1994), 28.

[5]Herbert I. Schiller, "Highway Robbers," *The Nation* (20 December 1993), 753.

[6]See for example, Ty Ahmad-Taylor, "Using Some of that Crazy Internet-type Stuff in Films," *New York Times* (9 October 1995), C5 for criticism of three films: "The Net," "Assassins" and "Hackers."

[7]Paul Kirvan, "Things You Can Do On the Internet," *Communications News* 31:4 (April 1994), 56.

Political analysts said the Web was capable of producing "an explosion of micro-democracy"[8] and venture capitalists fought over trendy Internet companies, turning college kids into millionaires overnight.

By 1999, visionaries were predicting the Internet would soon be a basic necessity. In fact by 2000, more than half of American households had at least one computer and more than 40% were connected to the Internet, according to a Census Bureau survey.[9] The founder of eBay, the online auction house, said that by 2002 the Internet would be "utility-like and recede into the background,"[10] taking its place among the other household appliances.

Some evidence suggests we have already reached a noticeable level of comfort and familiarity with the Internet. Most major newspapers now have regular sections devoted to coverage of technology and the telecommunications industry, and dozens of Internet-related magazines flourish on the stands and online. Sales of online books, considered a revolution in publishing just five years ago, have leveled off.[11] The Internet has become an accepted area of academic study, evidenced by the increasing number of publications and conferences devoted to new technology.[12] And, claiming that it has become "part of the everyday universe," a University of Pennsylvania professor has begun an effort to de-capital-ize the Internet.[13] "It's part of everyone's life, and as common as air and water," he told a *New York Times* reporter. "The moment is right to treat the Internet the way we refer to television, radio and the telephone." Indeed, a recent court decision stated the Internet was "as vital to everyday existence as the telephone."[14]

Although the dot-com bubble burst rather dramatically in 2000, the Internet at thirty-something is well on its way to becoming the world's biggest and most popular repository of information. The wealth of information available now, representing an impressive range of perspectives, will continue to proliferate. Developments in the technology progress at an impressive pace, suggesting future trends will free the Internet of its desktop confines once and for all. But even as the world is transformed, little things still mean a lot. Fancy wristwatch computers aren't worth the time of day if we can't use them to find the information we're looking for.[15]

In writing this book, my intention was to level the playing field, to pass along the computer-assisted research skills I've learned as a reporter to anyone who spends

---

[8]Howard Fineman, "Who Needs Washington," *Newsweek* (27 January 1997), 50.

[9]U.S. Census Bureau Current Population Survey Report, "Home Computers and Internet Use in the U.S.," August 2000.

[10]Ed Sussman and Lan N. Nguyen, "Visions: The Internet in 2002," *Worth* (November 1999), 154.

[11]David D. Kirkpatrick, "Sales Growth in Books Online is Leveling Off," *New York Times* (16 April 2001), C1.

[12]See for example, Andrew J. Flanagin and Miriam J. Metzger, "Internet Use in the Contemporary Media Environment," *Human Communication Research* 27:1 (January 2001), 153–181.

[13]John Schwartz, "Who Owns the Internet? You and I Do," *New York Times* (29 December 2002), 4:3.

[14]Matt Ritchel, "Courts Split on Internet Bans," *New York Times* (21 January 2003), A1. See also David Ho, "Notorious Hacker Allowed to Surf Internet," *Toronto Star* (2 January 2003), E4. Convicted hacker Kevin Mitnick told Ho that being denied access to the Internet during his five-year imprisonment, was tantamount to "not being allowed to use a telephone."

[15]Elisa Batistia, "Bill Gates' Watch: Your Next PC?" *Wired* (9 January 2003), www.wired.com; Kuriko Miyake, "Is That a PC on Your Wrist?" *PC World* (11 October 2001), www.pcworld.com.

time online, regardless of age or skill level. Whether you use the Internet for business, research, recreation, or any combination, whether you access the Internet from home, office, school, or a mobile phone, the techniques I've outlined in this book are intended to make your time online more productive and rewarding. Importantly, I've shown you ways to make search engines find the information you want, rather than the information advertisers and other corporate interests want you to have. A grasp of Boolean logic, applied to search queries, will serve users well into the future, as commercial entities will surely vie for your attention more often and more insistently. Understanding domain names further minimizes the time between searching and locating information on the Web. Remember, you don't need fancy equipment to navigate the Web, just know-how.

Even as the technology progresses, some attributes are sure to remain—such as lingering threats to users' privacy. The federal government will certainly continue post-September 11 surveillance projects in the name of national security. Those efforts include monitoring of private communications and the removal of many public records from Web sites.[16] In 2001, the government spent $1.8 billion to protect our computer networks, but a $59 billion budget proposal in 2003 included a 10% increase in spending on computer security and $5 billion for information technology related to the war on terrorism.[17] Such initiatives will keep privacy advocates and legal scholars busy for years figuring out the constitutionality of it all.

Laws are only one part of the equation. Protecting sensitive information online is a personal responsibility, too. Many private details about individual lives are made available unintentionally, by Internet users themselves. A colleague recently told me about receiving "instant messages" from people who had read her member profile, the personal details she provided to her ISP upon subscribing. Member profiles were available to all of the ISP's subscribers, who could use the directory to discover another user's name, age, gender, interests, and location. My colleague was annoyed but also somewhat frightened by men who approached her online to engage her in conversation or arrange meetings. My reaction to her was to ask why she provided the ISP with those personal details in the first place. "I thought I had to," she said. I suggested she edit or delete her profile immediately, and soon she reported the intrusions had ceased.

Such inadvertent personal details have already figured in cases of divorce, kidnapping, identity theft, and even murder. Throughout the book, I've shown you ways to safeguard yourself and your family. Internet users can take simple steps to avoid putting themselves or others at risk. Besides providing a measure of security, refraining from disclosing personal information online will also work to minimize unwelcome junk mail. Participating in an online community does not require you relinquish either your privacy or peace of mind.

Paid ad placement is another likely mainstay. Allowing Web sites to buy their way to the top of search engine results may be good business practice for site

---

[16]See for example, Robert O'Harrow Jr., "Hearings Sought on Data Agency," *Washington Post* (14 January 2003), E5.

[17]Rachel Conrad, "Government Proposes $59 Billion Technology Budget," *Washington Post* (20 January 2003), www.washingtonpost.com.

owners, but it's the bane of online research. Many Internet users rely on search engines to locate information, only to end up at sponsored sites hawking products. In this book, I've described how to identify and avoid sponsored sites, and ways to form alternate strategies for more directed searches.

Newspapers report daily the advancements in the development and use of new technology, and they continue to amaze. For example, as I completed this manuscript a Swiss town initiated the first legally binding Internet vote. The Estonian government plans to allow online voting in the 2003 general elections and Germany announced citizens will be able to vote online by 2006.[18] Microsoft has just entered the wireless business and ordinary cell phones are becoming essential, multipurpose communications devices, providing e-mail, messaging, audio and video functions, and Internet access.[19] The wireless household is quickly becoming a reality.

Even more encouraging is the news that open-source software like Linux has become a conventional technology and by 2005 will be "a mainstream choice" according to analysts.[20] And as the availability of high speed Internet connections becomes more pervasive and affordable, Web users can expect more choices and more control over what they see and how they search.

Certainly there is much work to be done before the Internet is the democratic haven that its early engineers visualized. Although some of us bemoan the fact we can't get a high speed digital connection, whole countries are denied Internet access. In some, despotic leaders continue to shield certain kinds of information from being sent or received by their citizens under penalty of law. Furthermore, we're leaving entire groups behind by failing to recognize their special needs or by neglecting the advancements in technology that would make their online experiences productive. For example, services for the visually impaired progress much too slowly. Socioeconomic factors and geographic location are still to blame for the distinction between the haves and have-nots of the Information Age.

Depending on how it is viewed, the predictable encroachment of corporate America is a threat to or an opportunity for the Internet. An influx of capital will help to improve and advance technology, but we must be wary of the corporate inclination to exert control over content and access. The techniques in this book offer a way to find meaningful information in a minimal amount of time, avoiding the commercial distractions that may put you off course.

The legal system continues to deliberate how laws will or will not dictate conduct in cyberspace, although in one of the earliest related decisions (ACLU v. Reno) the Supreme Court ruled the Internet should be preserved as a "wide open space." There are many promising indicators that Internet users take that notion seriously. For example, the overwhelming indignation among users of Napster's music site, when the owner was sued and forced out of business, along with the proliferation of new file-sharing sites, suggested users will not relinquish control

---

[18]"Swiss Town Leads Way with Internet Vote," *CNN* (20 January 2003), www.cnn.com; Dermot McGrath, "Europeans Eye E-Vote Eventuality," *Wired* (22 April 2002), www.wired.com.

[19]"Microsoft's Next Frontier: Wireless," *CNN* (19 January 2003), www.cnn.com.

[20]Steve Lohr, "As Linux Nips at Microsoft, Its Advocates Talk Numbers," *New York Times* (20 January 2003), C1.

of the Internet easily. Also, the momentum and commitment of so many people to the open code movement suggests democratization of the Internet may still be a viable goal. Innovations can't be improved on and can't be made more functional unless ideas are shared. As Lawrence Lessig has written, "The freedom to tinker is an important freedom."[21]

The Internet is fundamentally about information and access. Yet if this is truly to be an information revolution, as many predicted in the 1990s, then the participation of everyday people is just as critical as is that of visionaries and benefactors. At the beginning of this book, I listed some of the ways that the Internet had changed facets of life. Where the technology will ultimately go is anyone's best guess, but as capable navigators, we're sure to have something to say about how we get there.

---

[21]Lawrence Lessig, *The Future of Ideas: The Fate of the Commons in a Connected World* (New York: Random House, 2001), 61.

Appendix A

Finding People

Service	Address	Residential	Business	Reverse Phone	E-mail	Reverse E-mail	Coverage	Notes	Fee
411 Locate	www.411locate.com	name, city, state	name, city, state, category, near	x	x	x	US, Canada, UK	link to some free and fee-based public records searches	
555-1212	www.555-1212.com	name, state, city, zip	name, address, category, distance	x			North America	maps, directions, zip codes, area codes, toll free, government directories, celebrities	Fee structure begins at $10 for 100 look-ups
AT&T AnyWho	www.anywho.com	name, address, city, state, zip	name, street, state, category, city; advanced allows "begins with" match for street, city, zip, categories, distance	x			US, UK, 30+ additional countries (mostly business listings)	toll free numbers, maps, directions	
Bigfoot	www.bigfoot.com	name, city, state	category, business name, address, distance, keywords; detailed search	x	x "find people"	US, Canada, UK, Germany, France	detailed search has zip code look-up, wildcard, maps, ranking by name or city		

Service	URL	Search terms	Search terms			UK	Coverage	Notes
British Telecom PhoneNetUK	www.bt.com	name, street, initials, postcode	name, street, town, postcode				wild card	no fee, but registration required for more than 10 searches daily
Canada 411	www.canada411.com	name, city, province	name, city, province				Canada	English, French, toll free numbers, postal codes
Infobel	www.infobel.com/world	name, city, state, country	name, category, city, state, near address	x		x	US, UK, 187 countries	maps, area codes, dialing codes, search site in six languages
Infospace	www.infospace.com	name, city, state, zip, country	name, category, city, state, zip, beginning with	x	x	x reverse allows domain search	US, UK, Canada, Caribbean	not all directories for all countries, area code
Search	www.search.com	name, city, state, zip	name, city, state, zip	x	x		US	metasearch can be customized, IM look-up
The Ultimates	www.theultimates.com	name, city, state	name, city, state, category	x	x	x	US	metasearch, maps. No charge for basic search, $12/year for faster version

Service	Address	Residential	Business	Reverse Phone	E-mail	Reverse E-mail	Coverage	Notes	Fee
WhoWhere	www.whowhere.com	name, city, state	name, state, category, distance	x	x advanced		US, Canada, links to international directories	maps, celebrities, wild card, toll free numbers	
World E-Mail	www.worldemail.com			x		US, UK, Canada, 100+ additional countries and territories	advanced search, maps		
World Pages	http://search.worldpages.com	name, state, country	name, category, state, distance	x		US, Canada, 100+ additional countries and territories	maps, directions, toll free numbers		
Yahoo People	http://people.yahoo.com	name, city, state	http://yp.yahoo.com; US and Canada	x advanced for domain, name variants	US, Canada, UK				

Appendix B

Internet Domains and Country Codes

Every site on the World Wide Web (WWW) is assigned an Internet Protocol (IP) address for identification. An IP address consists of a unique series of numbers, but as you can imagine, an Internet user would have a difficult time finding or returning to a site based on a lengthy numerical address. For that reason, Internet domain names are substituted for a computer's identifying numbers.

Companies or organizations typically choose trade names or recognizable words as domain names, to distinguish themselves from others and to lure traffic to their sites. Until recently, trademark law did not extend to the Internet, so any individual could register a trademark as a domain name. For example, John Smith could register the site www.mattel.com even if he did not hold the trademark to that name. Then he could try to sell it to Mattel, the toy manufacturer. The practice is known as "cybersquatting."[1]

Top-level domain names are limited and provide us with one of the best ways to identify a site. Second-level names are unlimited. The introduction of seven new domain names in 2000 marked the largest structural change to the Internet since the early 1980s.[2] The not-for-profit board that oversees the Internet's addressing system is known as *Icann*, the Internet Corporation for Assigned Names and Numbers. There are millions of Internet addresses (URLs) in circulation; the ".com" domain alone has more than 20 million names.

Some engines allow you to search by domain names or country codes. This information is typically embedded in a URL, or it appears as a suffix. For example, in the address www.whitehouse.gov, "gov" is the domain, indicating this is a non-military government site. In the address www.amazon.co.uk, the "uk" is the

---

[1] Rebecca W. Gole, "Playing the Name Game: A Glimpse at the Future of the Internet Domain Name System," *Federal Communications Law Journal* (March 1999), 403.

[2] Chris Gaither, "Seven New Domain Names are Chosen to Join the Popular .com," *New York Times* (17 November 2000), C4.

country code for United Kingdom. The second-level domain names in these URLs are "whitehouse" and "amazon," respectively. Searching by domain is one way to narrow a search, and a familiarity with domains will also help you verify the credibility of a Web site.

The following list includes top-level domain names and country codes as of January 2001, arranged alphabetically.

Top Level Domains

.com	Commercial corporations or establishments
.edu	Educational institutions
.gov	Nonmilitary government organizations
.mil	United States military organizations
.net	Internet resource companies, networks, ISPs
.org	Not-for-profit organizations

The following domains were accepted by Icann in winter 2000 and were in limited use by mid-2001:

.aero	airline groups
.biz	general use
.coop	business cooperatives
.info	general use
.museum	museums
.name	personal web sites
.pro	professionals

Country Codes

AC	Ascension Island
AD	Andorra
AE	United Arab Emirates
AF	Afghanistan
AG	Antigua and Barbuda
AI	Anguilla
AL	Albania
AM	Armenia
AN	Netherland Antilles
AO	Republic of Angola
AQ	Antarctica
AR	Argentina
AS	American Samoa
AT	Austria
AU	Australia
AW	Aruba

AZ	Azerbaijan
BA	Bosnia-Herzegovina
BB	Barbados
BD	Bangladesh
BE	Belgium
BF	Burkina Faso
BG	Bulgaria
BH	Bahrain
BI	Burundi
BJ	Benin
BM	Bermuda
BN	Brunei Darussalam
BO	Bolivia
BR	Brazil
BS	Bahamas
BT	Bhutan
BV	Bouvet Island
BW	Botswana
BY	Belarus
BZ	Belize
CA	Canada
CC	Cocos (Keeling Islands)
CD	Democratic Republic of Congo
CF	Central African Republic
CG	Congo
CH	Switzerland
CI	Ivory Coast
CK	Cook Islands
CL	Chile
CM	Cameroon
CN	China
CO	Columbia
CR	Costa Rica
CU	Cuba
CV	Cape Verde
CX	Christmas Island
CY	Cyprus
CZ	Czech Republic
DE	Germany
DJ	Dijibouti
DK	Denmark
DM	Dominica
DO	Dominican Republic
DZ	Algeria
EC	Ecuador

EE	Estonia
EG	Egypt
EH	Western Sahara
ER	Eritrea
ES	Spain
ET	Ethiopia
FI	Finland
FJ	Fiji
FK	Falkland Islands (Malvinas)
FM	Micronesia
FO	Faroe Islands
FR	France
GA	Gabon
GB	Great Britain (also UK)
GD	Grenada
GE	Georgia
GF	Guiana
GG	Guernsey
GH	Ghana
GI	Gibraltar
GL	Greenland
GM	Gambia
GN	Guinea
GP	Guadeloupe
GQ	Equatorial Guinea
GR	Greece
GS	South Georgia/Sandwich Islands
GT	Guatemala
GU	Guam
GW	Guinea Bissau
GY	Guyana
HK	Hong Kong
HM	Heard and McDonald Islands
HN	Honduras
HR	Croatia
HT	Haiti
HU	Hungary
ID	Indonesia
IE	Ireland
IL	Israel
IM	Isle of Man
IN	India
IO	British Indian Ocean Territory
IQ	Iraq
IR	Iran

IS	Iceland
IT	Italy
JE	Jersey (Channel Islands)
JM	Jamaica
JO	Jordan
JP	Japan
KE	Kenya
KG	Kyrgyz Republic
KH	Cambodia
KI	Kiribati
KM	Comoros
KN	St. Kitts Nevis Anguila
KP	Korea (North)
KR	Korea (South)
KW	Kuwait
KY	Cayman Islands
KZ	Kazakhstan
LA	Laos
LB	Lebanon
LC	Saint Lucia
LI	Liechtenstein
LK	Sri Lanka
LR	Liberia
LS	Lesotho
LT	Lithuania
LU	Luxembourg
LV	Latvia
LY	Libya
MA	Morocco
MC	Monaco
MD	Moldova
MG	Madagascar
MH	Marshall Islands
MK	Macedonia
ML	Mali
MM	Myanmar
MN	Mongolia
MO	Macau
MP	Northern Mariana Islands
MQ	Martinique
MR	Mauritania
MS	Montserrat
MT	Malta
MU	Mauritius
MV	Maldives

MW	Malawi
MX	Mexico
MY	Malaysia
MZ	Mozambique
NA	Namibia
NC	New Caledonia
NE	Niger
NF	Norfolk Island
NG	Nigeria
NI	Nicaragua
NL	Netherlands
NO	Norway
NP	Nepal
NR	Nauru
NU	Niue
NZ	New Zealand
OM	Oman
PA	Panama
PE	Peru
PF	Polynesia
PG	Papua New Guinea
PH	Philippines
PK	Pakistan
PL	Poland
PM	St. Pierre and Miquelon
PM	Pitcairn
PR	Puerto Rico
PT	Portugal
PW	Palau
PY	Paraguay
QA	Qatar
RE	Reunion
RO	Romania
RU	Russian Federation
RW	Rwanda
SA	Saudi Arabia
SB	Solomon Islands
SC	Seychelles
SD	Sudan
SE	Sweden
SG	Singapore
SH	St. Helena
SI	Slovenia
SJ	Svalbard and Jan Mayen Islands
SK	Slovakia

SL	Sierra Leone
SM	San Marino
SN	Senegal
SO	Somalia
SR	Suriname
ST	St. Tome and Principe
SU	Soviet Union
SV	El Salvador
SY	Syria
SZ	Swaziland
TC	Turks and Caicos Islands
TD	Chad
TF	French Southern Territories
TG	Togo
TH	Thailand
TJ	Tadjikistan
TK	Tokelau
TM	Turkmenistan
TN	Tunisia
TO	Tonga
TP	East Timor
TR	Turkey
TT	Trinidad and Tobago
TV	Tuvalu
TW	Taiwan
TZ	Tanzania
UA	Ukraine
UG	Uganda
UK	United Kingdom
UM	U.S. Minor Outlying Islands
US	United States
UY	Uruguay
UZ	Uzbekistan
VA	Vatican City State
VC	St. Vincent and the Grenadines
VE	Venezuela
VG	Virgin Islands (British)
VI	Virgin Islands (US)
VN	Vietnam
VU	Vanuatu
WF	Wallis and Futuna Islands
WS	Western Samoa
YE	Yemen
YT	Mayotte
YU	Yugoslavia

ZA	South Africa
ZM	Zambia
ZR	Zaire
ZW	Zimbabwe

Appendix $\mathbb{C}$

Useful Web Sites

The volatile nature of the Internet, evident in the ebb and flow of Web sites, is both a blessing and a curse. New Web sites may appear without fanfare and reliable ones can vanish without a trace. You can find Web sites using the search techniques outlined in this book, including tapping knowledgeable sources through newsgroups and mailing lists. Most site developers want to be found, and their URLs often reflect a degree of logic, www.whitehouse.gov, for example, for the official site of the President of the United States. Bookmark the sites you return to often, using the pull-down menu on your browser. Should a site move or change its URL, a considerate web master will always direct traffic to the new address.

This list is intended to help you locate sites that might be useful to you, although between the preparation of this manuscript and its publication, the sites could have closed down or relocated. I've tried to include sites that have a track record, as much as that is possible in this new medium. Check your local library or bookstore for Web site directories, targeted to general or specific interests.

SEARCH ENGINES AND DIRECTORIES

Below are search engines and registries (or directories) listed in alphabetical order. Where appropriate, the URL for the advanced search option is listed. The compilation is by no means exhaustive, although I've favored sites that offer advanced search options. As more sites are bought up by larger companies, search engines that go by different names end up searching through the same data as the companies that own them. WebCrawler, for example, is owned by the Web portal Excite, so I've listed one and not the other. HotBot is owned by Lycos, and the latter is listed here.

| AltaVista | www.altavista.com |
| AltaVista Advanced | www.altavista.com/web/adv |

185

Ask Jeeves	www.ask.com
Excite	www.excite.com
Euroseek	www.euroseek.net
Go (formerly Infoseek)	www.go.com
Google	www.google.com
Google Advanced	www.google.com/advanced_search
Ixquick Metasearch	http://ixquick.com
Lycos	www.lycos.com
Lycos Advanced Search	http://search.lycos.com/adv.asp
MSN Search	http://search.msn.com
MSN Advanced Search	http://search.msn.com/advanced.asp
Teoma	www.teoma.com
WiseNut	www.wisenut.com
Yahoo	www.yahoo.com
Yahoo Advanced	http://search.yahoo.com/search/options

BUSINESS AND FINANCE

It seems as though every business is headed toward the Web, and the Internet is truly a great place for keeping up with breaking business news and the ups and downs of the stock market. Small business owners can find ample support from Web sites that provide tax advice to mailing list support groups.

Australian Accounting Standards Board	www.aasb.com.au
Bankrate	www.bankrate.com
Better Business Bureau	www.bbb.org
Dow Jones and Company	www.dowjones.com
Dun and Bradstreet	www.dnb.com
Financial Times (London)	http://news.ft.com/home/us
Hoover's Online	www.hoovers.com
Internal Revenue Service	www.irs.ustreas.gov
International Organizationof Securities Commissions	www.iosco.org/iosco.html
Quicken	www.quicken.com
Securities and Exchange Commission (SEC)	www.sec.gov
Small Business Advisor	www.isquare.com
Tax Sites Directory	www.taxsites.com
UK Accounting Standards Board	www.asb.org.uk
US Small Business Administration	www.sba.gov
Working Solo	www.workingsolo.com
World Investor Link	www.worldinvestorlink.com

DATA SOURCES: GOVERNMENT

Many government sites are organized according to their acronyms, followed by the "gov" domain. For example, the United States Environmental Protection Agency site is located at www.epa.gov. If you don't find what you're looking for on this list, try searching that way. For government agencies outside the U.S., try specifying the country code in your search—(house of commons) and domain:uk, for example. The FirstGov site (www.firstgov.gov) is intended to be a directory to all government sites online. You might also take advantage of some of the government Web directories available now, either at your local library or bookstore.

Administration on Aging	www.aoa.dhhs.gov
CIA World Factbook	www.cia.gov/cia/publications/ factbook
Department of Information Technology	www.doit.ca.gov
Department of Energy	www.energy.gov
Environmental Protection Agency	www.epa.gov
Equal Opportunity Employment Commission	www.eeoc.gov
Federal Communications Commission	www.fcc.gov
FirstGov	www.firstgov.gov
General Accounting Office	www.gao.gov
Government Information Sharing Project	http://govinfo.kerr.orst.edu
Government Printing Office	www.access.gpo.gov
House of Representatives Inspector General Reports	www.house.gov/IG
Library of Congress	http://lcweb.loc.gov
National Weather Service	www.nws.noaa.gov
Occupational Safety and Health Administration	www.osha.gov
OpenGov.UK	www.open.gov.uk/
Social Security Online	www.ssa.gov
UK Home Office	www.homeoffice.gov.uk
UK House of Commons	www.parliament.the-stationery- office.co.uk/pa/cm/cmhome.htm
UK House of Lords	www.parliament.the-stationery- office.co.uk/pa/ld/ldhome.htm
UK Parliament	www.parliament.the-stationery- office.co.uk
U.S. Agency for International Development	www.usaid.gov
U.S. Census Bureau	www.census.gov
U.S. General Services Administration	http://policyworks.gov

U.S. House of Representatives   www.house.gov
United States Postal Service   www.usps.gov
U.S. Senate   www.senate.gov

DATA SOURCES: NONGOVERNMENT

A considerable amount of data is compiled by not-for-profit organizations and research or educational institutions. Should you conduct a search, you might want to narrow your search parameters accordingly, by adding the syntax "domain:org" or "domain:edu."

Sheffield ChemDex Chemistry   www.chemdex.org
  Resources
Envirolink   http://envirolink.org
Foundation Center   http://fdncenter.org
Freedom of Information Center   http://web.missouri.edu/~foiwww/
Funding Information Center   www.fic-ftw.org/index.htm
Genealogy Resources   www.genhomepage.com
Investigative Reporters and Editors   www.ire.org
MegaSources   www.ryerson.ca/~dtudor/
      megasources.htm
National Academy Press   www.nap.edu
National Food Safety Database   www.foodsafety.org
NGO Global Network   www.ngo.org
U.S. GenWeb Project   www.usgenweb.com/index.html
Volunteer Match   www.volunteermatch.org

DICTIONARIES AND REFERENCE TOOLS

Many of the dictionary sites listed next include links to international dictionaries, as well as translating tools. Take care with any translator, as it may translate words correctly but fail to convey the meaning of a text.

AllWords   www.allwords.com
Brittanica   http://brittanica.com
Cambridge Dictionaries   http://dictionary.cambridge.org/default.asp
Computer Hope Directory   www.computerhope.com/jargon.htm
Dictionary   www.dictionary.com
Law.com   www.law.com
MacQuarie Dictionary   www.webwombat.com.au/reference/
      macqdict.htm
Medical Dictionaries   www.libraryspot.com/
      medicaldictionaries.htm
Merriam-Webster   www.m-w.com/dictionary

OneLook Dictionary	www.onelook.com
Research It	www.itools.com/research-it
Rhyming Dictionary	http://rhyme.lycos.com
Roget's Thesaurus	www.thesaurus.com
Webopedia Internet Terms	www.pcwebopaedia.com/
West's Legal Dictionary	www.lawoffice.com
Wordsmyth	www.wordsmyth.net

JOBS AND CAREER

Building a personal Web site is one way to show off programming skills to potential employers, or just display your resume. Some sites work as matchmakers, forwarding your resume to headhunters, or alerting you to job openings. Newsgroups and mailing lists are good ways to network within certain industries or professions. Often, job openings will be discussed informally in those settings before an official job search is begun.

6FigureJobs	www.6figurejobs.com
CareerBuilder	www.careerbuilder.com
Career Resumes	www.career-resumes.com
CoolJobs	www.cooljobs.com
Exec-u-Net	www.execunet.com
Headhunter	www.headhunter.net
Monster	www.monster.com
Techies	www.techies.com

LEGAL

Few legal matters can be solved entirely without professional advice, and it's certainly tempting to seek it online rather than pay a hefty fee to consult with a lawyer in person. But approach online lawyers or law-related sites with caution. Laws can differ by jurisdiction, for example, and you want to be sure you're getting advice that fits your situation. Furthermore, you will not enjoy a privileged relationship with an online lawyer, for that you'll need to meet face-to-face. Check a lawyer's credentials on the American Bar Association site (www.abanet.org) or the Martindale-Hubbell site (www.lawyers.com). Don't forget newsgroups and mailing lists as potential sources of legal advice, but always be careful about what you post in either forum.

American Bar Association	www.abanet.org
American Judges Association	http://aja.ncsc.dni.us
Free Advice	www.freeadvice.com
International Courts Directory	www.ncsc.dni.us/court/sites/
	courts.htm#international

LawGuru	www.lawguru.com
LawSmart	www.lawsmart.com
Lawyers	www.lawyers.com
National Arbitration Forum	www.arb-forum.com
State Court Directory	www.ncsc.dni.us/court/sites/ courts.htm
U.S. Federal Judiciary	www.uscourts.gov
U.S. Supreme Court	www.supremecourtus.gov/index.html

MAPS

Many portal sites offer links to maps or driving directions, as do most of the phone and e-mail directories online. Appendix A lists these sites and their search options. In addition you can find maps in the following places:

MapBlast	www.mapblast.com
MapMachine	www.nationalgeographic.com/resources/ngo/maps
MapQuest	www.mapquest.com
Maps.com	www.maps.com
MultiMap	http://uk2.multimap.com
Rand McNally	www.randmcnally.com
Tiger Map Server	http://tiger.census.gov
Yahoo Maps	www.yahoo.com/maps

MEDICAL AND HEALTH

Seeking medical advice online is a risky endeavor; studies have shown that much Internet-based information is inaccurate. Yet, as a place to find support during temporary or chronic illness, the Web is a wonderful gathering place. Look for sites maintained or endorsed by established organizations and check a doctor's credentials before taking any advice. Online medical advice should be something to enhance, not substitute for, the guidance you get from your personal physician.

Alternative Health News Online	www.altmedicine.com
Alzheimer Page	www.biostat.wustl.edu/alzheimer
American Academy of Pediatrics	www.aap.org
American Dental Association	www.ada.org
American Diabetes Association	www.diabetes.org
American Heart Association	www.americanheart.org
American Medical Association	www.ama-assn.org
Arthritis Foundation	www.arthritis.org
Benefits Check-up RX	www.BenefitsCheckUpRX.org
The Body: AIDS & HIV Information Resource	www.thebody.com

Boston Women's Health Collective	www.ourbodiesourselves.org
Centers for Disease Control	www.cdc.gov
Dept. of Health and Human Services (U.S.)	www.os.dhhs.gov
DocNet	www.docnet.org.uk
Health Grades Physician Ratings	www.healthgrades.com
Healthy Ideas	www.healthyideas.com
HIV/AIDS Surveillance Report	www.cdc.gov/hiv
Internet Grateful Med	www.igm.nlm.nih.gov
National Alliance of Breast Cancer Organizations	www.nabco.org
National Health Organizations	www.the-hip.com/Org-NHO.htm
National Institutes of Health	www.nih.gov
National Institute of Mental Health	www.nimh.nih.gov
National Library of Medicine	www.nlm.nih.gov/locatorplus
New England Journal of Medicine	www.nejm.org
Partnership for Caring	www.dyingwell.org/PFC.htm
Pediatric AIDS Foundation	www.pedaids.org
Planet RX	www.planetrx.com
Planned Parenthood Federation	www.ppfa.org
Science News Online	www.sciencenews.org
Support Groups	www.support-groups.com
Women's Cancer Network	www.wcn.org
World Health Organization	www.who.int

NEWS

Most major newspapers have an online presence, as do the major networks. Try entering the name of the publication or network followed by ".com" in your browser's address box to find a media organization not listed here. For directories of news-related sites try Newslink (http://newslink.org), the American Journalism Review (www.ajr.org), or World Newspapers (www.scaruffi.com/politics/wnewsp.html). Home Town Free Press has links to some 5,000 U.S. newspapers (www.hometownfreepress.com).

ABC News	www.abcnews.com
Afghan Online Press	http://www.afghan-web.com/aop
American Journalism Review	www.ajr.org
Cairo Times	www.cairotimes.com
Chicago Tribune	www.chicagotribune.com
China News Digest	www.cnd.org
CNN	www.cnn.com
Daily (Electronic) Telegraph	www.telegraph.co.uk
Der Spiegel	www.spiegel.de/spiegel

El Pais	www.elpais.es
Environmental News Network	www.enn.com
Hong Kong Standard	www.hkstandard.com
Indonesian Observer	www.indoexchange.com/ indonesian-observer
Iran Press Service	www.iran-press-service.com
Iraqi News Agency	www.uruklink.net/iraqnews/ eindex.htm
Irish Times	www.ireland.com
Japan Times	www.japantimes.com
Jerusalem Post	www.jpost.com
Le Monde	www.lemonde.fr
London Guardian	www.guardian.co.uk
Los Angeles Times	www.latimes.com
Montreal Gazette	www.montrealgazette.com
Newslook (Nepal)	www.newslookmag.com
New York Times	www.nytimes.com
Ottawa Citizen	www.ottawacitizen.com
Radio Locator	www.radio-locator.com
Russia Online	www.online.ru
Wall Street Journal	www.wsj.com
Wired	www.wired.com

RELIGION

Quite a few religions are represented online, as clearinghouses of information or individual facilities of worship. For example, Beliefnet (www.beliefnet.com) is a site with links to news related to many of the world's religions. The Vatican even has its own Web site, and recently named a patron saint of the Internet. Most religious organizations are not-for-profit, so if you're using a search engine you may want to use the "domain:org" inquiry.

Buddhist

DharmaNet International	www.dharmanet.org
Tricycle: The Buddhist Review	www.tricycle.com

Catholic

Catholic Information Center	www.catholic.net
Catholic Online	www.catholic.org
The Catholic Pages	www.catholic-pages.com
The Vatican	www.vatican.va

Hindu

Hindu Resources Online   www.hindu.org
Hinduism Today   www.hinduismtoday.com
Himalayan Academy   www.himalayanacademy.com

Islam

IslamiCity   www.islamicity.com
The Islamic Network   www.isnet.org
al-Muslim   www.al-muslim.org
Muslim World Yellow Pages   www.muslim-yellowpages.com

Jewish

Aleph   www.aleph.org
Cyber CAJE   www.caje.org/
Shamash: The Jewish Network   www.shamash.org
Torah.org   www.torah.org
Torah From Dixie   www.tfdixie.com

Mormon

All About Mormons   www.mormons.org
The Latter-Day Messenger and   http://members.ldscity.com/LDMA
    Advocate
The Official Site of the Church of   www.lds.org
    Jesus Christ of Latter-day Saints
Bienvenue Chez Les Mormons   http://le-village.ifrance.com/mormon

Protestant

Baptists Today   http://baptiststoday.org
Charisma and Christian Life   www.charismamag.com
Desperate Preacher's Site   http://desperatepreacher.com
Ecunet   www.ecunet.org
Episcopal News Service   www.ecusa.anglican.org
Evangelical Lutheran Church in America   www.elca.org
Worldwide Faith News   www.wfn.org

Unitarian and Universalist

The Journal of Liberal Religion	www.meadville.edu/jlr.htm
Unitarian Universalist Association	http://uua.org
UU News	www.pbat.com/uunews1
Unirarios Universalistas	http://uuhispano.tripod.com

TRAVEL

The major airlines have Web sites now (type the airline name plus ".com" in your browser's address box) and often recommend travelers make reservations on-line to avoid delays. Using the many travel-related sites such as Travelocity (www.travelocity.com) or Microsoft's Expedia (www.expedia.com), you can compare air fares, make rental car arrangements, book hotel reservations, check the weather forecast for your destination, and much more.

Access-Able	www.access-able.com
Adventureseek	www.adventureseek.com
Amtrak	www.amtrak.com
BizTravel	www.biztravel.com
Bureau of Consular Affairs (U.S. State Department Travel Advisories)	http://travel.state.gov
CDC Travel Information	www.cdc.gov/travel
CitySearch	www.citysearch.com
Concierge	www.concierge.com
Fodor's	www.fodors.com
Great Outdoor Recreations Pages	www.gorp.com
Hiking and Walking Homepage	www.teleport.com/~walking/hiking.html
Hyperski	www.hyperski.com
Lonely Planet Online	www.lonelyplanet.com
Pollen Forecasts	www.allegra.com/pollen/pollenframe.htm
Society for Accessible Travel and Hospitality	www.sath.org
Travelocity	www.travelocity.com
U.S. Customs Service	www.customs.ustreas.gov

VIRUS INFORMATION

A computer virus can hide anywhere a computer stores information. Often, they're executable attachments mailed with e-mail messages and they can do all kinds of damage. Most new computers include antivirus programs. If yours does not, make it the first thing on your shopping list. Once the software is installed, it is essential that you update your program, as new viruses are detected regularly and your initial program may not be equipped to detect and eradicate them from your computer's hard drive. A good antivirus program offers downloadable updates through the Internet.

To reduce the chance that your computer will become infected, never open an e-mail attachment from someone you don't recognize. Also, check your antivirus software manufacturer's Web site often to keep up on what's going around and for instructions to clean your hard drive when it does become infected. Several antivirus sites follow:

Datafellows	www.europe.datafellows.com/news/ hoax.htm
Hoaxbusters	http://hoaxbusters.ciac.org
McAfee	www.mcafee.com
Safety Net Security Cafe	www.safe.net
Symantec Anti-Virus Research Center	www.symantec.com/avcenter/index.html
Trend Micro Virus Information Center	www.antivirus.com/vinfo

Appendix D

Glossary of Terms

Bandwidth: The maximum capacity of a network or modem connection. The higher the bandwidth, the faster you can send or receive information. The bigger the file, the more bandwidth it requires.

Bookmark: A placeholder for a Web site, set into your browser so that you can return to it easily. Also called "favorites."

Boolean: Named for the English mathematician George Boole, Boolean logic allows users to search the Web using the operators "and," "not," "or," and "near."

Broadband: Also called wideband transmission, refers to telecommunications that provide a variety of data over a single communications medium. DSL and cable represent two types of broadband technology.

Browser: Program that allows you to view graphics and text on the World Wide Web.

Cookie: A text file entered into the memory of your browser as you view certain Web sites. Cookies allow the site owner to record your comings and goings, preferences, and logon information to quicken or customize your browsing experience.

Cyberspace: The collective places or locations created by computer networks.

Database: A collection of data or files organized for easy search and retrieval.

Dial-up access: Describes the way some users connect to the Internet by dialing a number through a computer to connect with an ISP. This is a standard phone line connection, as compared to a connection via broadband or other high-speed access lines.

Domain: Part of an Internet Web site's address that indicates what kind of site it is. For example, ".edu" indicates a site originating from an educational institution, ".mil" a U.S. military site, and so on.

Download: Transferring files to your personal computer from a computer you have contacted through an Internet connection.

E-mail: Short for electronic mail; messages that are sent electronically across phone lines and networks.

Emoticons: "Emotional" icons, a kind of e-mail slang which uses icons or acronyms to show emotion. For example, "LOL" means "laughing out loud," "BTW" is "by the way." A colon and right parentheses suggests a smiling face when rotated 90 degrees clockwise.

File format: Indicates with what program a file was created and can be read or viewed. A file extension indicates format. For example, a ".txt" file is a text file.

Flame, flaming: A message that attacks another message or its author in a derogatory way.

Hacker: A cyberspace safe cracker, someone who breaks into secure Web sites to access information or content. A hacker can use his prowess for good or evil.

Hard drive: The part of your computer that stores information.

Home page: Also called a Web site or another way to refer to the "welcome" page of one.

HTTP: Acronym for hypertext transfer protocol, the network data communications specifications used on the World Wide Web.

Hypertext: Appears as highlighted or underlined text, or icons on a Web site. Clicking on a hyperlink allows you to move around among various parts of a Web site.

Internet: Vast, worldwide Web of connected computers allowing access to information and services.

Icon: A graphic symbol used to enhance a Web site, often used to represent a hyperlink.

Instant messenger: Known as IM, a software utility that allows users connected to the Internet or a network to send messages and files quickly to one another.

Invisible web: Also called the hidden Web, the documents or pages which cannot be reached by search engines.

IP address: Short for Internet Protocol, this is the numerical address of a computer on a network.

ISP: Acronym for Internet Service Provider, a company that provides Internet access to consumers.

Kbps: Stands for kilobits per second, typically a measure of modem speed. The higher the number, the faster your computer can upload and download information.

Link: The connections between hypertext pages, clicking on a link allows you to move around a Web site.

Listserv: Also called mailing lists, a software program that allows subscribers to communicate with others on a topic of interest. Messages are conveyed through e-mail to the subscriber list.

Metasearch: A service that allows users to search using multiple engines and directories simultaneously.

Metatags: The HTML coding for a Web page that allows the author to enter information that is not shown in a browser window. Metatags may include the search terms used to find the page, the date the page was created, and contact information.

Modem: Short for modulation/demodulation, a modem is the device used to connect two computers so they may communicate. Modems range in speed, which is specified as a baud rate (bps) or kilobits (kbps).

Netiquette: Good manners, proper mode of behavior, or communication online.

Network: Smaller than the Internet, a system of connected computers arranged to share information and other resources.

Newsgroup: Also called Usenet, BBS, or electronic bulletin board, a newsgroup is a forum centered on a specific topic where like-minded people can post and read messages.

Online: The state of being connected to the Internet.

Open source movement: An organized effort to assure that source code is freely distributed, so that it can be customized and improved on. The acronym OSS stands for open source software. The Open Software Foundation is dedicated to finding alternative operating systems.

Pop-up ad: An advertisement that appears as a new window during a browsing session. Advertisements can also take the form of "pop unders," windows that open under the screen currently viewed.

Post: (n) A message on a newsgroup, mailing list, or other forum; or (v) to compose and send a message.

Search directory: A limited, searchable database of Web sites. Also called a subject directory.

Search engine: A vehicle with which to search information held on the World Wide Web. Search engines strive to be comprehensive, and attempt to compile every Web site on the Internet.

Server: A computer designed to send information to client computers, host of Web sites, and databases.

Shareware: Software distributed by its programmer available for trial period free of charge, but the program's author usually asks for a small amount of money if a user decides to continue using it.

Spam: Junk mail sent through electronic mail.

Upload: Transferring data from your computer to another through a modem or other transfer system.

URL (uniform resource locator): The Web address for a Web site. For example, the URL for the Library of Congress is http://lcweb.loc.gov.

Virus: A program typically sent as an e-mail attachment that can harm your computer's hard drive, the degree to which depends on the intent of the developer.

Web site: A destination on the World Wide Web, composed of "pages" which may contain text, graphics, sound, video, or any combination of these.

Wireless: Technology that allows computers and/or devices to communicate without the use of wires.

World Wide Web: Also called WWW, or W3, the Web is the interactive version of the Internet. You access and view hypertext pages on the World Wide Web using browser software.

Screen Capture Information

FIG. 1.1. Anatomy of a Web site.
URL: www.whitehouse.gov
Date captured: 16 August 2003
United States Government Site (not copyrighted)

FIG. 1.2. Before maximizing the browser screen.
URL: www.ire.org
Date captured: 15 January 2001
Reproduced with permission from Investigative Reporters and Editors, Inc.

FIG. 1.3. After maximizing the browser screen.
URL: www.ire.org
Date captured: 15 January 2001
Reproduced with permission from Investigative Reporters and Editors, Inc.

FIG. 1.4. Setting the home page.

FIG. 1.5. Bookmarking or designating a "favorite" Web site.

FIG. 2.1. Yahoo subject directory.
URL: www.yahoo.com
Date captured: 17 August 2003
Reproduced with permission from Yahoo! Inc.

FIG. 2.2. AltaVista simple search for "architecture."
URL: www.altavista.com
Date captured: 17 August 2003
Reproduced with permission from AltaVista Company

FIG. 2.3. Results of an AltaVista simple search for "architecture."
URL: www.altavista.com
Date captured: 17 August 2003
Reproduced with permission from AltaVista Company

FIG. 2.4. Google simple search for "hillary rodham clinton."
URL: www.google.com
Date captured: 7 November 2002
Reproduced with permission from Google Inc.

FIG. 2.5. Results of a Google simple search for "hillary rodham clinton."
URL: www.google.com
Date captured: 7 November 2002
Reproduced with permission from Google Inc.

FIG. 2.6. Google advanced search.
URL: www.google.com
Date captured: 17 August 2003
Reproduced with permission from Google Inc.

FIG. 2.7. Results of a Google advanced search.
URL: www.google.com/advanced_search
Date captured: 17 August 2003
Reproduced with permission from Google Inc.

FIG. 2.8. Boolean search using AND.
URL: www.altavista.com/web/adv
Date captured: 17 August 2003
Reproduced with permission from AltaVista Company

FIG. 2.9. Detail of a Boolean search using AND.

FIG. 2.10. Boolean search using OR.
URL: www.altavista.com/web/adv
Date captured: 17 August 2003
Reproduced with permission from AltaVista Company

FIG. 2.11. Detail of a Boolean search using OR.

FIG. 2.12. Boolean search using AND NOT.
URL: www.altavista.com/web/adv
Date captured: 17 August 2003
Reproduced with permission from AltaVista Company

FIG. 2.13. Detail of a Boolean search using AND NOT.

FIG. 2.14. Boolean search using NEAR.
URL: www.altavista.com/web/adv
Date captured: 17 August 2003
Reproduced with permission from AltaVista Company

FIG. 2.15. Université Laval Web site (Quebec, Canada).
URL: http://etudiants.fsa.ulaval.ca/projet/gie-64375/us_anglo/histo.html
Date captured: 6 February 2000
Reproduced with permission from Dr. Gerard Verna

FIG. 2.16. Université Laval Web site, translated into English.
URL: http://etudiants.fsa.ulaval.ca/projet/gie-64375/us_anglo/histo.html
Date captured: 6 February 2000
Reproduced with permission from Dr. Gerard Verna

FIG. 2.17. Boolean search using "sorted by."
URL: www.altavista.com/web/adv
Date captured: 17 August 2003
Reproduced with permission from AltaVista Company

FIG. 2.18. Results of a Boolean search using "sorted by."
URL: www.altavista.com/web/adv
Date captured: 17 August 2003
Reproduced with permission from AltaVista Company

FIG. 2.19. Nesting commands in a Boolean search.
URL: www.altavista.com/web/adv
Date captured: 17 August 2003
Reproduced with permission from AltaVista Company

FIG. 2.20. Detail of a Boolean search using nested commands.

FIG. 3.1. Google advanced search by domain.
URL: www.google.com/advanced_search
Date captured: 8 November 2002
Reproduced with permission from Google Inc.

FIG. 3.2. AltaVista advanced search by host.
URL: www.altavista.com/web/adv
Date captured: 17 August 2003
Reproduced with permission from AltaVista Company

FIG. 3.3. Results of advanced search by host.
URL: www.altavista.com/web/adv
Date captured: 17 August 2003
Reproduced with permission from AltaVista Company

FIG. 3.4. AltaVista search for image.
URL: www.altavista.com/image/default
Date captured: 17 August 2003
Reproduced with permission from AltaVista Company

FIG. 3.5. Results of AltaVista search for image.
URL: www.altavista.com/image/default
Date captured: 17 August 2003
Reproduced with permission from AltaVista Company

FIG. 3.6. Results of Google search by file type.
URL: www.google.com
Date captured: 8 November 2002
Reproduced with permission from Google Inc.

FIG. 3.7. Results of a meta search.
URL: www.vivisimo.com
Date captured: 23 May 2002
Reproduced with permission from Vivisimo Inc.

FIG. 4.1. Searching for mailing lists or listservs.
URL: www.lsoft.com/lists/list_q.html
Date captured: 10 October 2002
Reproduced with permission from L-Soft international, Inc.

FIG. 4.2. Mailing list search results.
URL: www.lsoft.com/lists/list_q.html
Date captured: 10 October 2002
Reproduced with permission from L-Soft international, Inc.

FIG. 4.3. Mailing list subscription information.
URL: www.lsoft.com/lists/list_q.html
Date captured: 10 October 2002
Reproduced with permission from L-Soft international, Inc.

FIG. 4.4. A search of mailing lists and newsletters.
URL: www.topica.com
Date captured: 7 October 2002
Reproduced with permission from Topica, Inc.

FIG. 4.5. Mailing list details.
URL: www.topica.com
Date captured: 7 October 2002
Reproduced with permission from Topica, Inc.

FIG. 4.6. Search of mailing list archives.
URL: www.mail-archive.com
Date captured: 16 October 2002
Reproduced with permission from Jeff Breidenbach

FIG. 4.7. A roster of mailing lists at The Mail Archive.
URL: www.mail-archive.com
Date captured: 16 October 2002
Reproduced with permission from Jeff Breidenbach

FIG. 4.8. An archived mailing list.
URL: www.mail-archive.com
Date captured: 16 October 2002
Reproduced with permission from Jeff Breidenbach

FIG. 4.9. An example of mailing list correspondence.
URL: www.mail-archive.com
Date captured: 16 October 2002
Reproduced with permission from Jeff Breidenbach

FIG. 4.10. An example of a mailing list thread.
URL: www.mail-archive.com
Date captured: 16 October 2002
Reproduced with permission from Jeff Breidenbach

FIG. 4.11. Searching mailing list archives at eScribe.com.
URL: www.escribe.com
Date captured: 17 October 2002
Reproduced with permission from Scott Paterson and Ron Theis

FIG. 4.12. A roster of archived mailing lists.
URL: www.escribe.com
Date captured: 17 October 2002
Reproduced with permission from Scott Paterson and Ron Theis

FIG. 4.13. Detail of an archived mailing list.
URL: www.escribe.com
Date captured: 17 October 2002
Reproduced with permission from Scott Paterson and Ron Theis

FIG. 4.14. Searching the text of an archived mailing list.
URL: www.escribe.com
Date captured: 17 October 2002
Reproduced with permission from Scott Paterson and Ron Theis

FIG. 4.15. A search of Google Groups for journalism newsgroups.
URL: http://groups.google.com
Date captured: 17 October 2002
Reproduced with permission from Google Inc.

FIG. 4.16. An example of a newsgroup message or post.
URL: http://groups.google.com
Date captured: 17 October 2002
Reproduced with permission from Google Inc.

FIG. 4.17. A response to a newsgroup post.
URL: http://groups.google.com
Date captured: 17 October 2002
Reproduced with permission from Google Inc.

FIG. 4.18. Google Groups advanced search.
URL: http://groups.google.com/advanced_group_search
Date captured: 12 November 2002
Reproduced with permission from Google Inc.

FIG. 4.19. Searching newsgroups using Google Groups advanced search.
URL: http://groups.google.com/advanced_group_search
Date captured: 12 November 2002
Reproduced with permission from Google Inc.

FIG. 4.20. Results of a Google Groups advanced search.
URL: http://groups.google.com/advanced_group_search
Date captured: 12 November 2002
Reproduced with permission from Google Inc.

FIG. 4.21. An advanced search of newsgroup messages at BoardReader.
URL: www.boardreader.com/advancedsearch.asp
Date captured: 19 November 2002
Reproduced with permission from Effyis, Inc.

FIG. 4.22. Results of BoardReader advanced search.
URL: www.boardreader.com/advancedsearch.asp
Date captured: 19 November 2002
Reproduced with permission from Effyis, Inc.

FIG. 4.23. An archived newsgroup message at BoardReader.
URL: www.boardreader.com/advancedsearch.asp
Date captured: 19 November 2002
Reproduced with permission from Effyis, Inc.

FIG. 4.24. Yahoo Groups Search Page.
URL: http://groups.yahoo.com
Date captured: 17 August 2003
Reproduced with permission from Yahoo! Inc.

FIG. 4.25. Results of a Yahoo Groups search for journalism newsgroups.
URL: http://groups.yahoo.com
Date captured: 17 August 2003
Reproduced with permission from Yahoo! Inc.

FIG. 4.26. Details of a Yahoo Group dedicated to journalism education.
URL: http://groups.yahoo.com/group/journalism
Date captured: 17 August 2003
Reproduced with permission from Yahoo! Inc.

FIG. 4.27. A Web log or blog search by URL at Waypath
URL: www.waypath.com
Date captured: 9 August 2003
Reproduced with permission from Think Tank 23

FIG. 4.28. Globe of Blogs.
URL: www.globeofblogs.com
Date captured: 9 August 2003
Reproduced with permission from H. Rawlinson and Jennifer M. Dodd

FIG. 5.1. Using a domain search to find people.
URL: http://kevdb.infospace.com/_1_25BGT9402941ZZI__home/wp/
    reverse.htm
Date captured: 17 August 2003
Reproduced with permission from InfoSpace, Inc.

FIG. 5.2. Results of a domain search at InfoSpace.
URL: http://kevdb.infospace.com/_1_25BGT9402941ZZI__home/wp/
    reverse.htm
Date captured: 17 August 2003
Reproduced with permission from InfoSpace, Inc.

FIG. 5.3. Yahoo advanced email search.
URL: http://email.people.yahoo.com/py/psAdvSearch
Date captured: 15 August 2003
Reproduced with permission from Yahoo! Inc.

FIG. 5.4. Yahoo advanced email search results.
URL: http://email.people.yahoo.com/py/psAdvSearch
Date captured: 15 August 2003
Reproduced with permission from Yahoo! Inc.

FIG. 5.5. Search for people by host on AltaVista.
URL: www.altavista.com/web/adv
Date captured: 17 August 2003
Reproduced with permission from AltaVista Company

FIG. 5.6. Results of a search by host.
URL: www.altavista.com/web/adv
Date captured: 17 August 2003
Reproduced with permission from AltaVista Company

FIG. 5.7. Finding a person using a link search.
URL: www.altavista.com/web/adv
Date captured: 6 December 2002
Reproduced with permission from AltaVista Company

FIG. 5.8. Results of a link search.
URL: www.altavista.com/web/adv
Date captured: 6 December 2002
Reproduced with permission from AltaVista Company

FIG. 5.9. Viewing a Web site's source code to trace a link.
URL: www.gti.net/mocolib1/kid/food1.html
Date captured: 6 December 2002
Reproduced with permission from Morris County (NJ) Library, USA

FIG. 5.10. Finding people using a syntax search for home pages.
URL: www.altavista.com/web/adv
Date captured: 21 August 2003
Reproduced with permission from AltaVista Company

FIG. 5.11. Finding home pages through an online community registry.
URL: http://homepages.whowhere.lycos.com/Online_Communities
Date captured: 21 August 2003
Reproduced with permission from Lycos Network, Inc.

FIG. 5.12. Using a WHOIS search to find out who's behind a Web site.
URL: www.networksolutions.com/en_US/whois/index.jhtml
Date captured: 14 August 2003
Reproduced with permission from VeriSign, Inc.

FIG. 5.13. Results of a WHOIS search.
URL: www.networksolutions.com/en_US/whois/index.jhtml
Date captured: 14 August 2003
Reproduced with permission from VeriSign, Inc.

FIG. 5.14. Finding people through public records at Search Systems.
URL: www.searchsystems.net
Date captured: 18 August 2003
Reproduced with permission from Tim Koster, Pacific Information Resources, Inc.

FIG. 5.15. Results of a public records search.
URL: www.searchsystems.net
Date captured: 18 August 2003
Reproduced with permission from Tim Koster, Pacific Information Resources, Inc.

FIG. 6.1. The Movie Review Query Engine is an example of an online database.
URL: www.mrqe.com
Date captured: 18 August 2003
Reproduced with permission from Stewart M. Clamen

FIG. 6.2. A partial list of databases available on the Washington University library
     Web site.
URL: www.wustl.edu/databases
Date captured: 18 August 2003
Reproduced with permission from Washington University Libraries, St. Louis, MO

FIG. 6.3. Finding databases using an AltaVista advanced search.
URL: www.altavista.com/web/adv
Date captured: 11 December 2002
Reproduced with permission from AltaVista Company

FIG. 6.4. Results of an AltaVista advanced search for databases.
URL: www.altavista.com/web/adv
Date captured: 11 December 2002
Reproduced with permission from AltaVista Company

FIG. 6.5. Results of a Google simple search by file type.
URL: www.google.com
Date captured: 18 August 2003
Reproduced with permission from Google Inc.

FIG. 6.6. Targeting a search by phrase and file type.
URL: www.google.com
Date captured: 18 August 2003
Reproduced with permission from Google Inc.

FIG. 6.7. A Google advanced search by file type.
URL: www.google.com/advanced_search
Date captured: 23 December 2002
Reproduced with permission from Google Inc.

FIG. 6.8. An AltaVista advanced search by file type.
URL: www.altavista.com/web/adv
Date captured: 23 December 2002
Reproduced with permission from AltaVista Company

FIG. 6.9. An MSN advanced search by file type.
URL: http://search.msn.com/advanced.asp
Date captured: 16 August 2003
Reproduced with permission from Microsoft Corporation

FIG. 6.10. The Government Printing Office (GPO) database search.
URL: www.gpoaccess.gov/serialset/creports/index.html
Date captured: 16 August 2003
United States Government Site

FIG. 6.11. Keeping up with new software releases on BetaNews.
URL: www.betanews.com
Date captured: 16 August 2003
Reproduced with permission from BetaNews, Inc.

FIG. 7.1. Web site for The Onion, a satirical newspaper.
URL: www.theonion.com
Date captured: 18 August 2003
Reproduced with permission from Onion, Inc.

FIG. 7.2. BBBOnline Reliability seal.
URL: www.bbbonline.com/reliability
Date captured: 7 January 2003
Reproduced with permission from Council of Better Business Bureaus, Inc.

FIG. 7.3. AltaVista search results indicate whether a site has been recently updated.
URL: www.altavista.com
Date captured: 7 January 2003
Reproduced with permission from AltaVista Company

FIG. 7.4. Google search results may include a cached version of a Web site.
URL: www.google.com
Date captured: 7 January 2003
Reproduced with permission from Google Inc.

FIG. 7.5. The National Center for Public Policy Research agenda is stated on its Web site.
URL: www.nationalcenter.org
Date captured: 7 January 2003
Reproduced with permission from The National Center for Public Policy Research

FIG. 7.6. Hoaxbusters, a site dedicated to investigating Internet hoaxes.
URL: http://hoaxbusters.ciac.org
Date captured: 15 August 2003
Reproduced with permission from University of California/CIAC/LLNL/DOE

Illustrations and Figures

Chapter 1: Getting Started

Chapter 2: When Seconds Count: Search Engine Strategies

Chapter 5: Finding Out About People

Chapter 6: Finding and Using Databases

Chapter 7: Evaluating the Information You Find

Author Index

Subject Index

A

Advertisements, 13, 22–23, 170

B

Blogs, *see* Web logs
Boolean expression, 28–40, 197
   searching with, 28–33, 38–40, 52–55
     and, 29–30
     and not, 30
     near, 31–33
     nesting commands, 38–40
     or, 30
Browser, 8–17
   defined, 2
   bookmarks, 16, 58, 62
   shortcuts, 12–17
   toolbar, 10–12, 59

C

Computer-assisted reporting (CAR), xi, 132
Cookies, 197

D

Databases, 131–154
   defined, 132, 197
   keeping up with, 145–146
   searching for, 135–143
     by file type, 137–141
     database services, 143
     peer-to-peer (P2P) networks, 143–145, 152
     with subject guides and directories, 141–143
   sources, 133–135, 146–152, 185–195
     business and not-for-profit, 150–151, 186, 188
     consumer services, 151
     government, 148–149, 187–188
     jobs and career, 189
     legal, 189–190
     libraries, 134–135
     maps, 190
     medicine and health, 150, 190–191
     newspapers and journals, 133–135, 146–148, 191–192
     polling and surveys, 152
     public records, 149–150
     religion, 192–194
Dictionaries and reference tools, 188
Domains, 43–46, 197
   credibility, 158
   cybersquatting, 44
   list of, 177–184
   registration, 115–117
   top-level, 44–46
   URL, 43, 200

E

E-mail, 1, 198
   credibility, 165–167
   privacy, 96–97
   spam, 99, 199
   telephone and e-mail directories, 101–108, 173–176
Evaluating content, 155–167
   accuracy, 159–160
   agenda, 164
   audience, 164–165
   authority, 160–161

221